EAT, DRINK AND BE WARY

A New Zealand Diplomat Looks Back

Remembering M

Jim Weir

EAT, DRINK AND BE WARY

A New Zealand Diplomat Looks Back

Jim Weir

May 2011

©Jim Weir 2011

Published in 2011 by
Dunmore Publishing Ltd
P.O. Box 25080
Wellington 6146
books@dunmore.co.nz
www.dumore.co.nz

All rights reserved by author. No part of this publication may be reproduced, stored in a retrieval system, or transmitted without permission in writing from the author.

Lay-up by A&V Design: avdesign@snap.net.nz

National Library of New Zealand Cataloguing-in-Publication Data

Weir, Jim, 1922-
Eat, drink and be wary : a New Zealand diplomat looks back /
Jim Weir.
ISBN 978-1877-399-602
1. Weir, Jim, 1922- —Career in diplomacy. 2. Diplomats—
New Zealand—Biography.
I. Title.
327.2092—dc 22

Contents

Preface	7
In the Beginning	
i. Some early New Zealand diplomats, their habits and habitat	9
ii. Strangers and journeys	26
Canberra, Port Moresby, Hollandia	
i. Seven suburbs in search of a city	50
ii. Leaving at first light in Papua New Guinea	57
iii. To Biak and back	65
Singapore at Sixes and Sevens	
i. A pre-eminent Prime Minister	74
ii. Farewelling a great empire	89
iii. Letters	104
Wondering About and Wandering in Burma	
i. Too good a country to ruin completely – but they're trying	110
ii. "Everybody doesn't like our government."	117
iii. A rough road to Nirvana	136
iv. Goodbye and good luck	143
Knock Five Times and Ask for the President or King	
i. The Italian job	147
ii. Yugoslavia	151
iii. Malta	153
iv. Egypt	155
v. Saudi Arabia	158
vi. Kissing hands	168
Departures	
i. A silence in Belgrade	172
ii. The lighter side of darkness in Cairo	178
iii. An unmarked Saudi grave	183
Italian Days	
i. Excerpts from a diary	184
Index	223

Standing orders were issued to grandchildren that, if they wished to play draughts with the policemen, "they should do so in a way which would never obstruct the arrival of ambassadors …"
                    Alister Horne, *Macmillan, 1957–86* (1989) p. 14

I myself have never met a man who lived abroad for any length of time who did not come to like and admire the people living in the country of his adoption.
                    Lord Cobham (1959), *Lord Cobham's Speeches* (1962) p. 187

To elevate into an Ambassador a modest gentleman who occupies a modest office, whose modest function is to attend to a few transactions of very ordinary business, is surely a highly ridiculous business.
                    The *Lyttelton Times* 27 December 1882

Our diplomats thought that telling the truth was an outrageous risk. They didn't advocate lying, but they advocated that the next best thing to not having a Prime Minister at all was to have a quiet one.
                    Former Prime Minister David Lange, September 2003

Preface

My book *Letters from Moscow*, published by Hodder and Stoughton in 1988, gave an account of my three years as New Zealand Ambassador in the Soviet Union, 1977–80, during the Cold War. The present memoirs begin by describing headquarters in Wellington when I joined the Department of External Affairs in 1947. I then give an account of overseas assignments, excluding Moscow and not including all the others. I've concentrated on things which seemed of general interest, some unusual experiences and some pioneering activity.

I've also been selective in accentuating the positive. Of course, there are difficulties in foreign service – bad patches, narks, apparent injustices, disappointments. That's so in most jobs, but it's worse, for instance, when you're dealing with a nark across several thousand miles and much, much worse if a nark is assigned to work in your own small office overseas. And, the foreign service can undoubtedly strain family relationships. For my part, I was very lucky, both in my personal and official life and not least in the country it was such a privilege to represent abroad.

The trouble with writing memoirs towards the end of a long life is that memory can play tricks. The dramatic incident, the colourful words, the outburst of temper, remain indelible. But when did that incident occur? What was that fellow's name? There has to be a protracted, sometimes tedious and always surprisingly time-consuming process of checking and filling in gaps.

Many have helped in this process. A few stand out. David Crooks, Air Vice-Marshall, RNZAF (Ret.) has been extremely helpful in all matters relating to aviation. Rob Laking has been equally good in saying how much so-and-so would have been in today's currency – or whether it could be said at all. Duncan Campbell very helpfully kept me from embroidering facts about the Chinese diaspora.

Former colleagues and others in what is now the Ministry of Foreign Affairs and Trade, most notably Peter Rider and Doug Law, have gone to no end of trouble in the search for relevant papers, which have often been elusive and, in a few cases, couldn't be found at all.

I'm especially grateful to Glenda Gale at the Alexander Turnbull Library. I put more questions to her than to all the others combined and she always came up trumps. I'm also indebted to the American, Netherlands and Thai Embassies in Wellington and the Australian, British and Canadian High Commissions.

Special thanks are due to Sarah Wild who used her word processor to put my untidy typescript into much better shape.

Above all, I am indebted to Sharmian Firth and Elizabeth Beattie of Dunmore Publishing, for their expertise and kindness.

In the Beginning

I. SOME EARLY NEW ZEALAND DIPLOMATS, THEIR HABITS AND HABITAT

On my first day, I reported to Ray Perry who was to be my immediate boss. He showed me to a desk in a room with two other fellows in it and, in what I suppose was my equivalent of today's 'orientation programme', Ray said, "Well, I think it would be a good idea for you to begin by reading the United Nations Charter." He gave me a copy of it, then added firmly, "… and preferably learn it by heart," – which I did.

That was the Department of External Affairs, Wellington, 1947. The United Nations was new and a major focus of work in the department. The Prime Minister, Peter Fraser, who was also Minister of External Affairs and whose office was just along the corridor, had played a significant part in drafting the Charter at the founding conference of the United Nations in 1945. And there was widespread public interest in it. Would it fare better than the League of Nations? Or would there continue to be a world war every generation?

Ray said the hours of work – which differed a little from one government department to another – were 8.30 am to five. But I found that when I arrived at 8.30, Ray was already there, as others were too. So I began catching an earlier tram. The result was the same. Ray was already there. So I caught an even earlier tram. But Ray was always in the office before me and always there when I left, beavering away – "getting down ten feet below bedrock," George Laking observed – notwithstanding that he lived a good half hour's train journey away, while I had only a ten-minute tram ride.

He was a prodigious worker, quick, decisive, judicious.

And I was astonished, one Saturday morning, in my very early days with the department, when a sleek black government car pulled up at our gate and the liveried driver brought in an envelope from Ray containing a draft telegram about something we'd been discussing the previous day. Ray now proposed to send off the telegram immediately to the New Zealand delegation at the United Nations in New York – if I agreed. If I agreed! Working on a Saturday! (We didn't have a phone and, in those days, it took six months to get one. We depended on neighbours for telephoning.)

The men's tea room was intriguing – the smallest room in that whole complex which had been hurriedly built to meet the greatly increased needs of the prime minister in wartime. It was on the flat roof of Parliament Buildings and the men's tea room had been the night-duty officer's sleeping quarters during the war and accordingly had a shower, in a recess – the only shower in that whole complex. As a tea room, it had a small, bench-high table where, at 10 am and 3 pm, the tea lady, operating from the women's tea room across the corridor, brought a large pot of tea. George and Wally played mother, as they said, and poured the tea. George and Wally, who were far older than anyone else – they were probably World War I veterans – worked as messenger/mail clerks. When the occasion arose, they would play a little game – I suppose it was a variation of the tin-kettling then practised in the rural areas of New Zealand – of passing increasingly suggestive remarks, to the embarrassment of anyone who had recently married. The victim would fairly quickly find this teasing more than he could take, and, grabbing his cup of tea, hurry away back to his desk, leaving everyone else to guffaw. At other times of the day, George and Wally were apt to slip down the back stairs for a quick one in Bellamy's bar. At lunch time they played cards with some of the young diplomats in the mail room.

Whereas the men sat on hard wooden benches in the confined space of their tea room, the women, mainly typists and filing clerks, had a room several times the size, with padded benches arranged over central-heating pipes which provided excellent under-buttock heating in winter; built-in couches where the women could lie down if need be at that time of the month; a built-in radio, especially to catch breaking news – the only radio in the department; wall-to-wall carpet and 'all-day sun', as a real estate agent would have claimed. When this room became the tea room for both men and women, and became known as the staff-tea room, there was always a knot of people with heads down in earnest discussion during the tea breaks but there was also constant laughter rippling from group to group. It could be raucous laughter, for instance when a young returned serviceman recalled, for men's ears only, "… on the way over, we got off the ship at a place called

In the Beginning

Colon, at the far end of the Panama Canal and ended up in a seedy dive, crowded with servicemen, and there was this sheila who walked down the aisle starkers, puffing a cigarette with the contractions of her quim and some cockney sailor brought the house down by leaning over towards her with an unlit fag in his mouth and shouting, 'Hey, luv, give us a light!' "

For the most part, of course, the talk was about things which probably remain standard fare during tea breaks in any New Zealand office. But there was one thing in the 1940s that was distinctly different. Not only the women but also the men swapped recipes and, with men, it wasn't food they had in mind but home brew – a passable drink which could be made for less than tuppence a large bottle. This was the heyday of do-it-yourself, when the top priority for young people was to buy a house, preferably with a copper to make the home brew in. Mortgages were available for, I think, a term of 25 years at a fixed rate of three or four percent. Ex-servicemen, as most of us were, had preferential rates. So – buy a house, do it up, start a family. These were the imperatives.

Every Wednesday at 11 am we queued to collect our pay packets, and continuing a practice begun during the war, we each had sixpence a week, or something of the kind, deducted from our pay to send food parcels to the locally recruited (British) staff at the New Zealand High Commission in London. (Rationing continued in New Zealand well into the post-war years, so that more food could be sent to Britain under bulk purchasing arrangements. And rationing in New Zealand meant, incidentally, that when your wife became pregnant and therefore entitled to an extra meat ration, the local butcher was among the first to know – and he passed the news on to your neighbours.) The local staff in London thanked the staff in Wellington for all those food parcels by sending out the print of a very English, very chocolate-box, scene, entitled 'Bluebells in the Woods', which was given pride of place, by the built-in radio, in the women's tea room.

Every second or third day, two of the girls from Records, Mary Seddon, a granddaughter of the turn-of-the-century prime minister nicknamed 'King Dick' Seddon, whose statue stood centrally in the grounds of Parliament Buildings, and Beverley Puttick, a daughter of Lieutenant-General Sir Edward Puttick, Chief of the General Staff during the war, would go into everyone's office, making a list of the files being held in case any of them were wanted urgently by someone else. Mary and Beverley were proud of their lineage but also very much individualists in their own right. Indeed, Mary Seddon was about as formidable in her way as her grandfather had been in his. And we thought it pleasantly ironic to have them as handmaidens when their forebears had lorded it over so many of us or our forebears.

Every year just before Christmas there was a late afternoon party in George and Wally's mail room, with jokey presents to tease selected victims. At the Christmas party in 1947 or '48 there were three notable resignations. One was Harold Evans (1916–2006), a lawyer in the department, who had been away on secondment as associate to Mr Justice Northcroft, the New Zealand judge on the International Military Tribunal for the Far East, which tried Japanese war criminals in Tokyo. While there, Harold met, fell in love with and married the daughter of a German admiral. In the climate of public opinion at that time, this marriage was regarded as tantamount to fraternising with the enemy, and unacceptable. Harold was obliged to resign from External Affairs through some of us thought this was taking things much too far. He spent most of his subsequent career as a magistrate in Christchurch but retained a lifelong interest in issues of international law.

Another to resign at that time was Dorian Saker (1922–95) who had already completed an MA degree in Latin and Greek and had become well known at university as a poet but now made a rather extraordinary career switch in opting to study medicine at Otago University. He subsequently spent his career as a GP in Wellington. Thirdly, John Woodward (1921–92) left the department to join the International Refugee Organisation in Geneva.

Every winter there was a dance – ladies a plate – in a dance studio upstairs in a building in Willis Street, where there were more of those long wooden benches set against the walls. We did the waltz, the foxtrot, the quickstep, the valeta, that sort of thing, but, strangely, not jive or jitterbugging which were then the rage. Perhaps there was an underlying problem that there were just too few people in External Affairs to muster enough of them for a dance. Anyhow, it was all rather dreary. But then Dick Hutchens and Peter Jeffery would sit down together at the piano and start playing duets. That was electrifying; they were remarkably gifted pianists who played in marvellous harmony with each other. We would all gather round and, when the singing began, it was led by Peter's wife, Margo, who used to sing regularly on radio with Peter as accompanist. With all this going on everyone forgot it was supposed to be a dance and no one wanted to go home. But, in reality, our social life was, for the most part, ruled by last trams leaving the city at 11 pm.

Whenever anyone was posted overseas, the rest of the staff passed the hat around and bought a hardback book as a farewell present. The recipient would then invite his colleagues home after work, to drink his home brew and eat his wife's sausage rolls and sandwiches. Not everyone was invited. Never the top brass. And not wives. But it was always a diverse mix of the people you worked closely with, including clerical staff and typists. It could be a bit of a crush but they all fitted happily into the modest-sized

In the Beginning

sitting room of our modest homes. There would be a similar party to wet the head of a colleague's new baby. Such a party at John Scott's home revealed something else to stick in the mind. Their house in Kelburn had a long, steep flight of steps and, at the entrance to the property, at street level, not a garage but a lockable shed for the pram.

But this is straying from the workplace. In 1947, External Affairs divided the world in three, like Caesar's Gaul. Tom Larkin did Europe, Rex Cunninghame Asia and Charles Craw Antarctica and Oceania, which somehow included trusteeship territories. The legal officer was Jack Northey. On the side, as befitted someone who later left the department and became a professor of law at Auckland University, he promoted the idea of making home brew in a completely unadulterated way, whereas Paul Gabites was an experimentalist who discovered, for instance, that if you put a few raisins in every large bottle as you capped it, the brew had a lot more kick. At that time, there was no economic section in the department – for the very good reason that there were no economists. Ray Perry, a lawyer by training, was in charge of the section dealing with the economic and social affairs of the United Nations and all the specialised agencies, as they were called, such as the International Labour Organisation. This work generated a great deal of correspondence, as well as many meetings, with other government departments, and instructions to be sent to delegations at overseas conferences.

Every day or so, Ray would make an appointment to see Mac, as everyone called Alister (later Sir Alister) McIntosh (1906–78), the head of the department. Only those close to him in seniority or age actually called him Mac to his face. Mac would deal with Ray's bundle of papers very expeditiously indeed. If I'd been involved in the drafting, Ray would take me along, too. "What's this about?" he would ask and Ray would give him a three-sentence summary while Mac glanced at the critical last paragraph and, as often as not, sign the letter or whatever it was before Ray had finished his explanation. If the issue were important enough, Mac put it in his tray of papers to take to the Prime Minister for approval. He also had another tray where he accumulated papers to go to the Governor-General for his background information. (Sir Bernard Fergusson, as Governor-General, described Mac as "the man who makes New Zealand tick" – he was also head of the Prime Minister's Department.[1])

Looking back now, more than 60 years later, it's rather astonishing to realise that one's diplomatic colleagues in Wellington were so young.

---

[1] Indeed, in those early days in the department, when telephoning anyone on official business, we all identified ourselves as, "This is so-and-so of the Prime Minister's Office."

Mac was 40, having become head of the department at what he later called "the ripe age of 37". The Deputy Secretary, Foss Shanahan (1910–64), was 37, George (later Sir George) Laking, Assistant Secretary (1913–2008), 35. Most of us were in our twenties. There was one notable exception, also an Assistant Secretary. J.V.Wilson (1984–1977) seemed incredibly old. Why, he'd been born in the previous century! In fact, he was 53. Apart from J.V. (as he was known with affection and respect), there were no grey hairs. Correspondingly, the retirement of a diplomatic colleague in Wellington, at the mandatory age of 60, was a rare event.

At the helm, Mac worked from a tidy desk in a methodical, calm, measured way. In apparent pursuit of this composure, he took a good breath of fresh air at lunchtime by walking up Bolton Street to his home in Wesley Road. And he similarly walked to work and then home again at the end of the day. It wasn't far as the crow flies but Bolton Street is very steep. (In the 'fifties, after he'd been ill, his wife usually came to collect him in the car. Like quite a few others, he never learnt to drive. Charles Craw and Tom Larkin both left driving to their wives.)

Mac also had a weekender, a retreat from the cares of the world, not least including the idiosyncrasies of New Zealand prime ministers. This was at Te Marua, about half an hour's drive from Wellington, beyond Upper Hutt. There, even in wartime, he refused to have a phone connected to disturb his peace when he was at the beck and call of the Prime Minister at least five days and nights a week. He loved to get out to Te Marua where there were about two acres with a small stream running through. On this land he made a beautiful garden, with many rhododendrons, camellias, azaleas and dogwoods growing under trees. On this property, too, he kept his household well stocked with vegetables. In the spring of 1958, during a meeting between Walter (later Sir Walter) Nash and his Australian counterpart, R.G. (later Sir Robert) Menzies – a meeting which achieved a lot in a very short time – Mac sighed despondently several times, "It's such a waste of time. I could be at home planting the potatoes," – which, in that era, was a quintessentially New Zealand way of measuring a waste of time.

Whenever you encountered him in the corridors of Parliament Buildings or nearby, Mac had his head cocked slightly to one side, his eyes cast down – thinking, worrying, his mind, it seemed, always on the job, mulling over issues big and small. In any such chance encounter there might be some opening pleasantry about the weather but he quickly brought you to the train of thought which had just been interrupted. He could then be astonishingly frank in talking to a junior officer. He once said, "You know, my biggest worry just now is …" and my mind raced through the drastic possibilities, but he added with a mixture of amusement and concern, "*wives*."

In the Beginning

And he went on to give eye-popping chapter and verse about recent occurrences. The wife of a very junior officer, for instance, had bailed up the Prime Minister at a reception in Australia and taken him severely to task. And Peter Fraser, who had assumed almost dictatorial authority during the war, didn't take at all kindly to such treatment from some whippersnapper – and a woman at that.

To Mac, External Affairs was not just a government department. It was his extended family. He knew all the diplomatic staff by their first names and what he didn't know about their relevant personal circumstances, Madie Browne, the head typist and departmental mother hen, filled him in on. In the 1940s, the department was very small and New Zealand had only five diplomatic missions, four of which seemed to be permanently headed by political appointees, some of whom hadn't the faintest idea what they were supposed to be doing and, if put in no doubt as to what this was, were incredulous. This was all the more reason for Mac to worry enormously, as one sensed he did, about the assignment of staff. Who would do the best job where? Who would be compatible with whom? (He was, said Doug Lake (1919–95), "as sensitive as a woman".)

As for the staff, those who had grown up during the Depression and had served in the armed forces during the war, could see it as a good steady job where they weren't being shot at. But it wasn't a notably well-paid job or even particularly reputable. Ministry of Works engineers building hydro dams and bridges, now they were greatly respected. But why on earth did New Zealand need its own diplomatic service? The British had been doing this sort of thing for centuries and for many years had been looking after New Zealanders who got into trouble abroad – and, moreover, doing it for nothing. So, following this trend of thought, when the government changed in December 1949, the diplomatic mission in Moscow was abolished (and not reopened for 23 years) and, at the same time, as a similar cost-cutting measure, the Consulate-General in New York was closed.

Cost was always a factor. If New Zealand was to have a diplomatic service, it had to be done economically. By comparison, Australian trainees began their diplomatic service with a two-year postgraduate course at university. Their New Zealand counterparts started work on day one and learnt by doing. Inch by inch, it seemed, as funds became available, more and more of that flat roof on the top of Parliament Buildings was covered over with a few more rooms of working space for External Affairs; more desks were moved into the bigger rooms (so that, when a few loud voices started talking on the phone all at once, the cacophony was appalling) and a couple of desks were even put into a sufficiently large wasteland of corridor. Financial resources were so carefully husbanded that if any money remained unspent at the end of a financial year, however small that amount of money might seem, it was cunningly 'saved' by buying open air tickets, to be locked in the safe for use in the following financial year.

Financial stringency, limited job prospects, the magnet of better-paid jobs elsewhere, meant it was never easy to recruit or retain suitable staff. There must have been times when it seemed like a losing battle. But there was an inevitability about the growth of the New Zealand diplomatic service, for instance to participate in the proliferation of international activity and notably aid programmes organised by the United Nations and the Commonwealth. Richer nations, including New Zealand, were expected to provide courses of study and technical expertise to poorer countries on a scale unthinkable before the war. And so it was that the first part of External Affairs to leave the nest and move out of Parliament Buildings was the Technical Assistance Unit, as it was called – relocated in Stout Street, along the corridor from the Research Unit of Treasury.

Apart from the inevitability of New Zealand becoming caught up in these currents of international activity, Mac himself was a magnet, attracting staff by his personal but unobtrusive interest in and concern for them and his ability to delegate authority to them surprisingly soon after they started work in the department. He was, moreover, a deep thinker – who could say at a staff meeting, after everyone else had had their say, "Well, I don't think any of you are right," and quietly proceed to explain why this was so. He was, moreover, a man of extraordinarily wide-ranging interests. Having started his career as a librarian, he was a bibliophile, as well as a wordsmith. He was an authority on early New Zealand art, buildings and history. And he could give better advice about plants and how to care for them than any modern multimillion-dollar garden centre.

In his own quiet way he was a good networker. He knew many of the parliamentarians – then limited to 80 – and perhaps had a special regard for the self-taught 'old hands' he had first encountered when working in the General Assembly Library. He was on excellent terms with newspaper editors and parliamentary press gallery journalists, to whom he would give extremely candid 'off the record' briefings and, as occasion demanded, enjoin them to be silent about this or that issue or fact, in the national interest. To my knowledge, none of them ever let him down. He made himself readily available to chat in his office with heads of diplomatic missions, although he carefully restricted his social activity with them. After J.V. Wilson retired in 1959, he came in almost every week for morning tea and a chat with Mac, not simply to get the news behind the news but also, I imagine, because Mac enjoyed the company of a man so full of such wise adages as "in international affairs 'never' means 15 years".

In the Beginning

At an earlier time, for nine years from 1943, when his predecessor as Secretary of External Affairs, Carl (later Sir Carl) Berendsen, was appointed as New Zealand's first High Commissioner in Canberra, Mac wrote, or rather dictated, a letter to him every week. These letters were the last thing Mac did before the diplomatic bag closed that week and were often hurriedly done and may well have included remarks which he later regretted. But the letters and Carl Berendsen's replies made up a remarkable historical record, taking us behind the scenes in times of disaster, during the war, and what, at times, could later be seen as naïve idealism, when New Zealand advocated the internationalisation of international air services (1944 and later), for instance, or the adoption of 'full employment everywhere' (Berendsen at the United Nations, 1949). The correspondence was based on a close working relationship and improbable friendship – Berendsen brilliant, theatrical, cantankerous, solitary; Mac self-effacing, steady, conciliatory, far more of an internationalist. They were bound together by equally dedicated pursuit of New Zealand interests, mutual respect and – when Sir Carl's duodenal ulcers and personal grievances allowed – by good humour. The correspondence continued until Sir Carl retired in 1952.[2] After that, they saw very little of each other.

In all his official activities Mac had the unstinting support of his wife. For instance, when Bethune's (Wellington) was to hold an auction which included early New Zealand art, Mac and his wife would go together to the preview, held after office hours, and then she would go to the auction and bid for early New Zealand watercolours in particular – acquiring many of them, on the department's behalf and for a fraction of their subsequent value. She received no recompense for this activity. Many of the watercolours bought in this way were sent to the New Zealand High Commission in London, although some were later transferred to Rome when Mac was appointed as the Ambassador there in 1966.

No New Zealand art was displayed in Mac's office or elsewhere in the department in his day. Indeed, the furnishings in his office remained the same for the 23 years of his occupancy. A leather-covered sofa stuffed with horsehair, which may well have come out to New Zealand with the first British settlers to arrive in Wellington, became increasingly anaemic-looking over the years as the colour of the ageing leather faded in the strong sunlight and seemingly pockmarked as idle hands at staff meetings plucked out more and more of the horsehair through holes worn in the leather. The only significant change in the furnishings in Mac's time was the addition

---

[2] A selection of these letters was published in *Undiplomatic Dialogue: Letters between Carl Berendsen and Alister McIntosh, 1943–1952*, edited by Ian McGibbon and published by Auckland University Press (1993).

of a large-scale map cabinet which was too big to fit in anywhere else in the department.

It was a mark of his humility that he calmly tolerated the inconvenience of having the departmental map cabinet in his office. And there were some rather unexpected things. When travelling overseas with the septuagenarian Prime Minister Walter Nash he was as solicitous as a son, ensuring that domestic staff anywhere in the world knew what an eggnog was – this being the Prime Minister's regular nightcap. And, in making a formal call on the Governor-General in Wellington, he was as deferential as a novitiate nun granted an audience with the Pope.

There was a remarkable simplicity in having External Affairs and the Prime Minister's Department combined and great advantage in being a few seconds away from the Prime Minister who was usually Minister of External Affairs as well. All this added to the interest, immediacy and sense of responsibility in our work, especially because we could be sure that any prime-ministerial press statement we had drafted would be published in full in that evening's paper or the next morning, as well as being given prominence on the radio news. The news media were far more deferential then, in the days before either television or inquisitional interviewing had arrived in New Zealand.

In Parliament Buildings we were very aware of being close to the centre of New Zealand power. We passed the politicians in the corridors every day and shared the lift with them – and it was possibly the slowest lift in the world. The prime minister I came to know best, partly through chatting in the lift, although mainly through his visits to Singapore when we were stationed there in the 1960s, was Keith (later Sir Keith) Holyoake. In Wellington, we seemed to leave the office at much the same time, around six, every evening. After going down in the lift together, we paused on the steps at the entrance to Parliament Buildings to exchange a few parting words – and at such times he always seemed full of the joy of living, whereas on his visits to Singapore, unable to stand the tropical heat, he was always grumpy. As I went to my car, parked in a vacant lot reserved for External Affairs, in what is now Kate Sheppard Place, I could see the Prime Minister sauntering to his home in Pipitea Street. As he went, he stopped to chat with the Chinese greengrocer and other shopkeepers in Molesworth Street, as well as any pedestrians he encountered along the way. This aroused some wonder. The President of the United States had been assassinated but there was the Prime Minister of our village democracy walking home alone, carrying his large briefcase of papers, completely unguarded, completely and justifiably confident that he would come to no harm. I'm sure he never gave the issue of his own security a moment's thought – and neither did anyone else.

In the Beginning

(Going walkabout was something he did in Singapore too, in a minor way. On his visits there in the 1960s he would go shopping at C.K. Tang's, a large department store, and my wife, Mollie [from here on referred to as M] would go with him to help. In fact, he very quickly became bored with the shopping and wandered off on a little walkabout, chatting with other shoppers or, rather, when he encountered a language barrier or ladies who knew better than to talk to strange men and anyhow hadn't the faintest idea who he was, he smiled broadly and bowed in a courtly manner, leaving a trail of bewildered little Singaporean Chinese women staring and giggling in his wake. Meantime, my wife got on with the shopping. This was the daunting, exasperating task of finding a small present for every member of the caucus – and there were about 50 of them – and it could not be something he had given them before, nor anything "gimmicky" [his word] and no item was to cost more than one Singapore dollar, which was then, if I remember correctly, worth about a quarter of a New Zealand dollar.)

Working in Parliament Buildings gave us a few perks. We could borrow books from the General Assembly (now called the Parliamentary) Library – slipping down the back stairs and changing books in about ten minutes. The best time for this was when most of the parliamentarians were away, during the recess. We then had first pick of books which the library had just acquired. And, for a Friday evening happy-hour, we could drink at a (duty-free) bar[3] in Bellamy's, a bar we shared with the parliamentary messengers – elderly men who picked, or made up – the gossip on their round of ministerial and other offices.

And when state lunches were held, the marvellous aroma of cigar smoke, as well as the smoke itself, drifted up the three and a half storeys, letting us know that the parliamentarians and others at the lunch would soon be back, soporifically, at their desks. In those days, before the Beehive had been built, state lunches were held in what had originally been the ballroom of Government House which had once been on this site – a wooden structure linked up to Parliament Buildings. Folding doors along one side of this large room opened on to a corridor so that, if you happened to go by when the speeches were being made, you could stop and listen – not that anyone bothered to do so apart from young egoists from External Affairs, wondering what the Prime Minister would do with the speech notes they had drafted.

(Would cigar smoke still smell pleasant? Almost certainly not now that everyone in his or her right mind has given up smoking, but, in the days of which I write, most men smoked. We had grown up before the medical

---

[3] A photo of this bar appears in John E. Martin's *The House: New Zealand's House of Representatives 1854–2000*, Dunmore Press, Palmerston North, 2004, p. 255. The photo, taken in 1968, is captioned, "The run-down, cubicle-like messengers' bar".

people discovered what harm smoking caused. During the war, every Red Cross or New Zealand Patriotic Fund parcel sent to us in the armed forces included two tins of 50 cigarettes, to calm our nerves – which they did. And these cigarettes were usually of the strong American kind – and more to our liking – if they were. Staff meetings in Mac's room were always thick with smoke, especially when Hunter Wade lit up a cigar. Mac himself didn't smoke but Foss Shanahan did, heavily.)

At the Bowen Street entrance to the old wooden structure which, in its prime, had been Government House, was the messengers' room, which had probably the last open fireplace in use in any office building in Wellington. On a cold, wet day it was good to be welcomed into the building by that cheerful fire in the grate and to be invited by the cheerful messengers to leave your overcoat there to dry off – or to park with them the shrub you had bought in Lambton Quay and were in the course of taking home in the tram. (Between Parliament Buildings and the far end of Courtenay Place there were seven shops selling plants. You could look them all over in a lunch hour, walking at a fast clip and getting the tram back.)

The messengers had no responsibility for security in Parliament Buildings. It was not part of their brief to vet people coming into the building. The underlying assumption must have been that all visitors were decent, law-abiding people and probably New Zealand electors, who were to be greeted and helped in finding whoever or whatever part of the building they were looking for, no questions asked. In pre-Beehive days the corridors of Parliament Buildings were corridors of power in a homely democracy. Anyone could walk in off the street and be directed to the minister or official he or she wanted to badger. (Guy Fawkes would have been treated courteously: "The basement, sir? Just take the lift down one floor.") They would be intercepted by a ministerial private secretary in an anteroom, of course, but there was nothing to stop them intercepting ministers in the corridor as they went about their business. When vetting was eventually introduced for visitors going to External Affairs, a trainee guard, on duty in a newly built cubicle in the corridor near the lift, rang Dick Sharp, the most considerate and caring of men, who was in charge of consular affairs, and announced, while a visitor stood beside him, listening, "There's a black man here to see you Sir," – which mortified Dick Sharp and, to put it mildly, didn't please the visitor one little bit. It was the High Commissioner for India.

Parliament Buildings was a wonderfully functional building. The Beehive, according to all those who work in it, as I never did, is just the opposite. It has, for instance, largely dispensed with corridors – places where, in the course of their day to day activity, ministers, officials and journalists, as well as members of the public, might interact without an appointment.

I began this chapter with Ray Perry and should say more of him. We were together again in Ottawa (1951–2), when T.C.A. Hislop, a former mayor of Wellington, was High Commissioner – the model of what a high commissioner should not be. When Ray returned to New Zealand he was Secretary of the Cabinet for nine years. After that, he became Deputy Secretary of Labour and stayed in that job until he retired in 1975. During these later years I had no official dealings with him and my wife and I were often on postings overseas. Meanwhile, however, he and his family came to live very near our home in Wellington and we and our families became close friends. When my wife died, Ray was the first on my doorstep.

When his wife died, Ray having pre-deceased her, I wrote to their older daughter.

26 October 2006
Dear Ann,

I have such happy memories of your mother's kindness to Mollie and our children. We met her first in 1948, I think it would have been, when we went to your home in Taita for dinner. Then, in Ottawa, you and Ellie would stand in your nighties on the stairs, shyly watching the guests arrive for dinner. Once, in Ottawa, when Mollie was wearing a flossy yellow dress, Ellie exclaimed, in wide-eyed admiration, "Oh, Mrs Weir, you look just like a fairy princess!" – a delicious compliment but somehow M didn't want to be a fairy princess and never wore that dress again!

Sometimes, it seemed your mother could tie-dye silk scarves in the morning, read an erudite book in the afternoon, play the piano, help someone in need, mind Marc [a grandson] and, in between times, cook a gourmet dinner for eight, including six guests, to be served in style and garnished with West Coast wit. Told in Ottawa that the New Zealand Chief of General Staff, General Weir (no kin of mine) would be coming for a weekend, she said instantly, knowing all too well what the routine would be, "Up the bloody Gatineau [river – meaning by road, a popular Sunday drive]!"

Recently, the happiness has been overshadowed by declining health but there must now be an aching void. Please find enclosed two big comforting hugs, one each for you and Ellie.

Ray and Agnes lived long, happy lives. Fate dealt a cruel blow to others. This was notably so with Adelina Davin, wife of Tom. I first met Tom in 1949, when he was briefly in Wellington. He was an older brother of Dan Davin, whose novel *For the Rest of Their Lives* had been published in London in 1947. Tom loved to be asked about this book but, in his engaging, dithery way, never knew whether to be proud or ashamed. The novel was a brilliant account of New Zealanders in action in World War II but it was controversial because it included thinly disguised, unflattering descriptions of senior New Zealand army officers and it was, moreover, I think, the first New Zealand book to include the f-word – and lots of it, at a time when it wasn't even in the dictionary.

Tom and Dan were opposites. Perhaps the only thing they had in common was that they both loved to sing and they both sang extremely well. Indeed, it might be said that the high point of Tom's career came in 1950 when he, Senator Sparkman, a member of the American delegation to the United Nations General Assembly – which, incidentally, he startled with a gaffe appealing to the Arabs and Israelis to settle their differences in a good Christian spirit – and Celeste Holm, now (2008) in her nineties and then the star of a musical comedy playing to packed houses on Broadway, got together as an impromptu trio at a large United Nations party in New York. Their frolicsome singing as a threesome, which had suddenly and unexpectedly somehow just coalesced, captivated everyone there. It was probably greeted with more thunderous applause than had ever been given to any speech in the United Nations and was talked about fondly long afterwards.

Then, some years later, when Tom was Consul-General in New York (1956–9), tragedy struck. One day, when Tom was at the office, Adelina thought she had discovered the Russian crown jewels in the grandfather clock in their apartment and, of course, reported this immediately to the White House. In truth, to put it bluntly, she had a nervous breakdown. That ended their postings abroad. Adelina, who when young had been a vivacious party girl, a notable singer, courted at one stage by Foss Shanahan, came to lead a reclusive life in Wellington and, for many years, never went outside the house. She died in 1989, Tom utterly devoted and caring till the end. After leaving Foreign Affairs, at the mandatory retirement age of 60, Tom worked for a law firm until he died suddenly, just before his 80th birthday. At the time of his funeral, his daughter, Antonia, remarked to me that he had been a civil servant of the kind born to make his own sandwiches and eat them at his desk in the office every working day. He had just recently decided, she added, to retire completely and she had been rather dreading the thought that he would take up some terrible hobby and pursue it with the same single-mindedness he had applied to everything else. All this said with a twinkle in eyes on the brink of tears.

A word about Foss Shanahan. My first encounter with him was when he interviewed me for entry to External Affairs. Well, there was an interviewing panel. There was someone else there, called McIntosh, but he just sat there quietly, smiling, while Foss had a conversation with me. (I think there was someone else on the panel, too, but it has faded from my mind although I do remember Frank Corner fluttering in the wings, organising an IQ test – the first time such a test had been given to applicants.) Noting that I was then working for the National Service Department's research unit, set up to consider ways of alleviating the heavy unemployment expected when about a hundred-thousand servicemen were demobilised at the end of the war, Foss remarked that, whereas there had been such unemployment after the First World War, we were lucky to have avoided it this time round. (In fact, there were so few unemployed – just a few dozen – it was jokingly said that the Prime Minister knew them all by name.) It was a great achievement, Foss said, to have full employment. The trouble was, I remarked, that we had over-full employment, causing all sorts of problems. And we went on in this vein.

I went home that day wondering if I'd been a bit too cocky in talking to such an obviously important man. But I really had no idea what the expectations of these External Affairs people were. Indeed, I had very little idea what they did. External Affairs was then so new and so small that not many people knew it even existed. My own interest had been aroused by just a few cryptic lines of fine print in a public service circular, indicating that the department was looking for staff.

As I discovered in due course, they were looking for 'personable young men': short back and sides, white shirt, a tie that was in no way garish, shoes that were not made of suede. Within this framework, there were graduations. On my first day I wore a suit. No one said anything but this was obviously viewed as uppity. Next day I was in the appropriate attire for my rank: sports coat and grey slacks. They were also looking for women graduates and were far ahead of other government departments in recruiting them.

There were other expectations, silently imposed by the diplomats themselves. The Government had decreed that, if there were to be a New Zealand diplomatic service, it had to be arranged as economically as possible. The diplomats determined that this service was to be as egalitarian as possible. No airs and graces. First off, New Zealand diplomats were not to call themselves diplomats, let alone diplomatists. They were simply civil servants working in External Affairs. That's how you described your job when other New Zealanders asked what you did for a living.

When you moved up in the world enough to rate an entry in *Who's Who*, the word 'diplomat' was never used. You simply gave name, rank and overseas assignments, sticking pretty closely to the name-rank-and-serial-number formula which covered all you disclosed if captured during the war. A bit of levity was permissible, even to be applauded if it hit the mark, as it had been during the war. In 1968, Paul Gabites, by then High Commissioner in Western Samoa, described himself as a 'licensed drainlayer' (Ottawa, 1955–6) – a qualification gained to overcome some local hindrance to his continuing do-it-yourself activity, by now requiring a degree of expertise several notches up from his home-brewing in earlier years. A New Zealand high commissioner qualified as licensed drainlayer! And, as well as being a university graduate! Diplomats from other countries could, at best, smile at the aberration. His colleagues – all New Zealanders – could glow with pride.

But I am straying much too far from Foss Shanahan. After joining External Affairs, I quickly found that he was very highly regarded in all sorts of quarters, especially in the military world, for his intellect, drive, boundless energy and capacity as a government trouble-shooter. I also found that it was better to avoid chance encounters with him. If you saw him just ahead of you in the corridor, going out to lunch, you stopped to look at something out the window, such as a blank wall six yards away. Otherwise, you would almost certainly get an extra job, which you didn't need and which would probably land you in trouble with your colleagues, because Foss had no great regard for the departmental schedule of how work was to be allocated, and you were likely to end up treading on other people's toes. For Foss, the over-riding consideration was that problems were to be solved and he could spot problems a mile off. And he had the answer to every problem. Moreover, in the course of his work, he dictated so much, so fluently and at such speed that, if you walked along the corridor with him and the conversation suggested there was a problem somewhere, Foss would pounce on it and almost automatically lapse into dictation mode. "Please draft me a memo to the Ministry of Works (or whatever). "You should say …" and off he would go, even putting in the punctuation, as for a typist, "…comma. No, make that a full stop." A workaholic, a powerhouse, a Brylcreemed charmer, indestructible. Then, tragically he was struck down by a brain tumour, aged 54.

(There was a poignant sequel. Foss's excellent typist, Wanee Rofe, kept in touch with his wife, Joan, throughout her long widowhood. Wanee took early retirement in 1973 and lived in a small house she had built in Tinakori Road, improbably opposite the Western Park hotel, now the Shepherds Arms. When Joan became confined to a nursing home in Karori, Wanee went to visit her every week, not taking the bus, as she might easily have done, but, as if on some medieval pilgrimage, walking, in her advancing years, up the increasingly steep hill to Ranui, the nursing home in Braithwaite Street, Karori. She would take yellow roses and other treasures from her tiny garden. These weekly visits continued well past the time when Joan could recognise her.)

I flew with Foss to New York in September 1949, he to be deputy to Carl Berendsen in the delegation to the United Nations General Assembly. I was joining the delegation, too, then remaining in New York on a posting. On the way, we stopped in Hawaii and stayed overnight at a hotel on Waikiki Breach. We swam there together before breakfast in the morning – disdainfully agreeing it wasn't nearly as good as many beaches in New Zealand. The next night we stopped in San Francisco. Such was the pattern of flights at that time. Then on to New York.

The next day, I think it was, I met Carl Berendsen at lunch with Foss and, to my dismay, found myself the latest and currently the most grievous on his long list of grievances with Wellington. They hadn't consulted him, he snarled, about my appointment to his staff. He was right with that fact. But was he justified in making it into a complaint? Wellington could well have wondered why on earth he needed to be consulted about the appointment of a lowly third secretary who was simply replacing another third secretary[4] who had come to the end of her term. On reflection, 60 years later, I wonder if it was his duodenal ulcers talking. It could be added though, that in those days the posting of a third secretary – the posting of anyone in fact – required the specific approval and the signature of the Minister of External Affairs. At that time I suppose there were only about six or seven postings in a year. In my case, the Minister's approval was given ten days before I departed. My wife followed a little later by sea.

---

[4] This was Helen Hampton (1921–71) who later became New Zealand Ambassador to the office of the United Nations and other international organisations in Geneva where she died, aged 50, after a short illness.

II. STRANGERS AND JOURNEYS

The first international conference I attended was in 1948, 29 November to 11 December. This was a meeting of the Economic Commission for Asia and the Far East (Ecafe), held at Lapstone, a small town in the Blue (so-called) Mountains of New South Wales, Australia. The Commission had been established in 1947 to devise ways of helping in the reconstruction of the region in the aftermath of war.

There was a continuing problem of who were to be members or associate members of the Commission. 'Associate members' were those not fully independent. At this time, 'decolonisation', in the modern era, had only just begun. The United Kingdom had granted independence to Burma, India, Pakistan and Ceylon (later called Sri Lanka) in the previous three years. The Netherlands (in the Netherlands East Indies which became Indonesia) and France (in Cambodia, Laos and Vietnam) lagged well behind.

At Lapstone the Commission considered once more the representation of the Netherlands East Indies. This had been hotly debated at the very first meeting of the Commission but no decision had been made, either then or at subsequent meetings. It had simply been left up in the air. At Lapstone the issue was more or less settled by a New Zealand resolution which proposed that "the Republic of Indonesia" – the increasingly large part of the country in which the Indonesians had asserted their authority in a long and bitter civil war – "and the rest of Indonesia" – meaning the area still under Dutch control – should both be admitted as associate members. This was accepted by eight votes to two (the Netherlands and the United States). The Netherlands delegation then promptly walked out – and stayed out, as I recall, for seven years.

The New Zealand delegation at Lapstone was led by Brigadier Les Hunt (1890–1989) (affectionately known as 'the Brig') with Treasury official Bert McGregor (known as 'Mac' or 'Wee McGregor') listed as alternate and, in the lowest possible ranking, I was adviser. The Brig was a rather remarkable man and an extremely good leader of the delegation. He had joined the regular army in 1905 and been badly wounded at Gallipoli. Indeed, as a result of that wound, he lost one lung. He nevertheless lived a long, happy and useful life. This included active military service in the Pacific in World War II. He died on his 99th birthday. As I encountered him, he was conviviality itself, a forceful, effective speaker in the Commission, quick-witted and a joy to be with.

On the bumpy, eight-hour seaplane flight from Auckland to Sydney he studied the brief while Mac and I drafted a short speech for him to make on every item of the agenda. (The Brig had looked at me hard and grinned,

"You don't want to waste your nights in Australia writing speeches, laddie.") Having previously been at meetings of the Commission in Baguio (The Philippines) and Ootacamund (India), he was well known and liked by many of the other representatives and members of the Secretariat – although some of them raised their eyebrows a little when he took egalitarianism so far as to include a few of the hotel chambermaids among his guests at a cocktail party.

The meeting at Lapstone was quickly followed by another meeting, this time of Ecafe's Committee of the Whole, held in Bangkok from 28 March to 5 April 1949. Wee McGregor was then the delegate and I was adviser. These two meetings considered a wide range of issues, some organisational, others about trade, industrial development, technical assistance, flood control and so on. The reports of the New Zealand delegation recorded all this earnestly – and, to the modern eye, quaintly, being typed double-spaced on foolscap. But these reports say not a word about the things which have remained in my mind, especially about the meeting in Bangkok.

First, there were the journeys. To get to Lapstone, we began by flying from Wellington to Auckland. In Auckland, we stayed overnight at the Railway Hotel and in the morning sauntered down to Mechanics Bay, a few minutes away, carrying our own baggage. This was where the seaplane was docked, by a ramp. It was a 30-seater, with two seats on either side of the aisle, arranged in foursomes with a table fixed in place between the seats – perfect for playing cards, as some passengers did.

One boarded the seaplane with the same pleasurable sense of anticipation as arriving at a party in a private home. And there were about the same number of people. But the airline officials (TEAL – Tasman Empire Airways Limited) were fussy about the load they were about to fly. Not only was every piece of baggage put on the scales, so were the passengers themselves. The airline was obliged to consider the limited load-carrying capacity of these planes. A flight from Sydney to Auckland a few months previously had turned back when one of the engines failed. To make sure they would get there – now flying into a head wind – all the baggage was jettisoned at sea.

The seating in these planes was, in effect, all first class – the seats wide and comfortable, with ample leg room. And the food was excellent. Having left from Mechanics Bay, close to the heart of the city, the plane landed in Rose Bay, about five minutes by car from the heart of Sydney. We stayed overnight at the Australia Hotel, then the best in the city, and my room cost ten shillings and sixpence.

A few months later, there was the journey to Bangkok. On the first day, we flew from Wellington to Auckland, the second to Sydney, as we had on the way to Lapstone. Then, on the third day, we went on to Darwin, the fourth to Singapore and the fifth to Bangkok. In other words, it took five days for a journey which can now be done in a day. It is now a much smoother flight, flying at a much higher altitude, above the turbulence. But, when flying in smaller planes at a lower altitude, you saw a lot more of what you were flying over. Nowadays, you scarcely see anything except in the ten minutes or so after take-off and before landing. (As I discovered in October 1967, there is no better way to see Mt Everest than to fly by slowly, watching from the cockpit of an RNZAF Bristol Freighter – which the Air Force lads described as "thirty thousand rivets flying in formation".)

Darwin provided my first experience of the all-enveloping, stifling heat of the tropics. (On the return journey, there was a memorable encounter with a dinkum Aussie Customs official in Darwin. While he searched assiduously through the soiled clothes in my suitcase, I pointed out, diffidently, that I had a diplomatic passport. He wasn't deterred for a single moment. "Diplomats!" he snorted. "They're the worst of the lot!" I suppose his superiors eventually caught up with him and ticked him off but, in the years which followed, I thought fondly of him when I came to see how right he had been when I heard diplomatic colleagues being impossibly precious about wine or some table-seating arrangement.)

To the tropical heat, Singapore added the smell of Asia – or, rather, the stench of it in such places as the very large monsoon drains where every kind of rubbish was discarded and rotted till washed out to sea by the next heavy rain. We stayed overnight at Raffles hotel. There were very few other hotels in Singapore at that time and the bedrooms were quite ordinary. But the service in the dining room was something else. Indeed, to young New Zealand eyes, it was downright astonishing. For every person at dinner there was a turbaned waiter hovering to attend to the diner's slightest wish. None of this modern nonsense of trying to catch the waiter's eye! He was paid to catch your eye! At the end of the meal I reached in my pocket for a packet of cigarettes and a waiter was instantly at my side, holding the flame of a cigarette lighter – or perhaps it was just a lit match – before I had time to get a cigarette out of the packet.

In Bangkok we stayed at the Rotanakosindr hotel, a hotel so new that there hadn't been time – or perhaps there just hadn't been enough money – to put in the lifts. So we spent a good deal of our time walking up and down the stairs to our room on the fifth floor. Nor was there any running water. Instead, the bathroom recess had a very large earthenware crock of water – which, in the tropical heat, soon became tepid – which you ladled over your sweaty body. As at Lapstone, Mac and I shared a twin-bedded room. In Bangkok, the beds were equipped with mosquito nets and, during the night, we heard the little blighters buzzing with irritation at their inability to intrude.

In the Beginning

After checking into our room we wandered downstairs and paused at the entrance where several young trishaw-riders were gathered, waiting for customers. One of the riders said, with a beaming smile, "Dancing girls?" Mac, who had been reading the tourist literature, cottoned on immediately. "Oh," he said, "you mean classical dancing?" The trishaw-rider beamed even more widely. So off he went with him to a large hall where the trishaw man indicated he would wait and take us back to the hotel. We went into a large hall packed with men and were ushered to the very middle of the front row, the only white faces in that crowd of several hundred. 'Classical dancing' my foot! In the performance which followed, the climax came when an evil-looking ringmaster brought on three stark-naked girls and put them through their paces. There was not the faintest glimmer of a smile from any of them. They were surely drugged. Even worse followed. The ringmaster invited Mac and me to participate in his proceedings by fondling the girls. We recoiled in utter revulsion, both muttering that we had to get out of the wretched place as quickly as possibly. The trishaw man was waiting for us, smiling more broadly than ever. Mac wagged his finger at him sternly and, on the way back to the hotel, gave him a piece of his Presbyterian mind, notwithstanding that the trishaw man didn't understand a word he was saying.

In the fullness of time we saw more than enough classical Thai dancing, as well as Thai kick-boxing. On the Sunday, the Thai Government took us all to Ayutthaya, the country's ancient capital, going north by train and back by river. And somewhere in Bangkok – I think in a public park – there was a flimsily built structure, several stories high, which, we were told, was to be the funeral pyre of the recently assassinated King. (When I came to check on these facts, I found a fascinating and very strange story. King Ananda Mahidol, aged 21, was murdered in his bedroom at the Palace in Bangkok on 9 June, 1946. The cremation, however, was not until 30 March, 1950. And not until 17 February, 1955, were the assassins – the late King's private secretary and two royal pages – executed.[5])

There was a distinctly New Zealand touch to the arrangements made for us in going to Bangkok. For such visits to the tropics, the Department of Island Territories held a small stock of suits made of white drill fabric, to be worn on formal occasions. These suits were in two sizes – too big and too small.

The following weekend, we went on an expedition organised by the British Embassy in Bangkok, flying to Siem Reap, in northern Cambodia, on a scheduled commercial flight, to see the nearby ruins at Angkor Wat, dating mysteriously from several centuries earlier and one of the wonders of the world. We stayed, I think, at the Grand Hotel in Siem Reap and

---

[5] Details may be found in *The Devil's Discus*, by Rayne Kruger, published by Cassell, London, 1964.

the thing I remember is the excellence of the breakfast, most notably the coffee – the first real coffee I had ever tasted, New Zealanders at that time having only 'essence of coffee and chicory' – and the freshly baked little loaf of bread – one was enough for most people, especially when served in the cool part of the day.

We travelled from the hotel in Siem Reap to the ruins at Angkor Wat by minivan with a jeep-load of armed soldiers going ahead of us and another jeep-load bringing up the rear. Actually, the most dangerous part of this little expedition was in flying back to Bangkok through a thunderstorm, in torrential rain with flashes of lightning every few minutes. I have never been so terrified.

* * * * *

I first met Sir Carl Berendsen early in 1948 when he was in Wellington on home leave. If I remember correctly, the travel component of this leave was paid by the United Nations as a means of ensuring that representatives 'permanently' at the United Nations got home occasionally to keep in personal touch with their governments. At that time, early in 1948, Churchill had just coined the expression 'the Iron Curtain', to describe the notional barrier between the Soviet bloc and the West. And Senator Joe McCarthy had not yet got into his stride in campaigning against alleged communists in the American State Department and almost everywhere else. Sir Carl was at the forefront of such thinking. In talking to the External Affairs staff in Wellington, he spoke in the same style as I later heard him use in speaking from the rostrum at the United Nations General Assembly – dogmatic, pugnacious, colourful – and concluding, in that rasping voice of his, with a peroration that sounds like a battle cry: the Russians were out to take over the world; only a bloody fool couldn't see that.

Then John Scott (1920–) promptly put the first question. He began, with a twinkle in his eye, "Sir, speaking as a bloody fool …" This incensed Sir Carl. The rest of us burst into hearty laughter which made Sir Carl almost apoplectic. Sir Carl was not to know – I don't think any of us did at the time, and anyway, it really wasn't relevant – that John Scott, who'd been in the navy during the war, had been on the Murmansk Run, as it was called, taking armaments to our wartime allies, the Russians. This was arguably the most dangerous of naval assignments in World War II. John Scott's question was not just a cry from the heart – as if protesting at the idiocy of contemplating another world war when we'd only just finished the last one. It stemmed from the optimism of the early post-war years and the healthy scepticism which came to permeate External Affairs, questioning

In the Beginning

every assertion and fact. Surely it was possible to overcome almost any problem in international relations, no matter how deep-rooted and serious the difficulties might be?

I saw much more of Sir Carl when I was posted to New York in September 1949; I then found him a more alarming character than any I've come across, before or since. And I tried to keep out of his way. Fat chance! For three months of the year, while the United Nations General Assembly was taking place, we drove together every workday to meetings at Lake Success or Flushing Meadow on Long Island, where all United Nations meetings were held before permanent United Nations buildings were constructed in Manhattan. So there I was, with three or four others, cooped up in a car with Sir Carl, while he held court for an hour at a time – and that was just one way.

Whenever he came to New York from Washington, which was usually by train, he expected to be met. He never came into the office. He expected the office to go to him. And it did. He established his lair in the Waldorf-Astoria Hotel – the best in the city – where he and his wife, his beloved Nellie, took a maisonette – a suite with a small galley kitchen. (The government paid for the accommodation and there was a set allowance, on a reasonably generous scale, for meals. By making maximum use of the kitchen in their maisonette, the Berendsens saved money. The rest of us delighted in the hundreds of good, reasonably priced restaurants in New York.)

Sir Carl set unrivalled standards: of commanding attention in the United Nations, with his histrionic performances and his brusqueness in chairing a committee (when he once chaired the disputatious Trusteeship Committee, it finished its work in record time); of distinguishing the wood from the trees and getting priorities right (his wood and his priorities); of expeditious report-writing: woe betide any of us who failed to meet his standing instruction that all report-writing, on a General Assembly lasting three months, was to be completed three days after the Assembly ended; of lucidity, punctuality ("When I say to come at nine o'clock, I mean five to"), parsimony and mordant wit. When Charles Craw went off to a Non-Self-Governing Territories meeting in Geneva in 1950, Sir Carl's parting shot was: "Well, just remember, whatever you do, it will be wrong!" – by which he meant it would be Wellington, not Sir Carl, finding fault.

At the outbreak of the Korean War in 1950, Sir Carl went straight into the State Department and asked, "What can we do to help?" Other ambassadors in Washington waited until they had conferred with their home governments. Not Sir Carl. Soon after the outbreak of the Korean War, I went to the Waldorf-Astoria with a draft telegram about the war. Sir Carl crouched over the draft, as intent as any lion on its prey, straining to get every element of the argument, every word and comma, right.

(Sir Carl's powers of intense concentration are illustrated by a story which McIntosh was fond of telling. When working as Carl's deputy in Wellington, Mac was conferring with him one day when they were interrupted by a phone call to say that Mac's son, James, had been born (1942). As Mac told it, Carl sprang to his feet, shook Mac's hand and said, "Congratulations. I'm sure it's the most beautiful baby in the world. Now let's get on with our work!") On this occasion, Lady Berendsen was having one of her quite frequent fluttering days, interrupting his train of thought. At last, Sir Carl could stand it no longer and roared, "For Christ's sake, Nellie, get out to the kitchen where you belong!" She forgave him as often as it was relevant. And they bickered happily ever after.

About once a month, at this time, when Wellington had once again exhausted his patience, he dictated an angry telegram saying, in effect, that, if the government did not come to heel, he would resign and pursue the issue publicly. None of these telegrams was ever sent, although Frank Corner once courageously put it to him, "But what would actually happen if you resigned and went public? It would hit the headlines in New Zealand for a couple of days but then that would be the end of it. Some other issue would take over the headlines." Sir Carl was unusually quiet, taken aback by this reality.

(Only very rarely did anyone dare to confront Sir Carl like this. But Bob Harriot, his dinkum Aussie driver in Canberra did, in a rather spectacular manner, when Sir Carl was there as New Zealand's first High Commissioner in Australia (1943–4), before being appointed as Ambassador in Washington. Both the Berendsens were highly practised and persistent back-seat drivers. Once, when going across the Sydney Harbour Bridge and running a little late for an appointment on the North Shore, the Berendsens pointed out opportunities for Bob to change lanes and make up a little time. Finally, the back-seat bombardment became too much. Bob stopped the car in the middle of Sydney Harbour Bridge and, as every driver behind them hooted disapproval of this, Bob took it a stage further. He got out of the car, tossed the car keys into the back seat and yelled, "Drive the bloody car yourselves!" As I came to know him later, Bob was an excellent driver and a splendid fellow. He took great delight in telling this story of how he had once brought the New Zealand High Commissioner to heel. It seemed to have been the high point of his career. He remained with the High Commission for about 20 years.)

About once a month, Sir Carl would reduce one of the girls in the embassy in Washington or the office in New York to tears (the stenographers then doubled as communications officers in every post except London). And when his fiery outbursts or scorching sarcasm provoked these tears,

In the Beginning

Sir Carl apologised for a month – which was worse. Shortly after the former Prime Minister, Peter Fraser, died (12 December 1950), Moira Barraclough reported to him, "Excuse me, sir. There's a letter come in for Mr Fraser. What shall I do with it?" Sir Carl blinked at her and snarled, "Send it on, girl! Send it on!" Then, after a moment's pause, he added, "And you'd better send it airmail!" (This may not sound very upsetting but remember he barked rather than talked and in a loud, rasping voice.) There were times when these girls were sorely tempted to 'make a mistake' and send on one of his tempestuous draft telegrams threatening to resign. Although it fell well short of this ambition, they nevertheless took a rather fiendish delight in putting his considerable volume of fanmail in a file labelled Odds and Sods. When he discovered this, he was, in fact, amused. Oh yes, he was human after all. This became much more evident in 1950 when the unthinkable happened, twice. Charles Craw's infant son, Billy, died with devastating suddenness, of meningitis, and at the funeral service Sir Carl wept.

Sir Carl could do a cocktail party in ten minutes. So loudly did he talk, so extravagantly did he flatter ("You look absolutely exquisite tonight, my dear – but then you always do! And that was a marvellous speech of your husband's this morning! Absolutely brilliant!"), so sardonic was his humour, so incontrovertible his opinions, that everyone in the room knew he was there, whether they met him that evening or not. And they felt better for it, not least when he left. In leaving, after the prescribed ten minutes, he would turn his back on the cocktail party and turn to his dear Nellie, whispering, "The silly bastards!" And Sir Carl whispered about as softly as a back-country musterer bawls at his dog on the next hill. Well, all that's a bit of an exaggeration – but not much.

When in New York, he and Nellie went regularly to newsreel cinemas which ran continuously, with a programme lasting an hour or so and constantly updated. And he watched a lot of television. He became an ardent, very knowledgeable, fan of American baseball. His keen interest in sport may help to explain why his speeches had a good deal of the racy, colourful, flamboyant style of American sports journalists rather than the more measured, less colourful style typical of New Zealanders.

I last saw Sir Carl at a lunch in Wellington in about 1971. I remarked then that it was a pity his memoirs had never been published.[6] (I have never read these memoirs but they were exceedingly long and every word devotedly typed by Nellie who, when young, had been a stenographer.) "Ah," he said, philosophically (at last), "they were too long and too hot for any publisher

---

[6] These memoirs were finally published, in greatly abbreviated form, as *Mr Ambassador: Memoirs of Sir Carl Berendsen*, edited by Hugh Templeton (VUP) in 2009, 35 years after Sir Carl's death and well over 50 years after the memoirs had been written.

to handle." "Well," I reflected, "as to the men you may have libelled, if that's what you mean by 'hot', surely most of them must now be dead and the dead can't be libelled." "Most of them dead now, eh?" he chuckled. "That's a nice thought." He himself died, in Dunedin, in 1973, aged 83.

* * * * *

During General Assemblies of the United Nations, the office hired a car with a driver named Max Gold. He hailed from the Bronx and belonged to that large, useful and proud class of New Yorkers who could get it for you wholesale, no matter what it was. In his more modest way, Max was almost as colourful as Sir Carl. Incidentally, he was completely and understandably mystified by the process which had made 'Mr Berendsen' into 'Sir Carl' and could not bring himself to be as familiar as this with such an obviously important man. Max always insisted on calling him 'Mr Sir Carl'.

In September, 1950, Max took me to La Guardia airport to meet Dick Collins (1921–2007), who was arriving from New Zealand for the General Assembly. Max drove up to the gate leading on to the tarmac at the airport. By chance, the gate – a high gate of hurricane wire, in a fence of similar construction – was open, although a guard was standing by, ready to shut it. Max hissed at me, "Just watch this!" and drove straight through the gateway on to the tarmac. As he did so he shouted at the startled guard, "Prime Minister of New Zealand!" What this was supposed to mean I haven't the faintest idea. But in this way, a third secretary – the lowest form of diplomatic life and now, I think, an extinct species – met another third secretary. Which indicates a bygone simplicity. There were few planes about, even in New York, 60 years ago and considerations of security were very limited.

What else stood out in New York at that time? First and foremost it was a shopper's paradise. New Zealand in 1949 was plagued with all sorts of shortages attributable to the war but New York seemed completely unaffected by it. From our office on the 60th floor – let me repeat that, the 60th floor – of the Empire State Building, we could see ant-like looking people going into Macy's, the world's largest department store, and emerge, like ants in real life, carrying parcels which appeared to be several times their body weight. Womenfolk fresh from New Zealand could spend a whole day there, "Just looking, thank you."

Skyscrapers were new in the world. The height of them and the speed of the express elevators – as Americans called their lifts – were real gobsmackers. The only time the height troubled me was when the window cleaners came round. They wore a wide, strong-looking belt with a clip on each side.

In the Beginning

When the cleaner had finished doing the window on the inside, he pushed up the bottom half of the window, which was moveable. Then he stood on the window sill, facing inwards, while simultaneously attaching the clips on his belt to metal eyelets embedded, at waist height, on either side of the window, on the exterior wall. Thus attached to the building, he leant backwards over the city far below. Mind you, I cannot be sure of the details of how all this was done because, before the process had been completed, I had to leave the room and loiter in the toilet for a few minutes, until the window cleaner had completed his task. (Actually, it wasn't called the men's toilet but the 'executive men's washroom' and we were each issued with a key to it.)

Another thing about the Empire State Building I cannot forget was that every Friday a large crowd of Irish Americans staged a vehement anti-British demonstration, with many placards and much shouting of slogans, at the Fifth Avenue entrance to the building, where the British Consulate-General was quartered. It was better to use another entrance at such times.

The Empire State Building was not air-conditioned; it had been completed in 1931, before air-conditioning became common. In mid-summer it was like working in an oven. Air conditioning was installed in the building after our time.

South Pacific was the current hit on Broadway in 1949–50 and, above the incessant noise of New York traffic, music from the show drifted marvellously, at high volume, from every gramophone-record shop in the city – "Bali Ha'i", "I'm gonna wash that man right out of my hair". We saw *South Pacific* with the original cast (Ezio Pinza and Mary Martin) after our first baby, Trudy, was born in February 1950. Such hit shows were booked out months in advance and it was touch-and-go whether the arrival of our second baby, in June, 1951, would interfere with our booking for *The King and I* (Yul Brynner and Gertrude Lawrence). In the event, the family planning was good. These musicals were immensely popular, not least with New Zealanders. George Laking went seven times to see Carol Channing in *Gentlemen Prefer Blondes*.

On arriving in New York, we were warned about all sorts of things. Top of the list was, "Don't go into Harlem," – the Negro quarter. The term 'Afro-American' had not yet been coined. The very idea that it could be dangerous to venture into this large part of the city seemed horrendous, and the big-city wariness of strangers was extraordinary. All eye contact was avoided in the street and, above all, in the subway. We didn't know whether to worry or be pleased that if, by some appalling mischance, one of our babies decided to arrive ahead of schedule and in the subway, no one, it seemed, would take any notice. No such calamity occurred and, in due course we were confronted with another fact of American life which we'd been warned about: when my wife came to, after each of the babies had been born, there, on the locker beside her bed, in one case, and on the pillow by her head, in the other case, was the hospital bill, or, to be precise, the balance of the hospital bill, a substantial part having already been paid in advance, which I was expected to pay on the way out.

Charles Craw showed me the ropes when I first arrived in New York: where and how to catch the subway, where our office (the New Zealand Mission to the United Nations) was and the separate New Zealand Consulate-General were, as well as the United Nations buildings at Lake Success and Flushing. When we came to the cavernous arena at Flushing Meadow where the United Nations General Assembly met in plenary session, with enough seating for all members of all delegation – although, in those days, there were only 56 member nations, compared with 192 in 2009 – I could scarcely believe my eyes when so many well known world leaders came drifting in at the beginning of a session. With a disdainful wave of his hand, Charles dismissed them all: "A pack of professional bastards!" On another occasion he declared: "When you've been in the diplomatic game long enough, you'll realise that everybody else is mad."

Shortly afterwards, it became my turn to show the ropes to an even newer arrival, Arnold Reedy. Apart from Sir Carl, ensconced in his lair in the Waldorf-Astoria, the New Zealand delegation stayed at Essex House, a hotel fronting on to Central Park. For a cheap and quick breakfast we went out the back entrance and across the street to the Carnegie Hall drugstore where the attendants at the food bar worked at amazing speed and used expressions which we were obliged to learn quickly to keep up with the play. "Sunny-side up," meant an egg fried only on one side. "Easy-over" meant an egg fried on both sides but not much. Customers sat on high stools at the counter where the attendants – always men – and I think Americans, called them short-order cooks, prepared the basic range of food, meanwhile exchanging banter with each other and the customers, many of whom were obviously regulars. It was fast food with a continuous, interactive floor show.

The conversation on my first morning there with Arnold went something like this:

"Eggs, mister?"

"Yes, please. Boiled."

"One or two?"

"Four."

"Oh, come off it, buster. I haven't got time for bad jokes."

"Now, listen to me, mate. My name's not Buster and when I say I want four boiled eggs, that's what I bloody well mean!"

"But *nobody* has *four* boiled eggs for breakfast!"

"Well, you've just met somebody who does! What's the matter with you, mate? Think I can't pay for four bloody eggs?"

So Arnold got his four boiled eggs, although not before his jaw dropped mightily when he saw the man scoop the eggs out of their shells and put them in an egg cup several times the size of a proper, New Zealand, egg cup. This deprived Arnold of the pleasure of opening his eggs, one by one, ensuring that the eggs didn't get cold. He muttered about all this as he ate them. Then he had lashings of toast and marmalade, followed by coffee after I'd told him what Americans did with tea. Then, as soon as we got out to Lake Success, Arnold made a beeline for the cafeteria and discovered they didn't have scones or pikelets like we had with a proper, New Zealand, morning tea. However, they had something he hadn't encountered before: Danish pastries. From there on he had two large pastries every morning. For lunch we went back to the cafeteria, which was blissfully self-service, so Arnold could help himself to as much as he liked for his three-course meal. Then, after Sir Carl had screeched, "I'll not have that man going to sleep behind the New Zealand nameplate in any meeting that's being televised!", arrangements were made for Arnold to have a siesta every day after lunch in the Red Cross Emergency Room. It was my job to rouse him just before the afternoon meetings began at three.

In a way, Arnold had been my idea and I was obliged to see it through which I suppose was fair enough. This arose because, at the meeting of the Economic Commission for Asia and the Far East held in December 1948, the Russians had launched a vicious, entirely unexpected and ill-founded attack on New Zealand for mistreating the Maoris. This accusation was rebutted swiftly enough because the Russians had used statistics from the turn of the century. Following this incident, the delegation's report (which I drafted) included the suggestion that the delegation to some future United Nations meeting include a Maori. This was earnestly questioned by the traditionalists in External Affairs – "A specimen Maori?" – but it appealed to the Prime Minister, Peter Fraser. So here now, in New York, was Arnold Reedy, a Maori from the backblocks of the East Cape, a farmer, kaumatua and aspiring politician. At the outbreak of war in 1939, he had enlisted immediately and had been a foundation officer of the Maori Battalion. He served in Greece and Crete, was captured in Crete and spent the next four years as a prisoner of war.

In 1949, when Arnold was 46, he was a member of the Labour Party and had come to the Prime Minister's favourable notice. Subsequently, he fell out with the Labour Party and unsuccessfully contested the Eastern Maori seat for Social Credit in 1957 and 1960 and for the National Party in 1963, 1966 and 1967. In short, he deserved top marks for trying, but never became a Member of Parliament. His surname, Reedy, came from an Irish grandfather who had married a Maori. He was the oldest of ten children and himself fathered ten children, a devout Anglican who firmly believed that children were the gift of God and nothing should interfere with this natural order of things. On his first night at Essex House in New York, when Arnold came across a cache of condoms in his bedside table, left behind by some previous occupant, Arnold was deeply shocked, as if he had arrived in Sin City.

During the weeks I knew him in New York, I became very fond of Arnold as a man of absolute integrity, old-fashioned values, a countryman at heart. And I like to think that we got on well. But there was one occasion when, for a few minutes, he could have thrown me to the wolves. The United Nations Third Committee was considering, clause by clause, a draft Convention on Traffic in Women and Children. Arnold, as delegate, sat in the front seat, behind the New Zealand nameplate and I sat behind him as adviser. At one point, after I'd advised him to vote against some particular wording, Arnold found to his dismay and extreme irritation, that he was the only one who had voted in this way. He turned round and began giving me a piece of his mind. While he was still at this, one of Eleanor Roosevelt's large phalanx of advisers came round and asked why the New Zealand delegation had voted in the way it had. I explained, over Arnold's deprecatory asides. A few minutes later, to my surprise and Arnold's astonishment, Eleanor Roosevelt intervened in the formal discussion to raise a point of order. She said she'd misunderstood the point at issue in the vote that had just been taken and proposed that the vote be taken again – a rare occurrence. First, there had to be a two-thirds majority in favour of having another go, before the vote could be taken again. Eleanor Roosevelt, a highly effective and widely respected representative, steered it all through. And perhaps, at that moment, Arnold and I became friends for life, although we never met again after those few weeks together in New York.

One Saturday, Eleanor Roosevelt invited two people from each of the 56 delegations on the Third Committee for lunch at the Roosevelt country home, near Poughkeepsie, about two hours' drive from New York City. The home was on a large, enchantingly beautiful site, sloping down to the Hudson River. The late President was buried there, with his full name and dates of birth and death inscribed on the marble slab on the grave. But it didn't stop there. Dear Eleanor's full name and date of birth were inscribed there, too, as if to remind her, every time she passed by, that this was where her future lay. Pretty crass, we thought. Then there was the lunch itself. Not to put too fine a point on it, there simply wasn't enough food to go round.

And Arnold compared that very unfavourably indeed with hospitality in Ruatoria. "And it's not as if she had to do any of the cooking herself!"

After my wife arrived in New York and we subsequently moved into an apartment, I didn't see nearly as much of Arnold. But at some point, well before the Assembly ended, Arnold threw down the gauntlet. He'd had enough, more than enough, of the United Nations and New York. He just wanted to go home. He *had* to go home. He was in tears. He missed his family too much. Perhaps this had something to do with his incarceration for those four long years during the war. Anxious telegrams were exchanged with Wellington. Arnold went back to New Zealand well ahead of schedule and I feel sure he never left his country again.

* * * * *

Early in November 1949 we moved into the apartment in the United Nations complex known as Parkway Village. This was near Jamaica, on Long Island, about 20 miles out of New York City and an hour's journey from our office by subway and connecting bus. It was close to Lake Success where the United Nations Secretariat was located and most United Nations meetings were held, before permanent quarters were constructed in Manhattan.

In Parkway Village we quickly found how agreeable it was to become detribalised – to succumb to the American way of life. Indeed, it was a way of life which in some respects was to be warmly embraced. It wasn't any trouble at all, for instance, to abandon the widely practised, tribal, New Zealand custom of home-brewing once you'd encountered the little man from a liquor agency who, once you'd signed up, came knocking on the door every couple of weeks or so. He didn't leave a crate of beer on your doorstep where it could easily be nicked but carried it into your apartment, put it in the appropriate cupboard and took away the empties in another crate. The beer, moreover, was of a light, lager kind and came in highly convenient small bottles which were not yet used in New Zealand. Better still, our apartment had a fridge, a rarity in New Zealand homes in 1949, and it didn't take any time at all to concede that an ice-cold Budweiser ("the beer that made Milwaukee famous," as their advertising jingle said) was better – far better – than tepid home brew.

In February 1950, we discovered 'the diaper service', unheard of in New Zealand, which led to another happy stride down the road to detribalisation. It meant casting aside the traditional New Zealand practice of washing nappies at home, putting them outside on the clothes line to dry, bringing them in, ironing them and then putting them in a warm cupboard to air. (Disposable nappies had not yet been invented.) For every new client, the American diaper service began when a little man delivered a stock of nappies, a pail with a lid and a bottle of disinfectant. From then on, all you had to do was rinse off the worst bits from soiled nappies, throw them in the pail, sprinkle them with disinfectant and put the lid on the pail. On his regular round, the little man followed much the same procedure as the Budweiser man: he knocked on the door, came into the apartment and restocked with a supply of clean nappies. He took away the soiled nappies and left a replacement pail.

Another attraction of the American way of life was to find that the bathroom in our apartment had not only a bath but also a separate shower unit, a rarity in any New Zealand home in 1949. There were also large, built-in wardrobes. Few, if any homes built in New Zealand before World War II included this useful arrangement. But perhaps the most attractive thing about the American way of life, as it impinged on our personal lives, was the bliss of central heating in winter. In Parkway Village the heat was pumped in from a central plant and there was no thermostatic control in the apartment. To lower the temperature, we had to open the double-hung windows a little. It was jokingly said that, in winter, other people could always tell which apartments were occupied by New Zealanders, as their windows were always ajar.

Just across the road from us was a supermarket, an institution which had not yet arrived in New Zealand. Moreover, whereas from 1920 to 1933 the United States had laboured under Prohibition, which prevented, or was supposed to prevent, the manufacture or sale of liquor, it was now open slather. American retail trading hours were also extraordinarily liberal by New Zealand standards. In New York, shops had their busiest day of the week on a Saturday, whereas no New Zealand shops were allowed to open on a Saturday apart from the corner dairy, and that was restricted to a small range of goods. American newspapers had a Sunday edition, and there was nothing like that in New Zealand. The Sunday edition of *The New York Times* was the biggest and best of the week: so full of good reading it could occupy a whole day.

One Sunday in 1950 I wandered across the street to get the paper at the drugstore, a distance of no more than 50 yards. On the way, a convertible car went by with the hood down and four or five attractive young ladies on board. When they saw me in shorts, which were commonly worn by men in summer in New Zealand, these American lasses startled me by bursting into a hearty chorus of wolf whistles. How about that! I hadn't realised that girls knew how to wolf whistle! It was, in fact, a sharp rebuff. By American standards, it was unacceptable to appear publicly in shorts like this, even in a quiet suburban neighbourhood. Thereafter, I always changed into slacks before venturing out. It was a rather curious difference between American and British (including New Zealand) habits, and the difference continues to exist. British, Australian and New Zealand servicemen have long worn shorts in summer or in the tropics, even in action in wartime. American servicemen, never.

Our apartment wasn't big. On the contrary, it was considerably smaller then the average New Zealand home. We had a double bedroom and a small single bedroom, a good-sized living room with a dining alcove, a kitchen and a bathroom. And that was it. Apart from the fridge and a stove, the apartment was unfurnished. For this, we paid US$117 a month. In 1949 the New Zealand pound was worth about four American dollars. By the time we went to New York all married staff posted to the New Zealand Mission to the United Nations took all their basic furniture with them – sofas, armchairs, beds, the lot.

If this left you short of a few things, you could readily find just what you needed, at a cost much less than you expected, in Macy's bargain basement. A collapsible (easily shipped) formica-topped table, with an extension leaf and four matching chairs – more stylish than anything available in New Zealand – cost US$100 and is still in use in Wellington. So is a small frying pan which M went out and bought impetuously at the hardware store across the street from Parkway Village. She bought this because she couldn't wait till our own things from New Zealand were unpacked, before getting to work on the more important job of cooking the first dinner in our new home. And it was a special occasion not just on that account: it also marked our second wedding anniversary. We were looking forward to a proper, New Zealand-style meal of home-cooked food after many weeks eating out or, in M's case, of eating for most of that time on board the *Aorangi*, crossing from Auckland to Vancouver and then by train to New York.[7] For our special dinner, M bought mutton chops. This was something which neither of us had found on any menu between Auckland and Parkway Village. M came back from her little shopping expedition thoroughly disconcerted. Contrary to expectations in New Zealand, the chops were not just expensive, they cost far more than the frying pan.

---

[7] Also on that sailing was Dr Val Armstrong, on his way to become Scientific Liaison Officer at the New Zealand Embassy in Washington. He was accompanied by his wife and, as M recorded in her diary, "two lovely kids, an 'Alice in Wonderland' girl of five and an absolute pet of a little boy aged ten months". This little boy emerged as Wade Armstrong, New Zealand Ambassador in various parts of the world. Another passenger was Bill Dawson, also on his way, with his wife to join the New Zealand Embassy in Washington where he was to ferret in American archives in the course of his work on New Zealand's war history.

Parkway Village, built in 1947, on 37 acres of rolling parkland, had 685 apartments, of two or three stories, in blocks of about a dozen. These were set out in roughly the laager formation of an encampment of wagons, surrounding an acre or so of lawn where there were young trees and a few sandpits, but no garden of any kind nor any clothes lines. Indeed, the tenancy agreements stated categorically that no washing was to be put up anywhere outside the apartment. Pets of any kind were strictly forbidden.

The New Zealanders in Parkway Village were a close-knit lot, baby-sitting for each other and partying together. The place was teeming with young children. This was the time of the post-war baby boom and there were enough babies being born in the village to attract an enterprising Karitane nurse to set up shop, as it were. This was Jean Peeper who, to abide by American work permit requirements from which diplomatic employers were exempt, worked exclusively on assignments with United Nations families in the village. It was a multi-national, multi-racial community and Jean was kept busy in jobs in a great variety of households. She was bright and breezy, highly competent and an ardent gossip. Living up to her name, she reported of one household, "Every night, my dear, and with the door wide open!" On another occasion and even more gleefully, "You know, my dear, when they went to Mexico on holiday he sulked all the time because she forgot to pack her contraceptive diaphragm!"

In our office on the 60th floor of the Empire State Building I sat at a desk facing Charles Craw at his. This was the only way that two desks could be fitted into such a small, square room. However, we didn't often have to look at each other at such close quarters, as we were usually away at separate meetings of one kind or another and Charles attended far more meetings than I. In Parkway Village, we were almost as close as we were in the office: our apartments were about 20 yards apart, across the lawn. His wife, Eve, and M dropped in to see each other almost every day and it was Eve who took M to see her gynaecologist on the first visit, introduced her at the hospital, told her about the diaper service and the Budweiser man and warned her about the flirtatious habits of the greengrocer across the street.

Eve and M remained close, lifelong friends, although the friendship was often tested by Eve's habit of invariably running late, up to an hour or more, although in a disarming way, seeming scarcely to notice that she was late. Perhaps the only occasion on which she was ever on time was in taking M to call on Lady Berendsen who shared Sir Carl's fanatical insistence on punctuality. And, just this once, Charles had no doubt insisted on it, too. After taking the bus and then the subway on the hour's journey from Parkway Village into Manhattan, Eve and M actually arrived at the Waldorf-Astoria Hotel *early* and had to wait ten minutes or so before knocking on Lady Berendsen's door.

In the Beginning

Charles was a man of great good humour and highly industrious. He got along exceedingly well with Sir Carl, which not many people did. This meant steering a careful course between 'shushing' and 'pushing' Sir Carl, who had classified all advisers as 'shushers' or 'pushers', just as he declared everyone in Wellington – which, in this context, was never clearly defined – as "either a knave or a fool". Sir Carl never needed much 'pushing' in the United Nations or heeded the 'shushing'. In attending United Nations meetings, Charles always carried an exceptionally large, exceptionally heavy briefcase, crammed with United Nations documents, copies of correspondence with Wellington, books – anything which might come in handy in the debate that day. This capacious briefcase became his trademark. J.V. Wilson once leant over the back of his chair at a United Nations meeting – I think this would have been in Paris in 1948 – and, with only the faintest glimmer of a smile, asked Charles, "Would you have the Magna Carta?"

On one occasion, when Charles was in charge of the office, he became very angry, taking a visiting fireman severely to task for sexually harassing one of the New Zealand girls who worked in the office. He was a New Zealand departmental head, no less, and should have known better. In a flood of tears the girl complained bitterly to Charles. I can still hear his voice, shouting in absolute outrage at a man old enough to be his father, but with the vehemence of a man protecting his own daughter and using language he had probably picked up in the Fleet Air Arm during the war: "For Christ's sake, man, don't shit in your own nest!"

Some years later, there was an equally memorable but entirely different and probably unique occasion. In 1958–61, Charles was *chargé d'affaires* at the New Zealand Embassy in Bangkok. His principal responsibility was to represent New Zealand on the (now defunct) Seato Council. For most of this time, Walter (later Sir Walter) Nash was Prime Minister, as well as Minister of External Affairs, and his views on Seato were equivocal, which may be putting it mildly. But Charles did a brilliant job, keeping within the framework of Nash's instructions and keeping New Zealand on side with Australia and the United States. Their governments took a more earnest view of Seato than Mr Nash, as did our own military people who were represented in force in Bangkok, breathing down Charles' neck. When he returned to Wellington, having travelled from Auckland by overnight train, so many people from External Affairs, led by Mac and Foss Shanahan, trooped over to the station to greet Charles and his family, that, for about half an hour, the department was left almost completely without diplomatic staff. I didn't go myself but so many joined the exodus, I remarked, "Well, someone had better stay to answer the phone!" But I knew that M was going to be at the station, the only departmental wife to be there, to greet Eve and the three young Craw sons.

Bill Sutch was in charge of the office, with the designation Secretary-General of the New Zealand Mission to the United Nations, working under the authority of Sir Carl who was Ambassador in Washington and concurrently Permanent Representative to the United Nations. Bill had been appointed to the job in New York because New Zealand had been elected for a two-year term (1947–9) on the United Nations Economic and Social Council and Bill's qualifications and experience made him pre-eminently suitable.

He lived with his family about 50 yards away from us in Parkway Village. His wife, Shirley, who had been a university lecturer in classics, was not a career woman in New York. Their daughter, Helen, who would have been about three when we arrived in 1949, eventually became a noted economist, working for a substantial part of her career with the International Bank, just as Shirley later had a distinguished career as a lawyer in New Zealand. (Mischievously, I have a fond memory of Helen as a little girl taking such strong exception to Jimmy Thorn – a dinner guest at the Sutches and, at that time, New Zealand High Commissioner in Ottawa, a portly, dignified, extremely pleasant man in his late sixties – that she tipped her dessert bowl of fruit salad over his head.)

I came to know Bill both as boss in the office and neighbourhood friend and I always found him even-tempered, amiable and easy to get along with – far easier than Sir Carl. He was not nearly as far to the left, I thought, as Sir Carl was to the right. On social occasions, Bill loved to toss ideas around and encourage lively discussion, but he never tried to ram ideas down your throat, as Sir Carl did. There was absolutely none of Sir Carl's "If something's 51 percent black and 49 percent white, then, for Christ's sake, its black!" Bill was far more critical of the United States than Sir Carl and I suppose most of us, and a good many Americans, thought there were, things to be justifiably critical about – in American race relations, predatory business practice, distaste for the welfare state, extraordinarily little concern for the underdog. Of course there have been great changes in the United States in the past 60 years. In 1949, it would never have crossed anyone's mind that an Afro-American could become president.

Yes, Bill was a good boss and he and Shirley became good, kind friends. He was an extremely effective participant in United Nations meetings, able to speak without notes, fluently, persuasively and, if need be, at length. Indeed, if I remember correctly, he rarely, if ever, spoke from, that is, read, a prepared text, as most speakers in the United Nations did except when making short interventions in the course of a debate.

But there were odd things about Bill, which wouldn't be worth mentioning now except to consider whether they could have some bearing on the issues which led to his sensational arrest and trial for spying (1974–5) – the only such case to have arisen in New Zealand. Consider, for instance, that he was a strict teetotaler but, rather oddly, took pride in being a connoisseur of wine although not a drop of it ever passed his lips. He claimed to judge the quality of wine and where it came from, simply by the bouquet. Others smiled and rolled their eyes disbelievingly, as they did, too, when he bought 2,000-year-old Egyptian antiquities in New York. Was there something of Walter Mitty – the James Thurber character who fantasised about a life more exciting and glamorous than his own, no matter how exciting and glamorous the reality was – in him? Why did he embellish the story of his extraordinarily adventurous journey in the Soviet Union and adjacent countries in 1932? What motivated his strange, clandestine meetings with the Russians in Wellington in 1974? And what motivated the Russians?

His trial and then his death which followed sadly, so soon after his acquittal, did not put an end to the case. Books continued to be written about it and interest was fuelled by incontrovertible evidence, caught on camera and shown repeatedly on New Zealand television, of Bill passing a package to the Russians at the top of Aro Street, Wellington, in the darkness of night. What was in that package? There has been plenty of speculation but nothing has become certain. Perhaps we shall never know.

Is it open for consideration whether there was something which happened during his visit to the Soviet Union in 1932 – reinforced, perhaps, during his visit there with Walter Nash, then New Zealand Minister of Finance, and others, in 1938 – which enabled the Russians to establish some lasting hold on him? On his own account, for instance, Bill trafficked quite blatantly in foreign currency during the visit in 1932. This was a serious offence at that time. But the amount of currency was relatively small and the practice of currency trafficking was probably fairly common. It has been suggested that he may have been encouraged by his success in 1932 to make a bigger investment in 1938. Now, so many years later, all this becomes so highly speculative as to seem not worth considering.

Other New Zealanders, who worked in the United Nations Secretariat, also lived in Parkway Village. The one we came to know best was John Male (1913–2003) who had a Chinese American wife, Hilda, who also worked in the Secretariat. It was a second marriage for them both. Some time after Mao Tse Tung came to power in China, he appealed to well-qualified members of the Chinese diaspora to go to China and help build it anew. Hilda and, I think, two of her sons by the earlier marriage, both of whom had become qualified engineers, responded to Mao's call. This eventually led to the dissolution of the marriage with John and he later married Cathy, a Canadian who had also been a colleague in the Secretariat.

As a young man in the 1930s, John had worked as a journalist in Auckland, alongside others who became New Zealand literary greats – Robin Hyde (1906–39) and Rex (A.R.D.) Fairburn (1904–57), the latter becoming a close, lifelong friend of John's. John joined the Secretariat in 1946. He was the kindest man I ever met, resolutely determined, in New York, to retain his New Zealand identity and New Zealand ways. In summer, he would pitch his tent for the weekend at Sag Harbour, on the tip of Long Island, where he'd found an estuary teeming with crabs which he and Hilda would catch and cook on an open fire. The first time we joined them there, we took our baby in her bassinet. One evening the following summer John took us to the hospital when our second baby was due to arrive, and, in fact, arrived so quickly that John and I had scarcely arrived back in Parkway Village than the doctor rang to report "another bonny wee daughter". The speed of her arrival led John to declare – this was long before political correctness had been invented – that M must have Maori blood and, he added, "I wouldn't be at all surprised to see her come riding home on a horse, bareback, first thing in the morning!"

John and Cathy took early retirement in 1964, having already bought a house which Rex Fairburn had found for them at Mahurangi Heads, north of Auckland. Actually, it was a converted church, which provided a very large, rectangular sitting/dining room. Along the length of the house was a deck which gave stunning views of the Mahurangi estuary and out to sea. John and Cathy lived the good life there for 35 years, growing their own fruit and vegetables, catching and smoking fish, gathering shellfish, sailing, making wine and beer and doing good works in the community. It was a place which acted as a magnet for a remarkable assortment of people: journalists, writers, poets, politicians, broadcasters, diplomats, people from throughout New Zealand, old friends from overseas and those sent by mutual friends to look up the Males, as a kind of highlight on the tourist trail. And I'm sure everyone enjoyed the New Zealandness of it all, the retirement life-style, the views, the abundant birdlife in the surrounding bush, as well as the joy of living which both John and Cathy exuded and John's endless fund of anecdotes (some bawdy). At 76, John dusted off and published his *Poems from a War* (1989) which he had been moved to write as a result of his service in North Africa and Italy during World War II. This marked him out as New Zealand's major war poet, as illustrated by a brief extract:

> … in the eyes of a young man trudging
> to the start line for the night's attack
> I saw fifty-seven centuries'

acceptance of the little man's
destiny to die this way[8]

In our time in New York, there were five other New Zealanders working as officials in the United Nations Secretariat. The youngest was George Barton (1925–) who, with his wife, Ailsa, lived in Parkway Village. George did not make a career of the United Nations, like some of the others, and after a couple of years returned to New Zealand where he became an eminent lawyer. Then there was Ian Berendsen (1919–2001), a son of Sir Carl, who stayed with the Secretariat throughout his working life, married an American who had several children by a previous marriage, and retired in the United States. Cedric Firth (1908–94) stayed only briefly with the Secretariat, working on large-scale housing schemes in Brazil and various parts of Africa. He returned to New Zealand where he became a leading architect of his generation.

Another was Ian Milner (1912–91), son of Frank Milner (1875–1944), Rector of Waitaki Boys' High School for the extraordinarily long term of 38 years and politically an extremely conservative man who would have been astonished by the course of his son's life. After a flying start as a Rhodes Scholar, Ian joined the Australian Department of External Affairs and then, in 1947, the United Nations Secretariat. On leave from the Secretariat in 1950, he took his New Zealand wife to Prague to get spa treatment for her rheumatism. Bizarrely – Prague was then behind the Iron Curtain – he never left Prague again, apart from brief absences outside the country. His marriage was dissolved in 1958 and he married a Czech. He became Professor of English at Charles University in Prague, immersed in teaching and the translation of modern Czech poetry, an erudite book on George Eliot (1968) and a fine biography of his father (1983).

Bruce Turner (1914–2000) had previously been a foundation member of the New Zealand Legation in Washington. He became Assistant Secretary-General and Controller (1955–72), responsible for administrative management, accounts, audit, budget, manning-tables, treasury and investments, one level below the top job. It was a position nicely described, tongue-in-cheek, in a book published to mark the centennial of his old school, as "akin to that of treasurer of the [Christchurch] Old Boys' Association – except that his club was the biggest in the world's history and probably the most expensive."[9] He remained determinedly a New Zealander, entirely

---

[8] From "Portrait of a young man grown old" in *Poems from a War*, Black Light Press, Wellington, 1989.

[9] Bruce Turner, *The Years Between: Christchurch Boys' High School 1881–1981* (Christchurch: Caxton Press, 1981), p. 334.

without airs or graces. His retirement dream was to buy a high-country sheep station in New Zealand, like Samuel Butler's Mesopotamia, as he confided when he came to have a drink the night before we left New York. By then he could have afforded such a property; Secretariat salaries were high and tax-free. But his circumstances changed. His New Zealand wife died in 1970 and he later married an American who had been Director of Recruitment in the United Nations Secretariat. They retired to live on Long Island but maintained an apartment in Auckland and usually escaped the New York winters by visiting New Zealand.

In December 1949, the government in New Zealand changed and, soon afterwards, the new government even-handedly, so it might have seemed, closed the Legation in Moscow and the Consulate-General in New York as an economy measure. Our United Nations Mission moved from the Empire State Building to what had been the New Zealand consular office in Rockefeller Center, on the fifth floor, overlooking Fifth Avenue, opposite St Patrick's Cathedral. These quarters were in every way superior to those in the Empire State Building, the rooms bigger, with more natural light. There was air conditioning and, as a bonus, an unrivalled vantage point to watch ticker-tape parades. Very quickly, however, it was decided there should be someone in New York to issue visas to all those well-to-do American tourists wanting to visit New Zealand.

So I doubled up, becoming vice-consul in a consular office which had just been abolished, as well as continuing as a third secretary doing United Nations work – two for the price of one. The consular work opened up a whole new world. The Consular Corps, having been in New York for generations, had long since become an honoured part of the City Establishment, whereas those United Nations people were controversial Johnnies-Come-Lately. (Right-wing Americans suspected the United Nations to be a hot-bed of communism.) As the only New Zealand consular representative in New York, I was invited, with my wife, to all sorts of exhilarating occasions. One of the first was a formal, black tie/long dress dinner, in a private dining room at the Waldorf-Astoria Hotel, to farewell the British Consul-General, Sir Francis Evans. (The Americans just adored those titles.) We arrived, in all our finery, and found what seemed to be the right room. To check this, I showed our invitation card to the man on the door, remarking apologetically, that we were a little late. The man took one look at the card and sniffed, "Sir, you are forty-eight hours and ten minutes late!" It was a salutary lesson. We never again made such a mistake.

In those days, the only consular instructions we had from Wellington relating to visas were on a single page of typing. For the rest, we relied on voluminous British consular instructions (*The Red Book*) as a general

In the Beginning

guide and, in emergencies, for us, as novices, on frantic telephone calls to former, locally recruited members of the staff, who had just been declared redundant, seeking their advice. And, as there was no one in Wellington expert in, or with much time to consider, consular problems, it was much easier to decide things arbitrarily on the spot. This did not come right till Dick Sharp (1908–95) was appointed to the Department of External Affairs in 1954 for the specific purpose of formulating New Zealand consular instructions and, with his background in law and compassion, he did an excellent job.

Sometimes it was a question of money. Later a 'Distressed New Zealanders Fund' was established but, in New York in 1950–1, it was far, far easier to fork out a bit of money from your own pocket rather than try to engage the sympathy of over-worked people, thousands of miles away, for compatriots who had got into difficulty and were sitting right there in the office waiting room, if not beside you. So I would lend money, never a large amount, and only once was this money not repaid. You could say that, in this exceptional case, it was my fault for becoming soppy about a New Zealand seaman who had strayed from a wealthy, highly respected and influential family, into the grip of alcoholism.

Canberra, Port Moresby, Hollandia

1. SEVEN SUBURBS IN SEARCH OF A CITY

In our retirement, people often asked, "What posting did you like best?" We could answer without a moment's hesitation, "Canberra". We were there from May 1956, for five years.[10] At that time, all Commonwealth High Commissions, as distinct from the embassies of other countries, had different designations for their diplomats. I was 'Official Secretary' – that is, No. 2 in the office – and, below me, there was an 'Assistant Secretary'.[11]

And, with the High Commissioner, that was the extent of our diplomatic staff in 1956.[12] It was a very small and very cheap establishment – New Zealand's cheapest diplomatic mission by far.

On arrival in Canberra, we experienced a bit of unexpected culture shock. Canberra then had a population of 36,000. It was, said the Australians, seven suburbs in search of a city. (The Indonesian military attaché and his wife lived next door to us when their son was born and they named him Narabunda Yarralumla, after two of the suburbs, followed by the surname which was something like Wadaminijojo.) The suburbs were scattered and separated from one another by a broad, low-lying valley where sheep grazed

---

[10] We had previously been in New York 1949–1951, Ottawa 1951–2 and then in the Department in Wellington 1952–6.

[11] These designations were phased out during our time in Canberra, as being altogether too confusing.

[12] There were also Trade Commissioners and New Zealand Government Tourist Offices in Sydney and Melbourne, as well as military liaison staff in Melbourne. The military people moved to Canberra during our time.

and the Molonglo River flowed through. In summer, it became more like a stream. This valley was later submerged under what the town planners had envisaged as Canberra's unifying feature, Lake Burley Griffin.

In our day it seemed that the seven suburbs searched rather despairingly for their city. Goods and services were extremely limited. On our first day in our new home, we went to the largest suburban shopping centre to stock up with food and other household supplies. After looking around, M said, wistfully and without expecting an answer, "If we have to lead this nomadic life, why do we have to go to a place that's so much like home – only worse."

But Canberra grew on us quickly. After the first few days, we both enjoyed every minute of the next five years, and it was by far our hardest posting to leave. New Zealanders and Australians spoke the same language. We knew their idiomatic expressions and their brand of swearing better than any other English-speaking people. For our children it was an easy transition. There was no significant difference in the school curriculum. They walked and later rode their bikes to the school nearby, just as they might have done at home. And they played with their school chums and neighbourhood children with the same easy freedom they enjoyed in New Zealand.

And for the children as well as for us, it was pleasant to find that in Canberra we could easily keep pets. First, we had two Muscovy ducks, won as third prize in a raffle – which was just the sort of thing to expect when Canberra was almost a rural community. Then there were chooks, bought impulsively when the children fell in love with them as day-old chicks in a pet shop window. It began as three chicks but one of them was loved too much. To be blunt, it was squeezed to death in four-year-old hands. The other two chicks thrived so much on being frequently cuddled, they cheeped piteously to be picked up for more. And this continued well into the adolescence of their henhood. By then, we kept them in a badly neglected, weed-infested clay tennis court in the grounds of the old house we were renting. The chooks kept escaping through holes in the rusted wire-netting of the tennis court enclosure and venturing into the house next door. To chooks with their upbringing, this must have seemed an even friendlier place than ours, because the back door was always open, as ours never was. So the open door was an obvious invitation to go in – and leave calling cards. It so happened that this house was occupied by the Japanese Embassy office. The staff picked up the chooks readily enough but didn't know they expected to be cuddled. They were simply picked up and promptly returned to us with indignation, which mounted with the number of these occasions. Finally, drastic action had to be taken.

Then there was a cat who loved this old house – the fourth we occupied in Canberra,[13] rented from Australians serving overseas and vacated when they returned – because there were large old trees and beautiful, white pouter pigeons living in a dovecote on top of the ivy-covered garage. In the time we were there, I think the cat killed six of these 12 pigeons we took over with the house. Until this happened we'd always prided ourselves in handing over these rented houses and their gardens in as good, if not better, condition than we'd found them. In our next house, incidentally, there were no trees at all. The cat hated it and persisted in going back to the place it loved. When it went missing, time after time, we always knew where to find it, about half a mile away. Finally, it went missing completely.

Lastly, but by far the best of our pets was a cairn terrier called Ming, which was the Prime Minister's nickname. We bought Ming as a pup and in no time at all he set himself up as our infant son's minder, following him everywhere he went, going from room to room and in the garden, sleeping by his cot, then his bed, never letting him out of sight. Then, one day, when our son was not quite three, he 'escaped', with Ming in tow, and wandered down the road and into the grounds of the Prime Minister's home, about a hundred yards away. The Prime Minister's wife brought them back, together with some of her grandchildren and two dogs on leashes. In the hand-over on our front doorstep, in an excited tangle of dogs and little children, to our great dismay Mrs Menzies broke a finger.

To go back to our earliest days in Canberra. We quickly found that, in the material and cultural wilderness that was Canberra at that time, the resourceful Australians made the most of it. They organised their lives round an occasional visit to Sydney or Melbourne to visit their parents – only rarely did you ever come across an adult in Canberra who had been born there – to do their Christmas shopping in Myers Emporium or watch their countrymen thrash the Poms at cricket. They made their own fun, played every possible kind of sport, excelled in making Canberra a garden city and developed repertory to a remarkable degree.

These amateur theatricals included writing the script, composing the music and staging a musical entitled *The Sentimental Bloke*, based on a book of verse by C.J. Dennis, published in 1915 and in its day about as popular in New Zealand as it was in Australia. The production in Canberra was very largely the work of a highly talented young Australian diplomat who wrote the script, staged the production and took the leading role. He was eventually obliged to resign from the Australian Department of External Affairs because the show became such a hit that it went on tour, which lasted, as I recall, for over two years, around Australia, in New Zealand and,

---

[13] Diplomats and military attachés compete with each other in counting the number of houses or apartments they have lived in.

Canberra, Port Moresby, Hollandia

I think, in London. In the course of this journey, he married his leading lady. Subsequently, he rejoined his old department.

There were several New Zealanders in the original cast of *The Sentimental Bloke* and some of them went on tour. New Zealanders blended into the local scene and were readily accepted. This included taking part in do-it-yourself activity, then in its heyday in both countries. In my case, a senior official from the Australian Prime Minister's Department, on a posting with their High Commission in London, was found to have a fast-moving cancer and was invalided home. Before he returned with his family, which included five or six young children, his mates (among whom I felt privileged to be included) painted his house, inside and out, although the exterior was mainly in brick.

New Zealand's relations with Australia, although nowhere near as complex as they are now,[14] were closer than the relationship of any other country represented in Canberra. Thanks to the cordiality established by the Canberra Pact of 1944, New Zealand diplomats stationed in Canberra were the only ones allowed – indeed, they were expected – to go round the Australian Department of External Affairs knocking on doors without an appointment, although we made appointments to see the most senior officials. I went to the Department almost every working day, as did the assistant secretary, Helen Hampton. We carved up the work between us.

And, incidentally, as if to emphasise how close the relationship between New Zealand and Australia was, Helen was being courted by not just one but two Australian diplomats. Eventually, both these courtships fizzled out. One was with Jim, later Sir James, Plimsoll (1917–87), who became head of the Australian Department of External Affairs, an ambassador in various major assignments and finally, Governor of Tasmania. He was arguably the most distinguished Australian diplomat of his generation. Behind his quiet good humour and unassuming demeanour, there was a man of steel, remarkably erudite, remarkably gifted in his ability to put complex issues into simple language.

Helen's other suitor was Max Loveday (1923–2005), an altogether different character; a wicked punster, an amusing fellow who made everybody laugh. At that time, he was head of the department's Defence Liaison Branch and I often went to see him in his office. He would greet me with, "Hello, you old bastard, and how are you today?" And, if there weren't some warm greeting of this kind, I came to realise he was signalling that something was amiss, and it had to be sorted out smartly. He always referred to the British as "the perfidious albinos", a malapropism coined during the

---

[14] In our time in Canberra there was about one New Zealand Ministerial visit to Australia each year. In 2008 there were 33 such visits.

Suez crisis which occurred soon after we arrived in Canberra in 1956. Some years later, when he came to see us at our home in Wellington, after a visit to Western Samoa, he summed it up: "Lazy bastards. They lie about in their fales all day and, in the evening, they roll over and make more Samoans."

During our first few weeks in Canberra, before taking delivery of our car in Sydney, I went to the Australian Department of External Affairs on a bike lent by Bob Harriot, our High Commissioner's driver. I would leave the bike unlocked, leaning against the wall near the entrance to East Block, where the Department was quartered. It was the only bike there. And I discovered later that, in biking to the Department in this way, I was following something of the pattern set by Paul Hasluck who had worked there in the 1930s, when Canberra was even more out in the sticks. He went on to become a parliamentarian, cabinet minister and finally Governor-General of Australia. In the 'thirties, he rode to work on a horse, which he tethered just outside the building, changing its grazing area during the day.

Incidentally, he was the only cabinet minister I ever chatted to in the buff. By coincidence, we both went to the Manuka public swimming pool (unheated) for a pre-breakfast swim around 7 am in the summer. At that time he was Minister of Territories and an eager-beaver in everything he did, and was only too happy to talk about Papua New Guinea as we dried off in the men's changing room after the swim. (Incidentally, as you entered the Australian External Affairs building in those days, the first room on the left was occupied by the Chief of Protocol, the incumbent in 1956 being the only person I ever came across who wrote with a quill pen.)

When we arrived in Canberra, our High Commissioner was Lisle Alderton (1888–1969), a political appointee who had been prominent in legal, business and National Party circles in Auckland. Before we went to Canberra, Alister McIntosh, the head of our department, gave me a remarkably succinct and accurate, if also acerbic, briefing: "He's got wonderful contacts but doesn't know what to do with them. She [meaning Lisle's wife, Biddy] has far more political nous."

He would come into the office about 10 am, read a selection of the latest inward and outward correspondence and telegrams, sign or approve things but never, in my experience, question any of it and certainly never draft anything himself, and never going to see anyone in the Australian Department of External Affairs or other departments. Unless there was some official or lunch engagement, he would go home around noon for lunch and a snooze, then return to the office about three, to see what we'd been up to, as he jokingly said. He would go home again about four and, if the weather and the season were favourable, would potter in the garden which extended to two acres or so. Most of the gardening was done by Bill,

Canberra, Port Moresby, Hollandia

husband of Cicely, who cooked and kept house. They were a live-in team.

Both the Aldertons were party animals and got on famously with the Prime Minister, Bob (later Sir Robert) Menzies and his wife (who became Dame Patti Menzies). I doubt that any New Zealand High Commissioner has ever had such a close friendship with an Australian Prime Minister. Whenever the Menzies were in Canberra on a Sunday – and they were quite often away in other parts of Australia or overseas – they had the evening meal together with the Aldertons, alternately in each other's homes. Sunday was the day off for domestic staff so the practice was to keep it as a very simple meal with the company confined to just the four of them. Sometimes there was the addition of the Menzies' daughter Heather, the apple of her father's eye, and her husband; and sometimes, when it was the Aldertons' turn to host the occasion, they included Helen Hampton who would regale me with her first-hand, delighted accounts. After dinner, there would be an unaccompanied sing-song, with the Prime Minister and Biddy singing duets with tremendous gusto, hamming it up with such songs as, "Get me to the church on time", from the current hit musical *My Fair Lady*. These were evenings of great jollity, the Prime Minister completely relaxed.

One might have wished to be a fly on the wall, listening to the Prime Minister – a pre-eminent Australian Prime Minister – yarning with the High Commissioner, drinking whisky while the wives prepared dinner – or even more when they chatted over the post-prandial brandy. It was against this background that Alister McIntosh once asked Lisle Alderton – and he would most assuredly have asked in the gentlest possible way – why he never reported anything of what the Prime Minister said on these or any other occasions. And Lisle Alderton retorted sharply, with words to the effect, "But he speaks to me frankly in confidence and he wouldn't if I passed on these confidences to other people!"

We were with the Aldertons for about a year before they returned to New Zealand on retirement. He was then 69 and not at all well. By then, he had given up driving and golf. It was a second marriage for them both but they had no children and doted on ours. When we returned to New Zealand after our five years in Canberra, we always went to see the Aldertons whenever we were in Auckland and Biddy always came to see us whenever she was in Wellington. Lisle didn't travel much beyond Auckland in his final years.

Lisle Alderton's successor as New Zealand High Commissioner in Canberra was Fred Jones (1884–1966), appointed by Walter (later Sir Walter) Nash's newly elected Labour Government. And there could scarcely have been a greater contrast than between these two men. Lisle Alderton left Canberra, in failing health, aged 69. Fred Jones began the job when he was 73. He was physically fit, although in recent years had no doubt led a more restricted, less stimulating life in Dunedin than he had enjoyed in the hurly-burly of Parliament where he had been since 1931 until he lost his seat in the general election of 1951.

While Lisle Alderton had the invaluable support of his wife, Fred Jones had been a widower for many years. And, while both the Aldertons were lively party animals from cosmopolitan Auckland – in the right company Biddy Alderton made an art form of the double entendre – Fred Jones was, by contrast, a political party animal from Calvinist Dunedin. And this is not to say he was churchy – indeed, when asked soon after he arrived in Canberra if he went to church regularly, he replied, with his disarming smile, "Oh, I go sometimes … if I get an invite." He was nevertheless, a man of very firm moral standards, with a rigorous sense of fair play – a thoroughly decent, homespun kind of man who had earnestly aspired to make life better for the people he represented in Parliament, as he had earlier in the trade union movement and on the Dunedin City Council.

Fred Jones had been Minister of Defence during World War II, although when Alister McIntosh briefed me, he said, in his usual succinct, accurate and acerbic manner, "In Peter Fraser's presence, he never opened his mouth." In other words, Peter Fraser, as Prime Minister in wartime, saw it as his principal responsibility to be, in effect, his own Minister of Defence, leaving Fred Jones with that designation but expecting him to undertake the lesser tasks – to be, for instance, a kind of welfare officer for the armed forces, an important enough job when there were 100,000 young New Zealanders in the armed forces. And, from my experience of him during his three years in Canberra, I'm sure he would have done his utmost for the welfare of the services, especially, as the former unionist, in speaking up for the 'other ranks'. And, as a moderate conciliatory man, he was probably just as good in sorting out differences over this or that issue or in settling clashes of personality. But, as McIntosh's words indicated, he was not a policy man.

About six months after arriving in Canberra, Fred was joined by his son, Arthur, an up-and-coming man in the New Zealand Post Office, together with his wife, who was to be the High Commissioner's official hostess, and their teenage daughter. Arthur, having taken two years without pay, got a job in a suburban post office in Canberra but it was nowhere near as high-powered (nor, I should think, as well-paid) a job as the one he had left behind in New Zealand. For the six months on either side of these two years, when Fred (on a three-year term) was without the support of his family, he had particular support from M, who sorted out differences between him and the cook, arranged the flowers (from his splendid garden) when he had a party, acted as his unofficial hostess on these occasions, and so on. And he was always tremendously grateful for anything that was done for him.

II. LEAVING AT FIRST LIGHT IN PAPUA NEW GUINEA

From 14 to 27 July 1959 I accompanied the High Commissioner, Fred Jones, on a visit to Papua New Guinea. We were the first New Zealand diplomats to visit the territory – at that time a Trust Territory, administered by Australia – so it was something of a journey of discovery. And, in many ways we found it to be the antithesis of Australia which is, in truth, geographically a rather boring country: the longest straight stretch of railway in the world, through many hundreds of miles with no sign of life except the occasional kangaroo; by far the greater part of it flat or gently undulating; and few rivers for its size. (The Australians, by contrast, are far from boring. They're larger than life.)

And we found Papua New Guinea a land of great diversity in almost every respect – a pocketful of surprises, beginning with all the women topless outside the main centres. Its most obvious geographical feature was a complex system of greater and lesser mountain ranges, with three peaks higher than Mt Cook and its mountains were interspersed with broad valleys and plains. One was seldom out of sight or sound of a river – the two main rivers, the Fly and the Sepik, navigable up their tortuous way for hundreds of miles, having spewed out a great delta, much of it swamp. Further variety was added by an extensive volcanic belt running through the islands off the northern coast where the most disastrous eruption occurred in 1951, claiming 3,000 lives.

We found, too, a surprising diversity of climate. Around Port Moresby, the administrative headquarters – and now the capital – it was relatively dry, with 50 inches of rain a year, the countryside arid, like much of Australia, with eucalypts dotted about. Across the mountains, in Lae and Madang, the air steamed with heat and humidity and the lush growth of thick forest was the response to 250 inches of rain a year. In Lae the people complained it had rained every day for three months. In Rabaul, they complained there had been no rain for three months.

At Goroka, in the Eastern Highlands, 5,000 feet above sea-level, we found the bracing climate of a Shangri-La – a perpetual, mild summer. In the garden of the District Commissioner's house, where we stayed – I don't think there were any hotels in Goroka – there were roses, violets, snowdrops, hydrangeas, gladioli, orchids, hibiscus and many other tropical and temperate-climate flowers, blooming in incredible variety and profusion throughout the year, immune to seasonal change. The District Commissioner's wife mused, "When do you prune roses if they never stop blooming?"

Geographic and climatic factors – a relatively flat, far-flung country, with readily forecastable weather even in pre-satellite days – made Australia, like the Soviet Union, a cradle of aviation. Australia, a young country in terms of European settlement and small in population, produced Qantas, an international airline which could do better than the airlines of the Great Powers, in being the oldest international airline and, in 1959, the only one with round-the-world traffic rights.

In New Guinea, by contrast, everything was against aviation: the high, rugged mountains, the density of cloud cover, unpredictable weather. So, at least in the 1950s when we were there, there was no night flying, airline schedules were literally as variable as the weather because they depended on it entirely, and connecting flights were upset by bad weather in remote places. For such reasons, our itinerary was often altered and we were very quickly acquainted with the need, as they said, to get away at first light. We could be stirred from bed to meet this deadline at the airport, only to find that some sudden, unexpected weather disturbance had delayed departure by one hour or several.

And we found, too, that strange things happened when flying in New Guinea. We flew, for instance, with the District Commissioner from Lae, on the coast, to Kainantu, 5,000 feet up, in a four-seater Cessna. On the return journey the Cessna couldn't take off at that altitude with four passengers, so the pilot took me out first, left me at an intermediate point, an isolated, emergency airstrip constructed by the Americans during World War II, went back to Kainantu for the High Commissioner and the District Commissioner, then returned to pick me up from my eerie isolation. This back-tracking took almost two hours. The emergency airstrip was in the broad, treeless, desolate Markham Valley, covered by kunai grass growing three or four feet high. We learnt subsequently that a fortnight or so before we were there, the grass had been cut for about six yards around the perimeter of the airstrip – which was about 300 yards long – and, in the course of this clearance, the workmen had killed 47 death-adders – which left me wondering how many others slithered away and had their eyes on me as I waited.

In a land so rugged that adjacent areas were shut off from one another by precipitous mountains and a network of rivers carrying off a greater rainfall than in any area of similar size in the world, it followed that the indigenous inhabitants would also be diverse. But we found the degree of difference little short of astonishing. There were, for instance, almost 500 languages and dialects. No one seemed sure exactly how many and the various authorities quoted different figures. The largest linguistic group was said to number 50,000 and some groups as small as 300 had their own language, unrelated to that of neighbouring tribes.

Equally we found a surprising variation in physical characteristics – skin colour, hair texture, contour of the face and stature. Those in the south, around Port Moresby, were of medium height, light brown in skin colour and adorned with a mop of frizzy hair. Those in the north had a darker skin, verging on black, with wavy or curly hair. The Kukukuku tribes in the central highlands were close to being pygmies. Other groups had reddish-brown skin.

To generalise roughly, they were all Melanesian, of good physique although they aged quickly, were physically less attractive than Polynesians and, especially because the Highlands were free of malaria and had a bracing climate, the people there were more vigorous than those living on the coast.

Social customs were similarly diverse, with considerable variation in rules of kinship, marriage, ceremonial events and so on. They were not a nomadic people, like the aborigines of Australia, but were – and remained when we were there – agriculturalists, cultivating, in a primitive manner, such things as sweet potato, yams, bananas, sugar and coconuts; collecting sago; and breeding a scrawny type of pig. Those on the coast added fish to their diet. Traditionally, the indigenous people also hunted and periodically burnt off tracts of forest or grassland for the snakes, opossums and other delicacies burnt alive.

It was a settled and highly introverted life. Inter-tribal skirmishing and cannibalism, once widespread, had been largely stamped out but, especially in areas which had only recently been brought under governmental control, there was, we were told, a considerable indifference to the value of human life, as well as considerable suspicion of any outsider.

The indigenous population, in 1959 numbering something not far short of two million – in an area about twice the size of New Zealand – was scattered throughout the Territory. Few areas were uninhabited. Indeed, Michael Leay, whose cattle ranch we visited some 50 miles from Lae, had discovered, with a companion, a pass into the Highlands of New Guinea – an area previously thought to be uninhabited but where lay the broad valley where Garoka now stands. There, in "the healthiest, most populous, most beautiful part of New Guinea," as Michael Leay put it, were "half a million people who weren't supposed to exist".

Some remote areas, we were told, had not yet been penetrated, let alone brought under government control, and pockets of indigenous people were still being discovered. At the other extreme, tribal groups in some of the coastal areas had been continuously influenced by Europeans for the greater part of a century.

The facts of history, like those of geography, were also divisive. The Dutch annexed the western part of New Guinea in 1828, mainly, it was said, to suppress piracy and slave-trading in an area adjacent to their rich Dutch East Indies (now Indonesia). Then, for 130 years – until November 1958, when a measure of liaison was established with the Australian part of New Guinea – the Dutch administered the west without reference to what was happening in the other, larger and more populous part of the island.

In 1884 Germany annexed the north-eastern part of New Guinea and major adjacent islands – and for 30 years administered them entirely without reference to what was happening in the west or south.

Also in 1884, the British annexed the south. This was handed to Australia in 1906 and then named Papua. When World War I began in 1914, Australian forces occupied German New Guinea and in 1921 this area was placed under League of Nations Mandate, administered separately from Papua. Not until 1946, under a United Nations Trusteeship Agreement, was the former mandate united with Papua for administrative purposes and made accountable to the United Nations Trusteeship Council.

A further divisive historical factor was the Japanese invasion during World War II. The Japanese occupied the main islands to the north and most of the coastal area of mainland New Guinea. Everyone we talked with on this subject, however, thought the Japanese had exerted little influence on the indigenous peoples except to antagonise them.

Something which impressed us greatly in New Guinea was the fine calibre of officer serving in the administration. One might have wondered whether Australian dealings with their own aborigines would have recommended them as colonial administrators. But the mistreatment of aborigines was at the hands of individuals – although there could well have been government connivance. Be that as it may, in dealing with New Guinea, the Australian Government appointed administrators with impeccable credentials, beginning notably with Hubert (eventually Sir Hubert) Murray, who served as Administrator in Papua for the extraordinarily long term of 33 years, from 1907 till his death in 1940.

The British had administered Papua for 20 years before handing it to Australia – and they handed over not just the territory but the pattern of British colonial administration. Hubert Murray inherited this pattern, confirmed it in essence and built on it.

When we were there in 1959, the senior officers in the administration were men who had served together in New Guinea during the war. Many had been in New Guinea before the war and stayed on throughout the war as 'coast-watchers', reporting home by radio on sightings of Japanese shipping, living lonely lives, always on the move, constantly hunted by the Japanese and depending utterly on the loyalty of the indigenous people to whom, one sensed, they retained a continuing debt of gratitude.

Canberra, Port Moresby, Hollandia

It seemed to us that the administration had benefited greatly from extensive introductory programmes for new recruits, established at the Australian School of Pacific Administration set up in Sydney after the war; extremely generous terms and conditions of appointment to the administration; a very high standard of housing provided for officials; and the Australian Government's undertaking to meet the cost of a prescribed number of domestic staff, ranging down from 12 for the Administrator's household. Even so, it was easy to imagine that a job in the administration, serving in the wilds of New Guinea, could prove not to be everyone's cup of tea and in fact, there was a shortage of staff because many had left.

But those who had found their niche in the Territory formed a very fine colonial service which had brought out all the best qualities of the Australian – initiative, drive, practicality, a great sense of humour – together with a surprising degree of sophistication in their personal lives and an admirable humility about the work they were doing.

We encountered absolutely no trace of arrogance such as might, perhaps, have emerged in officials exercising great authority over primitive people. On the contrary, the relationship with their charges was firmly paternalistic but in no way autocratic. For instance, during a formal dinner given in our High Commissioner's honour by the Administrator Brigadier Cleland at Government House (as it was called) in Port Moresby, a small child of the household staff fell and cut his forehead – although not badly, as it turned out. The parents of the bawling toddler instantly brought him to the wings of the great dining room, respectfully keeping their distance while a waiter whispered to the Administrator's wife what had happened. She immediately excused herself from the table, went out and gathered up the child in her comforting arms, applied a band-aid to the wound and kissed it better, whereupon the bawling ceased – as some of us could observe as well as hear as we sat at the dining table. When she returned, Mrs Cleland reported to us all that the child was Don So-and-so – and she laughingly explained that all boys born to the household staff were named Don, in honour of her husband, whose first name it was.

Similarly, when we were staying with the District Commissioner in Goroka, the 'house-boy' – a man in his mid-thirties – interrupted us when we were having afternoon tea with him and his wife to report plaintively that he couldn't find his kitten. The Commissioner's wife explained to us that the 'boy' regarded the kitten as his most precious possession. It slept on his feet and kept them warm in the chilly nights in the Highlands. Then the Commissioner and his wife went off to help in the search which eventually ended when the kitten was found inadvertently locked in a garden shed.

We found other characters in the cast of New Guinea affairs, most obviously Chinese, numbering about 3,000, living in the north, the former German colony to which their forbears had originally been brought as indentured labour. In the course of several generations, the Chinese had set up as shopkeepers, acquired land, graduated from university and, in a few cases, joined the administration. They lived mainly in Rabaul and Madang and were, by all accounts, highly industrious, extremely law-abiding and apolitical but were playing a significant part in the economic development of the territory.

Other characters in the cast of New Guinea affairs were missionaries. Indeed, missionaries had been active in New Guinea before the British and German annexations. It was said there were so many of them that, until just a few years ago, there were more missionaries than administrators. Generally, the missionaries were well regarded by the administration people for being dedicated and often courageous men and women who had done much to establish contact with the indigenous people and extend to them something of the ethical and moral values of Western civilisation. Their material rewards were insignificant. At the outpost of Kaiapit, in the Markham Valley, we met a Lutheran pastor who, as a hobby, was compiling a dictionary of the local language which was spoken, he said, by some 15,000 people; he had already assembled 5,000 words and reckoned there were probably about 5,000 more. He and his wife had been on home leave only once in ten years. Their children were at school in Germany and they had not seen them for several years.

While administration officials and others invariably gave the missionary his due, in the next breath there was criticism. It was said they took too narrow a view, saving souls for the next world, with too much fire and brimstone, and making theology the core subject in mission education to the neglect of secular studies such as manual skills which would have assisted the native people in improving their lot. It was also a common criticism that the missions engaged in dubious business practices. Some, for instance, owning copra plantations, had found it paid off to be an incorporated company – 'The Society of the Holy Ghost and Company Ltd'" – which divested them of liability to pay taxes for which lay enterprises, of exactly the same type, were liable. Michael Leay, for one, was hot under the collar in telling us that the milk he supplied to Lae was subject to sales tax while that supplied by his only competitor, a Lutheran mission, was not.

It seemed understandable that the missionaries had branched out into commercial activity to supplement the slender and uncertain financial support from their home countries. Such commercial activity also advanced the welfare and widened the horizons of the native people in their care. But it was said that some missions had taken commercial enterprises so far that they had not only become financially self-sufficient but paid a dividend to the Church at home. This could have just been gossip. But we heard so much criticism of the missionaries, they were obviously the subject of controversy and a source of some discord in the community.

The cast of characters in New Guinea also included resident outsiders, almost entirely Australian, making a living as planters and farmers (coffee, copra, rubber, cocoa, peanuts, cattle), traders and those providing such services as transport, banking, hotels and shops. Among these people there were some with a sense of service as dedicated as that of any missionary and who, after living in the Territory for many years, thought of it as home – would never have dreamt of living anywhere else. And some of them were straight out of Somerset Maugham.

There was, for example, the widow, an Australian, who managed the hotel at Lae. She had lived in the Territory for over 30 years – had left it once, thinking it would be for good, but was back within three months. She had grown used to the trying climate, to the problems of staffing and of coping with the unquenchability of Australian thirst in the tropics – it was said that more liquor was consumed per head in the Territory (Europeans only) than in any other country in the world. It still remained surprising that she accepted so affably the duty, which she regarded, no doubt correctly, too responsible to delegate, of personally wakening hotel guests at five o'clock in the morning so they could get to the airport to catch a plane leaving at first light. And this meant going around knocking on doors – there was no such thing as a telephone in every room – and making sure you were awake. You were considered to be awake if you'd turned on the light in your room but she'd pop back to make sure if you didn't appear for the early breakfast they served.

We encountered some stirring of political life, in which the planters and traders were playing a leading role, as far to the right of the political spectrum as it was possible to get – questioning the administration at almost every turn and, in particular, always declaring that any talk of political advancement for the indigenous people was utter nonsense. These well-to-do planters and traders had incongruous company in redneck 'poor whites', the ones with less responsible jobs which they saw as under threat from the indigenous people. The Australian head-waitress at the hotel in Lae complained raucously and repetitively that "the natives were getting uppity". "When they get to talking English, they think they're as good as us." Similarly, the Australian barmaid in Lae fumed at me when, in my innocence, I gave money with my order to her native assistant. "*They* don't handle money!"

Yet it seemed incredible that, when many of their families had been in contact with Europeans for generations, spoke English fluently and had become well educated, the indigenous people should have so little say in the government of their country, as indicated by the fact that they were allocated only three seats in a Legislative Council of 29 established in 1951.

Looking back now, in 2010, it is also remarkable how quickly political advancement of the indigenous people occurred after we were there. The first House of Assembly opened in 1964, with 64 members who included an elected indigenous majority and only ten nominated official members. And, only 15 years later, in September 1975, Papua New Guinea became fully independent.

I don't know for sure but I imagine that a good deal of the impetus for this rapid advance came from the administration in Papua New Guinea. When we were there in 1959, I asked the District Commissioner in Lae whether he found the 'back-room boys' in the Department of Territories in Canberra "a bit starry-eyed – long-haired idealists". He replied instantly, "Good God, no. That's what they think of us!"

III. TO BIAK AND BACK

I went to New Guinea again, this time by myself, from 27 November to 17 December 1960, spending eight days (3–11 December) on the Dutch side and the rest on the Australian.

The itinerary included Rabaul, Lae and, on the Dutch side, Hollandia, the capital, Biak, Manokwari; then west to Sorong, within sight of Indonesia; then back, on the Australian side, to Lae, Wau, Goroka and Port Moresby. About a third of the daytime was spent in flight or getting to and from or waiting at airports for planes which never seemed to leave or arrive on schedule. Flight was mainly by DC3, unpressurised, although often at great height. In the heat of summer it was an exhausting journey.

The Dutch DC3s seemed to be an especially doubtful proposition. There were endless delays while mechanical faults were fixed up. And the Dutch had a nasty, phlegmatic habit of pulling their planes to bits, putting them together again, then trying them out while prospective passengers watched. Another habit of these tough Dutch colonialists was not to serve meals on their planes. So the 800-odd miles from Sorong to Hollandia or from Hollandia to Lae, was, with touch-downs, a long day's journey by DC3 – and one got nothing but a cup of coffee and a piece of sodden cake. The Australians also put passengers to the test at Wau, where the airfield was one of the steepest in the world, with a grade of one in six, and where the latest wreck was left at hand for unavoidable inspection.

My itinerary was determined largely by airline schedules – to the extent that planes stuck to them – and, in particular by the fact that there was only one service a week between Dutch and Australian New Guinea, run alternately by the Dutch and Australians.

For the rest, the programme was left in the hands of the administration on either side. And the result was an interesting contrast. In effect, the Australians were saying, "Look at what we're doing!" and the Dutch, "Listen to what we're thinking!" The Dutch had organised all manner of opportunity for discussion. For the Dutch, the material achievements were rather incidental things to be seen on the way to another discussion. Every evening of the eight days of my visit there was a gathering in the home of some Dutch official, either with other Dutch officials or businessmen or, usually, with a mixture of them and prominent Papuans – political aspirants, civil servants, clergymen, trade unionists, entrepreneurs and teachers. None of these seminars ended before midnight and, in addition, there were usually one or two discussion groups during the day.

Every one of these discussions was lively and uninhibited. The Dutch were all fluent in English and I talked to the Papuans through a Dutch official – all their officials seemed to have the knack – who acted as interpreter in an admirably self-effacing way, showing only mild amusement when he was obliged to interpret statements critical of the administration. In the case of English-speaking Papuans and most notably Nicolas Jowve, a timber merchant married to a Eurasion lawyer, and Herman Womsiwor,[15] also a timber merchant with an interest in the salvaging business (retrieving ships or planes shelled, wrecked or shot down during World War II), I was left alone with them to talk as long as I wished. None of this was organised at my request. It was arranged by the Dutch on their own initiative. They were, moreover, well aware that Womsiwor was openly critical of the administration for alleged mishandling of salvage arrangements with the Japanese.

There was none of this kind of discussion on the Australian side of New Guinea. The closest I came to it was when an Australian official took me to meet three local government councillors in Lae. We met at the Council House, an open-sided building where no seating was arranged for us. So we stood about awkwardly, looking more at our shoes than each other, in a conversation which everyone assumed would be brief and perfunctory, as it was.

Educated Papuans spoke to Dutch officials as their equals, cracking jokes and questioning opinion. The Dutch were perfectly at ease with all this – in having these Papuans in their homes for an evening's drinking and talking. There was nothing like this on the Australian side. Why? I suppose it was relevant that so few of the Australian officers out in the field were university educated – apart, that is, from those technically qualified, such as agricultural scientists. Indeed, I never met one. By contrast, all the Dutch officials I encountered were university men. For the Dutch, a university degree was the prerequisite to promotion. As the Dutch saw it, the advancement of a native people, especially when approaching self-government, was a highly complex, politico-sociological-anthropological problem requiring years of study – and not, they sneered, short pressure-cooker courses such as the Australians ran at their School of Pacific Administration in Sydney. From this studious background, the Dutch attitude to the indigenous people emerged as more thoughtful, more deeply concerned, more tolerant, more optimistic and, in personal terms, more familiar. I wondered, however, whether it was a recipe for paralysis by analysis.

---

[15] Womsiwor seemed like a character in a far-fetched Hollywood movie. As a boy during the war, he'd been 'smuggled' out of New Guinea by an American Negro soldier. Womsiwor was denied entry to the United States but stayed for several years with the American Occupation Forces in Japan where he became fluent in both English and Japanese. (The word 'Negro' fell out of favour in the 1960s.)

The Dutch attitude was surely accentuated by the strong Eurasian presence in the Dutch administration. Many Dutch officials – the Australian Liaison Officer in Hollandia put it as high as 50 percent – had Eurasian or Indonesian wives or were themselves Eurasian. In Australian New Guinea, I didn't come across a single Australian official of mixed blood or with a marriage involving it.

Another thing making for an easier relationship between the Dutch and the indigenous people was that the natives were allowed to drink liquor – only beer and a weak brew at that, being only about half the strength of beer on the Australian side, but it was the same beer as the Dutch themselves drank – and they drank together.

The Dutch saw the indigenous people as victims of their environment. Time and again I heard some such reassurance as, "There's nothing wrong with these boys' minds, given a chance. If anyone lived in their mountains for any length of time, out of touch with the rest of the world, they'd quickly find themselves thinking differently, with a different sense of values, a different perspective."

And this is precisely what seemed to have happened to some of the Australians living in the Territory – planters, patrol officers – only tenuously in touch with the rest of the world. Even as a visitor, I began to feel immensely out of touch with what was happening elsewhere.

Again by contrast, the Dutch were only too well aware that they were administering a disputed land. The Australians were free of any such burden. The Dutch had the Indonesians breathing down their necks, led by the flamboyant President Sukarno who was making headway in his campaign to win international support for his claim that Dutch New Guinea was rightfully Indonesia's to inherit, just as the Netherlands East Indies had become Indonesia. The Dutch were accordingly highly sensitive about world opinion.

The widely divergent attitude of the Australians and the Dutch towards the indigenous people was the most apparent contrast for an outsider. And, in this respect, the Dutch seemed to be on the side of the angels. But, in matters of material achievement, the Australians left the Dutch far behind.

The two territories were roughly the same size, with roughly the same kind of rugged topography and much the same indigenous people. Government expenditure in the two territories was also roughly the same, although the native population on the Dutch side was less than half that in Papua New Guinea. But the contrast in what was done with government expenditure was extraordinary:

	Papua New Guinea	*Dutch New Guinea*
Number of native pupils	170,000	35,000
Number of airfields	154	25
Number of road miles	5,918	250

(Many of the Australian roads were very rough and only negotiable by four-wheel-drive vehicles. The Dutch concentrated on beautifully sealed roads that came to a dead end on the outskirts of town. And they drove like lunatics.)

How did this extraordinary contrast come about? Perhaps the Dutch were fettered by their careful, intellectual background – foreseeing all the difficulties and dangers, as well as the advantages, in any course of action, and apt, therefore, to do things the hard way or not do them at all, spending too much time and money on feasibility studies. The Australians prided themselves on being "Bachelors of Experience, not Bachelors of Engineering", to quote the words of a district commissioner about their achievements in roading. They were cheerful amateurs, giving it a go, full of pioneering enthusiasm, getting things done pragmatically with ingenuity and vigour.

A Dutch official told me that while visiting Papua New Guinea he had been shown around by an Australian district officer when they came across some natives working a tractor to clear land but not doing it properly. The Australian promptly got out of the car, jumped up on the tractor and, with a barrage of blasphemous exhortation, spent the best part of an hour showing the natives how it should be done – and doing a good part of the job himself. The Dutchman thought the Australian domineering, bruising the natives' ego and encouraging the natives to think that the white man would always be around to help them out of any sort of a jam. But I wondered about this. It seemed far too convoluted a view. As I imagined it, the Australian was doing what seemed to him the obvious, practical thing. And had he, in fact, impressed the natives? Here he was, a big boss, regarding them as more important than his visitor, another big boss, who was being neglected on their account. And their big boss was not afraid to get his hands dirty and, to judge by his grin, enjoyed what he was doing. And wouldn't the natives have grinned too, and enjoyed the occasion?

A further illustration of the contrast between the Dutch and Australian approaches was provided in a scheme, some 50 miles out of Rabaul, to develop native cropping on a substantial area of unused land. Most of the land was being leased to Europeans but part of it was being cut up into 20-acre blocks, allocated by ballot to indigenous people for growing cocoa. The idea was that a native settled on this block of land, erected a temporary

Canberra, Port Moresby, Hollandia

shelter, immediately cleared enough land to start growing vegetables for his family's use and then also to sell to neighbouring European planters for their 'labour lines'. With the help of outside native labour and advice from the administration's agricultural scientists, he then planted the rest of his block in cocoa. From what I heard and could see for myself, the scheme was working well.

So, when on the Dutch side, I asked if they had any scheme of this kind. They said there was a proposal 'on the books' but it had not yet got under way. It would entail the expenditure of A£5,000 for a block of about 12½ acres (compared with the Australian expenditure of A£144 for a 20-acre block). Development costs would involve a mechanical clearing of the jungle and access toads (in the Australian case, this expense had been borne by a timber lessee); the erection of a house (whereas the Australians expected the native to build his own temporary shelter from undergrowth left by the (Australian) timber merchant lessee who had cleared the jungle of millable timber); and the loan needed to be enough to tide the native over until his cocoa came into production. There were no nearby planters, they said, to whom he could sell quick-growing vegetables in the interval. So, although the two cases were by no means parallel, they were sufficiently similar to suggest that the Dutch were taking too paternalistic an approach. They declared, moreover, that an obvious flaw in the Australian approach was that, if a native employed other natives to help him clear his land and plant his cocoa, they would inevitably come back when the cocoa came into production, demanding 'their' share of the profits from the trees they had helped to plant. (When I mentioned this later, the Australians said "Bullshit!")

Another example of the enterprising, practical, cost-conscious Australian approach was provided at technical schools for natives at Rabaul and Lae. These were in fine modern buildings set in beautiful, extremely well-kept grounds. The buildings had been largely erected and the building and grounds were being fully maintained by student labour. The Australian headmasters maintained that the boys were, indeed, happy in their work, despite being roused at daybreak to mow lawns and dig the garden. They had developed a great pride in the school. It meant much more to boys in a carpentry class to be given some meaningful job such as helping to build extra accommodation for the school than, say, being shown how to make beautiful bookends to take home to a village with no books.

At a similar technical training institute in Biak, but in extremely unkempt grounds, I asked the Dutch headmaster if the boys took any part in the erection or maintenance of the buildings. It was obvious the thought had never occurred to him. As I could see, the boys' handwriting was in impeccable copperplate and they made wonderfully good copies of technical drawings which the instructor drew on the blackboard. And they made beautiful bookends. Similarly, native students in Dutch New Guinea learnt German and French as well as Dutch and English, like the Dutch living at the crossroads of Europe. And these languages, of course, were in addition to their mother tongue.

It seemed that a significant factor contributing to Australian material achievement was the presence of the private (Australian) entrepreneur. Private enterprise scarcely existed in Dutch New Guinea, where it was confined to oil production (rapidly declining in 1960); an international airport and hotel built by KLM at Biak; a timber concession recently acquired by an Australian company on an island to the south; and import/export firms. Apart from the one hotel in Biak, all hotels were government owned. On the Australian side, all the hotels were built and run by private enterprise. Planters in Dutch New Guinea could, it was said, be counted on the fingers of one hand. In Papua New Guinea, planters abounded. They accounted for by far the larger part of production, in 1958–9 producing 75 percent of the copra, cocoa and coffee and practically all the rubber (although the proportion of native production of cocoa and coffee was steadily increasing).

The mere presence of the Australian planter seemed to contribute a good deal to the atmosphere of vigour and initiative, infecting both the administration and the natives. The planter seized any opportunity to make money – and did. A planter near Rabaul said it cost A£100 an acre to clear land and bring it into production in cocoa; after five years, the return, even on prevailing low prices, was A£50 an acre a year. Coffee came into production in a shorter time. It was only to be expected, therefore, that the planter went about with a grin on his face, full of vigour and enthusiasm. Nor was it surprising that a significant number of senior officers in the administration had resigned to become planters, despite the generous treatment they received from the administration.

Moreover, the sight of the Australian planter's material rewards and the first-hand experience which a native could get on a white man's plantation before giving it a go himself, must have provided a far more pertinent object lesson than any to be gained from the impersonal government 'pilot project', to which the Dutch were obliged to resort in the absence of Dutch planters.

Why were there so few Dutch planters? In earlier times, there had been no inclination on the part of the Dutch to settle in West (Dutch) New Guinea rather than in the Netherlands East Indies (which became Indonesia) where the land was more fertile; access to the interior far easier; and labour far more abundant and amenable. And once the Indonesians had gained their independence, Dutch planters had little incentive to move next door to territory which the Indonesians claimed and which therefore had a very uncertain future.

In our discussions, the Dutch officials brooded incessantly about this Indonesian claim which they said retarded all development. As long as the future ownership of the territory was so much in doubt, overseas investment from any private quarter was frightened away. The only exceptions were a few projects with a quick return – oil, salvage and one timber concession.

The Dutch were caught in a quandary. They had good reason for wanting to get out of Dutch New Guinea. It was costing them more and more money and it was losing them friends. Moreover, if they did strike it lucky and find nickel, cobalt or other minerals which might help them out of their financial difficulties, the Indonesians would want the place even more.

Another factor impeding development was the scarcity of native labour. The population of Dutch New Guinea was only about half that of Papua New Guinea, although the two territories were about the same size. But the terrain in Dutch New Guinea was more inhospitable – the mountains were rugged, the interior more impenetrable, the swamps more widespread. Even the freewheeling Australians, who, in a kind of mission impossible, had put a road through from the coast to the eastern side highlands of Papua New Guinea, reckoned it really would be impossible to put a road from the coast to the interior on the Dutch side. And it was in that interior that half the indigenous population lived.

The economic and other prospects in Dutch New Guinea seemed so bleak, one wondered why the Dutch had held on to the territory. Why hadn't they called it a day at the time of Indonesian independence and handed over Dutch New Guinea as well? In part, there had been altruism. The indigenous people of Dutch New Guinea were racially quite different from the Indonesians and far more primitive. Indeed, Indonesians couldn't be called primitive at all. They had been under Dutch 'tutelage' for three centuries. There had been very little such tutelage in Dutch New Guinea. The indigenous people there needed to be treated in a different, preferential way. Self-determination had become an overarching doctrine of the modern world. As cynics – or perhaps they were realists – said, good government was no substitute for self-government. If given a chance, for instance, the people of Dutch New Guinea might opt to set up a separate state of their own or federate with Papua New Guinea.

Was that all? Two of the Dutch officials, independently of each other, said Dutch New Guinea was retained primarily as a haven, a bolt-hole, for the half million Eurasians living in the Netherlands East Indies at the time it became independent as Indonesia. It was assumed that many of these people would want to stay in a tropical climate, close to Indonesian relatives but not themselves wanting to stay in that country after the Dutch had gone. In the event, some 300,000 of these Eurasians had migrated to the Netherlands legally and another 200,000 had gone there illegally. Few had gone to Dutch New Guinea and, of those who did, many were drifting away, worried about the future of the place.

Another Dutch official, who had been serving in Batavia (renamed Jakarta when the Indonesians took over) at the time of independence and during the negotiations leading up to it, took me aside and said, in confidence – which, at this distance in time might reasonably be broken – that to his certain knowledge the decision to retain Dutch New Guinea had been taken on the insistence of the Americans, who wanted it kept in friendly hands as a base from which to operate if things went badly wrong in Indonesia (which sounded rather fanciful) and, more importantly, as part of the strategic chain arching east to include Papua New Guinea and north to Formosa, Japan and South Korea, with an eye to the containment of communist China. (During World War II, the American General Douglas MacArthur, who had been Commander-in-Chief of Allied Operations in the Pacific, had his headquarters in Port Moresby and later in Hollandia.)

Be all that as it may, the Dutch, having accepted the doctrine of self-government, were obliged to follow through. And circumstances – Indonesian pressure, the increasing financial burden, increasing Dutch unpopularity, especially among the 'non-aligned' – dictated that this should be done in a hurry. At the time of my visit in 1960, the Dutch were, therefore, proposing to set up a New Guinea Council, which was to have a majority of indigenous people. Privately, Dutch officials said the council would be a political instrument rather than an instrument with which to govern. It was intended that as soon as possible the council would declare itself to represent the will of all the people of Dutch New Guinea. And the will, the wish, of those people would be to have self-government in some shape or form – except that no one, of course, would want to have their future tied up in any association with Indonesia. This, said the Dutch officials, would be the Dutch answer to the Indonesian claim to Dutch New Guinea. One could only listen in silence, bewildered, thinking of the 'buts' … But this council would claim to represent constituencies which had never heard of the council. And, similarly, there would be quite a few members of the council who had never been to their constituencies. Moreover, here was a territory, being given the appearance of self-determination – taking a kind of referendum – when over a third of the indigenous people had not yet been brought under control of the administration.

With elections to the New Guinea Council in the offing, various political parties had suddenly sprung into existence in recent weeks and I was taken to meet most of the party leaders. The party with the largest membership, EPANG, formed in September, by December had 1,200 members. Their main plank was union with the Netherlands while aiming for independence within 15 years. A related party, PONG, which confined itself exclusively to membership by indigenous people (while EPANG included Eurasians, Dutch and other residents, as well as the indigenous people), had 197 members.

Meanwhile, at Biak the jet-fighters were taking off on their daily practice runs – disturbing one's early morning sleep. The anti-aircraft guns at Biak and presumably elsewhere seemed to be manned, at the ready, continuously. And a very high proportion – it seemed to be over 75 percent – of the air travellers within Dutch New Guinea were military personnel. These were reminders, too, of the dangers which could lie ahead.

* * * * *

In the following years, events moved swiftly. In April 1961, just three months after I was there, the New Guinea Council was set up to prepare the way for the Territory to become an independent state. Later that year the newly devised flag of this state-in-waiting was hoisted. To President Sukarno it was like a red rag to a bull. He threatened to take the Territory by force and the Soviet Union backed him. Worried by the mounting tensions, the United Nations took up the issue and the eventual outcome was an agreement brokered by Robert Kennedy, brother of the American President, and Attorney General in his cabinet, whereby the Territory was put into the care of the United Nations for a cooling-off period. The agreement was signed, then ratified, by the Netherlands and Indonesia in August–September 1961. In 1963, Indonesia took over control of the Territory and in 1969 it formally became a region of Indonesia, now known as West Papua (Papua Barat) – and one of the most unvisited and unvisitable places in the world.

Singapore at Sixes and Sevens

I. A PRE-EMINENT PRIME MINISTER

MILITARY PEOPLE like to test the mettle of diplomats. When we went to Singapore early in 1966, for instance, they warned me that Indonesian airspace was only three seconds away. Later in 1966, when I visited New Zealand forces then deployed in Sarawak, I'd no sooner arrived than their commander, Brian Poananga, tried me out on the rifle range and quite rightly sniffed at my performance. Later still, in Singapore, the British military police, at the instigation of the fleet commander, the British admiral in charge of the naval base, took me on a tour, checking 'doctor cards' and so on, in Singapore's brothels and catamite dens. This was an experience which sent me looking up words that were unfamiliar to me but which stood me in good stead when I came to be involved in dealing with the case of a senior New Zealand Army officer (now deceased) who had taken indiscretion rather too far in one of those catamite dens, leaving behind a briefcase of classified papers.

The warning about Indonesian airspace was, in fact, rather irrelevant by the time we arrived in Singapore. By then, Indonesian relations with Malaysia and Singapore were settling down fairly quickly. But two Indonesian infiltrators, saboteurs, had, on 10 March 1965 let off a bomb in the stairwell of the building where the Australian High Commission had its quarters (and which I passed every day on my way to and from our office). The bomb was the 29th and most serious of such bombings in Singapore and had killed two people and injured at least 33. The infiltrators were arrested and, despite loud Indonesian protest, were subsequently hanged

Singapore at Sixes and Sevens

on 17 October 1968. A hundred-thousand British, Australian and New Zealand military personnel remained in Malaysia and Singapore, having lately helped repel Indonesian 'Confrontation': limited Indonesian warfare against Malaysia, the formation of which President Sukarno of Indonesia had declared would perpetuate colonialism in a different guise. On the contrary, the British aimed to divest themselves of responsibility for all the territories incorporated in the new Federation of Malaysia: the Crown colonies of Sabah and Sarawak and the self-governing colony of Singapore, now being attached to Malaya which had become independent in 1957.

I went to Singapore to become New Zealand's first high commissioner after Singapore had, in effect, been expelled from the Federation of Malaysia to become an independent state. When I paid my introductory call on the Prime Minister, Lee Kuan Yew, he emerged from his inner sanctum and greeted me warmly but, when we sat down to chat, I might have wondered whether he too, was testing the mettle of a newly arrived diplomat. His opening gambit was, "The trouble with New Zealand is that you've got the Maoris." Perhaps I could have smiled foolishly and let it pass. But Lee was not about to let that happen and I suddenly found myself locked, not just in a lively exchange but what could only be described as a heated, if not full-blooded, argument. Eventually, the conversation moved on to other topics, but I left Lee's office that day feeling miserably worried that I'd mucked things up before I'd really begun, by putting myself offside with the Prime Minister.

But he never again referred to that heated exchange, or the Maoris, and I soon learnt that my Australian colleague, Bill Pritchett, who subsequently became Australian Secretary of Defence, had been far rougher with Lee than I had been, and, by his own account, my British colleague, John Rob, could be coldly dismissive with him. So, if Lee thought about it at all, he probably concluded I was pretty mild. Anyhow, in the five years which followed, we developed a close and easy relationship. Pritchett and Rob soon moved on to other assignments and I outstayed their successors. So I probably saw more of Lee, in those five years, than any other outsider. The presence of our forces gave the British, Australian and New Zealand high commissioners highly preferential access to the Prime Minister. Defence issues were by far the most important part of our relationship.

I talked with Lee in his office at least once a fortnight, together with one or both my British and Australian colleagues, alone, with visiting New Zealand cabinet ministers, or on social or public occasions. In most capitals this would be an unusually high level of contact with a head of government. Only very rarely did we get to chat about anything personal. It was almost two years before he opened the door on his own past. He did so with a characteristically grand sweep: "The first generation of migrants makes money. The second squanders it … Thank God there was enough left to put me through Cambridge [University]. The third generation tries to fit into place but we're too raw, too intense. We depend on the fourth generation to be properly rounded." Then the door to his past closed as suddenly as it had opened.

Several months went by before he opened that door again. He said his paternal grandfather had come up from nothing to be managing director of a shipping company based in Singapore. One branch of the family settled in Indonesia and the servants in his grandfather's household, in which Lee spent his early years, were Javanese "because they were cheaper than local servants … Until I was about ten, I was brought up by Javanese amahs and spoke almost no other language but theirs." This was leading up to the point that he knew his Indonesians: knew that to give way to them under pressure would be taken as showing weakness. And, in particular, he went on, he would not intervene in the judicial process which had decided that the two Indonesian infiltrators who had killed two Singaporeans, should be hanged, whereas the Indonesian Government was now strongly urging the Government of Singapore to intervene and grant the men a pardon.

Lee regarded himself as a third-generation Singaporean. On his mother's side – although in Chinese reckoning this did not count – he was seventh generation. She came from a family that had intermarried with Malays. As she put it neatly, "I am half-past eleven Chinese." His mother, to use her own words, "left school at standard five, was booked to marry at 13, formally engaged at 14, married at 15 and bore Lee Kuan Yew at 16. And I didn't marry my husband. I married my mother-in-law – but I was trained to take it."

In our time in Singapore, Lee's father worked behind the counter of de Silva's jewellery shop in High Street. He seemed a good companion of a man but to his son he was a ne'er-do-well. Perhaps Lee got some of his charisma from his father but Lee would have reckoned, tartly, that he didn't owe him much else nor, for that matter, set much store by charisma. Lee's drive certainly owed a good deal to his mother, a lively, energetic, warm-hearted woman, full of impish good humour and such challenging maxims as, "There's no such word as 'can't'."

From an early age, Lee aimed to get on. Neither the honours board at Raffles Institution (the English-language secondary school he attended) nor (so the headmaster told me) the school magazines of the time, made any mention of him except scholastically. To his contemporaries at Raffles (University) College, including Tun Razak, who became Prime Minister of Malaysia (1970–1976), and several of his own cabinet colleagues, he was a know-all, as they were wont to say, albeit fondly, reminiscing over the brandy. He capped his university days in Singapore by winning a Queen's Scholarship, one of only two given each year. The other recipient that year was the woman who became his wife. They both went on to take a double first in law at Cambridge. (One brother became a police inspector, another a lawyer, the third a doctor. His only sister married the son of a Chinese rubber plantation millionaire.)

While still in his early thirties, Lee founded a lucrative law practice from which he could have enjoyed an easy life. What prompted him to go into public life and work so hard for such little material recompense? By the standard of any head of government, he was poorly paid in the 1960s, although his pay greatly improved when the economy of Singapore boomed. He lived in his own modest house rather than the spacious house officially provided for him. This was Sri Temasek, once the residence of the colonial secretary. In Lee's day as prime minister it was used extensively for government dinners. At other times, he spent many evenings there, away from family noise, doing his "homework". Even so, he used to refer to his home disparagingly as "a fortress". Everywhere he went he had a heavy guard. When he once dined with us, there were more guards in the grounds than guests at the table.

Lee first found the attractions of power – and found the power of his tongue – as an advocate of union causes. He went on to acquire political power partly in the anti-colonialist cause but mainly to lead the local revolution of expectations. Inspired and schooled by his British Fabian friends, he promoted such a wide range of welfare state measures in less than a decade that *Time* magazine, in 1968, called him "The Prophet of the New Asia" – although, as a socialist, he was somewhat further to the right than most conservatives parties in the West.

His relations with the British were so good in my time in Singapore, it seemed scarcely credible that he had once vociferously advocated the anti-colonialist cause. He could be cynical about the British Labour Party, whose principles, he thought, had been trampled on by "an inward-looking trade union movement" and its philosophy so reduced to emphasis on "more pills for the people", as he found during his visit to London in January 1968, and subsequently observed to me, "forfeited the loyalty of its intellectual elite". He was disturbed in 1967 and angered in 1968 that his old friends in London had let him down by proposing to cut their ties east of Suez.

He admired the initiative, industry and self-confidence which had built the British Empire – and Singapore a bastion of it – first to break the Dutch mercantilist grip on their East Indies (now Indonesia) and then to secure the sea lanes to China. As he saw it, the Empire was not exclusively to British benefit; they gave it up before they needed to and, more than any other imperialists, they educated men like him to take over. But for British determination and skill in two costly campaigns, Malaysia and Singapore could have fallen into communist or Indonesian hands. These were hard and real debts and he was not in any way coy about them. When a new British high commissioner arrived in Singapore in 1968, Lee put on a dinner for him to meet members of the Government and senior officials. No other head of mission received such preferred treatment. Throughout my time in Singapore, he saw more of the British High Commissioner officially than all other heads of mission put together.

The grandfather in whose household Lee grew up wanted him, the oldest grandson, to be educated like an Englishman. As a child, he was 'Little White Boy'. His given name was Harry and one brother was named Dennis and another Freddy. He was not generally known as Kuan Yew and he did not master the Chinese tongue until it became important in his political career. His years at Cambridge could not have been in greater contrast to the immediately preceding cruel and sterile years of the Japanese occupation to which 50,000 of his civilian countrymen in Singapore fell victim. At Cambridge, the other occupying power could teach the intellectual elite of its subject people to think and dream. They were heady years, following the war, when young Englishmen could be as confident of a new order as their forbears had been of the Empire.

Every year since 1959, when he had come to office as prime minister of the self-governing colony of Singapore, aged 35, Lee went back to Britain at least once. Few, if any, people outside Britain — and not too many in it — followed the British press as closely as he did or knew the domestic politics of that country as well, or the processes by which British policy was formed. He was probably on first-name terms with more British politicians, Conservative and Liberal as well as Labour, than anyone else outside Britain. A British public opinion poll rated him television personality of the year in 1968. An (unpublicised) address he gave to a Far East Air Force (RAF) dinner in April 1968 was greeted with thunderous applause. What other Afro-Asian leader could arouse such a response from the RAF? Indeed, he was, perhaps, more at home with a British than a Singaporean audience. Did he, in fact, end up as 'an Englishman with a Chinese face' — the conceit of some Englishmen?

Oddly enough, most of the diplomats in Singapore in our time saw Lee as first and foremost Chinese, and scoffed at the idea — or those who maintained, as I did, that there was something in it — that, like a New Zealander, he could be as different from his forbears as a New Zealander from his. New Zealand, they would say, is an obviously separate country with identifiable indigenous influences which made a manifestly distinctive people. Until fairly recently, they would argue, Singapore was essentially a migrant community where no one who could help it chose to end their days.

As I saw him, Lee was a man of two heritages which, in some measure, coincided. As he said himself, "The British and the Chinese, I think, have a certain affinity of soul." In different lights and to different people, he could be seen as 'insular', 'cold', 'arrogant', 'hypocritical', 'cautious', 'cunning' and 'pragmatic' – the terms in which Dennis Bloodworth saw the British and Chinese contemplating each other.[16] Lee Kuan Yew knew he was right and it was the Mandarin, as much as the Raj, telling you, telling anyone. To paraphrase the advice he gave Washington: 'Well, frankly, Mr President, you won't get anywhere until you find a Vietnamese like me, ready to push my kind of policy'. The stoicism of the Chinese and the British stiff upper lip taught him to knuckle down to it, work hard, face adversity and adjust to change. It had been the habit of Chinese in the tropics, far longer than of Englishmen, to go out in the noon-day sun.

In our day in Singapore, he was cut off from China except in trade and he severely squashed Chinese chauvinism in Singapore. But he could no more ignore his Chinese origin than a New Zealander his British heritage. When the Chinese exploded their first nuclear device, he could say privately, with a mischievous grin, "Some of the glory rubs off on us," and when, during Mrs Gandhi's visit to Singapore in May 1968, someone noted the warmth of the welcome given to her by the Indian community in Singapore, he retorted, privately, with the same roguish grin, "It's nothing compared with the reception Mao would get."

The Chinese and British influences established the parameters. Within them, his most notable quality was his intenseness. Though, on every occasion, he could break into that captivating grin as he was nevertheless apt to take all things seriously, even such small pleasures he allowed himself. At golf, he was out to win. He was a born worrier: "That's what I'm paid to do." His thinking provided for the worst contingency and, in any lesser eventuality, there was a windfall.

As a conversationalist, he was criticised for talking far more than he listened. But he was such a brilliant talker that he outmatched most of those who conversed with him and their interventions usually served no greater purpose than to stimulate his flow. It was always purposeful conversation – no small talk – or at least that is the way he liked it. Probably on the assumption that it would lead to small talk – although I was also inclined to think there was more shyness in him than most people would have thought possible – he steered clear of conversation with women. When I called on

---

[16] Denis Bloodworth, *Chinese Looking Glass*, (London: Secker and Warburg, 1967) pp. 13–14.

him in his office, alone or with others, I reckoned that the time he would allow for pleasantries would be about ten seconds, although the call would often last upwards of an hour. When he went to the airport in September 1968 for a ceremonial welcome to the Prime Minister of Japan, he shook hands with heads of mission while we were lined up waiting for the Japanese plane to arrive and, by chance, he ended up in a group standing beside the French chargé d'affaires. Within the prescribed ten seconds, Lee was away on a marvellous comparison of French and British colonialism.

He came nearest to relaxing completely when, on an evening with two or three men he trusted and a whisky or Campari and soda in hand, he lapsed into talking about people he had encountered. At such times, he could be hilarious, especially in mimicry. No one was spared. At these and other private times, he could be a devastating critic. He found Indira Gandhi "unimaginative and ill-informed", President Eisenhower "eight tragically wasted years", Walt Rostow[17] "more mind than judgement". His unkindest cuts were for the Malaysians, especially because his remarks had a racist slant. Speaking of Commonwealth defence arrangements in Singapore and Malaysia, he said privately, more than once, "We must remember that one party to these arrangements is less than adult." In March 1968, he went on to say, when talking about his discussion with Tun Razak the previous day, "The main thing about the Malays is that they want to be happy. So I kept the issues very simple and he understood them and he was happy."

It would be put as a statement of indisputable fact which would be obvious to any intelligent person. But the discussion of personalities was softened by the grin, the disarming gesture of helplessness. It related to the resolution of problems. Nothing was ever said of any man's private life, nor of any woman not in public office. He could be harshly critical but also magnanimous. He found in Robert McNamara, American Secretary of Defence, 1961–7, "one of the finest minds I ever encountered." When Dean Eyre, New Zealand Minister of Defence, 1960–6, deeply offended other Asians by suggesting publicly that "a basinful of bombs" was needed in Vietnam, Lee said to me only, "Made a gaffe, eh? I like him – hearty, blunt, earnest," and then passed on quickly to the next topic.

Sentiment was not for display, palaver inadmissible. The only time he ever spoke crossly to me was in the latter part of 1966 when, just after returning from a visit to London, he plunged into the problem of restoring formal relations with Indonesia. He called in my Australian colleague and me and, as we entered his inner sanctum – which visitors were only rarely

---

[17] Walt Rostow, 1916–2003, throughout the 1960s, a close adviser to American presidents John F. Kennedy and Lyndon Johnston; one of the principal architects and most passionate defenders of the Vietnam war.

invited to do – I remarked, "Welcome home." Although I was within the prescribed ten seconds, he snapped, "No time for pleasantries." He almost never commented on the weather or sport and certainly never inquired about one's health or family, nor buss any woman on the cheek nor any baby. Nor did he ever pay anyone a compliment to his (let alone her) face. The only exception I recall was a gentle compliment to Sato, Prime Minister of Japan, who, Lee said, had taught a young man (meaning himself) old wisdom about relations among states.

R.H. (later Sir Robertson) Stewart, a New Zealand industrialist, liked to tell the story of being in Singapore with a trade mission in 1964 and, encountering Lee at a reception, waxed eloquent about the dynamic approach and material achievements of his government and finally said, "You know, we should swap governments for a while." Lee replied, "That may be all very well for you but what about us?" Early in 1968, the Canadian High Commissioner, based in Kuala Lumpur, went to see Lee to say they were thinking of giving further aid to Singapore under the Colombo Plan. Lee heard him out and, when the pause for gratitude came, Lee said, "It's not enough."

But Lee was certainly not cold or aloof or deliberately abrasive. I never had the slightest difficulty in getting an appointment to see him, although one obviously exercised restraint in asking. As a rule, I could set my watch by the time he received me for an appointment. There was always a welcoming grin and a warm handshake. Time was never grudged. When the secretary interrupted to remind him of his following appointment, he made a little play of keeping the next fellow waiting. The issues were always gone over fully. There were only two occasions when I spent less than half an hour with him. The first was when we were wanting something: to clear our (RNZAF) practice of staging through Changi to Vietnam. The issue was disposed of in less than five minutes, to our complete satisfaction.

The second occasion was shortly after the race riots in Kuala Lumpur in May 1969 when I accompanied the New Zealand Minister of Defence, David Thomson,[18] and Chief of Defence Staff, Sir Leonard Thornton,[19] to call on Lee. The previous day, a Sunday, we had taken them on a family picnic at Snake Island in Johore Strait, a popular place for waterskiing. At one point, when the minister was out of earshot, I said worriedly to CDS, "You know, I don't think he really understands what's been going on in Kuala Lumpur." CDS looked at me hard and said in his admirably decisive military fashion, "Well, I've tried to tell him and you've tried to tell him. So

---

[18] 1915–99, Minister of Defence 1966–72 and 1978–84.
[19] 1916–99, Chief of Defence Staff 1965–71.

now it's on his head." It was. Next morning, when we called on Lee and the minister gave him a contrary view of the race riots, Lee scarcely bothered to conceal his anger. We were dismissed in less than five minutes.

When his son, Hsien Loong, then a teenager, returned from an extended visit involving a lot of work for many New Zealanders, not a word was said to me so, finally, one evening, on a social occasion, I raised the subject myself. "Oh," said Lee, "Melbourne was best. He stayed there longest, got to know his hosts best and they got to know him. He enjoyed the rest of it, of course, but it was too flitting from one place to another to mean much." (Hsien Loong became Prime Minister of Singapore in 2004, aged 52.) There was not a word of thanks. But thanks, to the Chinese, is for the butcher, the baker. In the next breath, Lee was expressing gratitude in his own way by sounding me out about going to New Zealand on holiday himself.

It fitted in with Dennis Bloodworth's finding: "The Chinese have a more delicate appreciation of personal relations simply because they also have a thick carapace of tough, almost cynical convention ... An intimate shows gratitude, he does not voice it. True sentiment is only shyly revealed."[20] The envoy of a friendly country was not to be treated like a tradesman or relative. Rather, the envoy was to be almost invariably singled out for conversation in a crowd and his correspondence answered within two days, often on the same day, delivered by hand. At first one missed, resented, the absence of pleasantries, but ended up wondering whether Lee was not more honest, more subtle, more civilized than most people – more a Confucian in his manner than an Englishman. But he did not fit neatly into this or any other category.

On most occasions and with most people, there was a notable element of reserve. Even among his own colleagues, Goh Keng Swee was the only one I ever heard call him Harry – at least in the presence of outsiders, the others avoided the point of whether it was to be Harry or Kuan Yew or anything else. He rightly expected a decent respect for the position he held. This was not tied to the smallness of a country where, as the Speaker once put it to me, every member of Parliament lived within a 25 cent bus ride of Parliament House. Lee rightly demanded decorum on public occasions. However, while on private, stag occasions, his colleagues – his countrymen – happily lapsed into a good run of bawdiness, and this was never, never done in Lee's presence. He had a strong puritanical streak. During the euphoria of capping week in 1967, some of the lads at the University of Singapore staged a rather feeble 'panty raid' on a women's students' hostel. Lee let fly with a volley of indignant anger. The Tunku, when Prime Minister of Malaysia, could refer understandingly to the 'womanising' of the Forces. It was the

---

[20] Bloodworth, op. cit. pp. 265–6.

kind of word that never passed Lee's lips. In private, he let 'bloody' drop now and then, but that seemed somehow contrived to put my Australian colleague and me at ease.

In my first three years in Singapore, Lee went only twice to a diplomatic home – once to put in a dutiful half hour at a garden party in Mrs Gandhi's honour and, secondly, when he rose to the occasion of our Governor-General's visit in 1966. (That evening was notable for the toasts. Lee proposed "The Queen" and Sir Bernard Fergusson responded by proposing "The President of Malaysia", then apologised for the rest of the evening.) He was not just keeping his distance. He was conserving his energy, reading omnivorously, pondering the problems before him, writing his own plethora of speeches, rearranging the world.

His severely restricted social activity reflected the priorities of a carefully ordered life. This included a concern for his health as intense as his concern for any other problem. "He's a tremendous fad about what he eats and drinks," Goh Keng Swee (who could live it up) counselled me when we first met. When the Speaker put on a dinner for a team of New Zealand parliamentarians in 1967, Lee let it be known that he would go (as he did) after he had dined at home. He drank in the most careful moderation. Once a heavy smoker (50 a day), he came to detest the habit. The annual pilgrimage to Britain followed a solemn ritual: before catching the night plane, there was a tiring game of golf, a hot bath, a good meal and then, on board, sleeping pills, eyeshade, earplugs. He had to be ready for those chaps – a favourite word – in Whitehall.

There could be odd spasms of anxiety about assassination, the kidnapping of his children or other breach of security. He was once pacing the floor of his office, the inner sanctum, while he talked to my Australian colleague and me, when he suddenly stopped, went to the drawn venetian blinds behind which he normally worked, tilted a few slats aside a little and looking down on the street below, said, "One of these days they'll get me." He then immediately resumed the conversation. Again, in November 1967, when I went to see him for the first time after his return from the United States, we talked initially about other things, then I asked how he'd got on with the President. Lee paused, rose abruptly to his feet and said, "Just a moment till I lock the door," and when he had done so, although there was always a guard outside the door, the conversation immediately resumed with merry normality.

These two minor incidents aside, I found him the most equable and mild-tempered of men, extremely easy to get along with. One had to acknowledge, of course, that this reflected New Zealand's special position. And things had been different in the hectic days of Separation, as the severance with Malaysia was called. At that time, the British High Commissioner, John Rob, was once received by an exhausted Prime Minister, reclining on a couch, his head wrapped in a wet towel. Those were, however, exceptionally excitable days when the concept of Malaysia, for which Lee had worked hard, came tumbling down. Separation, moreover, left him with an army composed mainly of Malaysian citizens and a police force that was predominantly Malay. He became Prime Minister of a predominantly Chinese city-state surrounded by mistrustful, if not hostile, Malays.

To preserve the image of Singapore as a multiracial society, he displayed specimen Malays in prominent positions, but no one got into the Cabinet except on merit. With acerbity matching Lee's, a senior Chinese official in the Ministry of Education once remarked to me, of Rahim Ishak, the Malay Parliamentary Under-Secretary for Education, that it was difficult to tell whether he was alive or dead. Within the Cabinet there was no pretence of being first among equals. He was pre-eminent in intellect and authority and he let this be known. At the end of the Speaker's dinner for New Zealand parliamentarians in August 1967, to which a majority of the local parliamentarians, including five cabinet ministers, turned up, Lee suggested to me that the New Zealanders leave first. He added, not solely for my ears, "I want to give the boys a pep talk."

He set the tone, devised the grand design, the philosophy. The British bases in Singapore represented a vital issue for him. On this, he, by and large, played a lone hand and accounted to his colleagues afterwards. There was nevertheless a substantial measure of threshing out all issues, at least within the inner Cabinet and there was certainly a full measure of collective responsibility. From time to time there were rumours of 'dissension' in Cabinet, in particular between Lee and Goh. It was a notion, I thought, aired by the British military intelligence wallahs second-guessing high commissioners – and non-sensical. Lee and Goh were very different men but they needed each other and complemented each other very well. It was only to be expected that they might disagree at times, honestly and fundamentally. That was healthy. But it was also to be expected that the disagreements would blow over quickly. And they did.

Government members worked as a team and it was not always Lee who led the way. With economic issues or new ideas of any kind, it was usually Goh. It was he who initiated the Jurong Industrial complex which cynics originally called "Goh's folly" but which soon paid off. It was Goh, too, who took the lead, when Minister of Defence, in planning the expansion of the Singaporean armed forces. The relationship among members of the Cabinet was solid enough for talk so straight and banter so vigorous that it could easily be misunderstood by outsiders. At a working dinner for the British Secretary of State for Commonwealth Relations, Sir Saville Garner, who, in January 1968 brought news of an accelerated withdrawal of their forces from East of Suez, Goh did most of the talking on the Singapore side – and he talked very vigorously, indeed. As the party was breaking up, Lee said of Goh, to Sir Saville Garner, and in Goh's presence, "I put him in to say the things which I wouldn't dare say myself. He's really a bit of a thug."

Over the years, I took many New Zealand Cabinet ministers to see Lee, or helped make the arrangements for others, such as parties of journalists, to call. Almost invariably they were captivated by him. The same held good of New Zealanders living in Singapore but who never met him and based their judgement on his speeches and interviews on television. A cool generation of New Zealand university students overflowed the halls to hear him speak on his visit in 1965. He was lionised in Britain, invited to address Labour Party rallies and international Socialist conferences: Stockholm in 1966 and Zurich in 1967. What was the attraction?

To begin with, Lee worked from a solid base. The strains of confrontation, separation from Malaysia and the impending British withdrawal from their bases in Singapore only spurred him on his way to weld a dynamic little nation out of rather unpromising material. Critics could say that his virtually absolute command of the electorate enabled him to do very much as he pleased. He could say, "Let there be trees," and within a year there were 15,000 and not the slightest murmur from anyone about the expense. But, a Socialist, he could also decide that wages must be strictly, ruthlessly, pegged to productivity – a concept which a community emerging from semi-literacy might have been expected to question as much as, if not more than, a literate society. He stoutly turned his back on what J.K.Galbraith called "the politics of convenience … the belief that the proper remedy for man's problems is whatever does not cause too much trouble". In an editorial on 2 May 1968, *The Far Eastern Economic Review* said, "Mr Lee knows that a politician's duty is not merely to represent the wishes of the majority but to provide a positive lead on issues, the rights and wrongs of which are beyond discussion." Singapore's growing prosperity, the manifest contentment of the people, the law and order, all showed that he was a man of action as well as words.

Lee's words could be dazzling, cutting to the heart of an issue in the shortest possibly order, the bon mots perhaps picked up from his highly literate mates at Cambridge. His mind was keenly analytical, the line of reasoning embedded in a sense of history and the realities of power. Alister (later Sir Alister) McIntosh, New Zealand Secretary of External Affairs, 1943–66, who, in his day, attended more Commonwealth Heads of Government Conferences than anyone else, thought Lee's intervention on Southern Rhodesia, at the meeting in Lagos in January 1965, was the most brilliant speech he had heard at any of these gatherings. After returning to Singapore, Lee said (privately) of this speech, "Harold [Macmillan, British Prime Minister 1957–63] put me on as a filler, you know, like they do on television when they've got nothing better to fill a gap. So I said my little piece and the white men cheered and the rest of them hated me for every word I said." This was only a matter of weeks after Lee had become Prime Minister (August 1965) and eligible to attend such meetings. The new boy could well have been silent on an issue relatively remote from his country's essential interests. Of course he enjoyed being in the limelight and it helped to have trained as an advocate and to have abounding self-confidence. But the essential ingredient in his ability to make a good speech such as the one on Southern Rhodesia was that he revelled in learning and in thinking through any problem that came his way. He was the kind of man who took a rather fiendish delight in finishing the cryptic crossword or a thousand-piece jigsaw puzzle after everyone else has given up.

One of the most pervasive problems in Lee's little city-state was how to achieve racial harmony among a very mixed bag of people with a history of erupting into communal strife. (During our early months in Singapore in 1966, the British military people – who had a kind of early warning system to keep their [and Australian and New Zealand] forces out of the way of race riots – would tip off our high commissions, too, when trouble was brewing.) The Government could encourage racial tolerance by exhortation but words were not nearly enough when racial feeling ran so deep. Nor was it enough to tell the police to get tough, bang a few heads together, when the heads could be those of the policemen's brothers. The only word which the English language adopted from Malay has been, tellingly, to run 'amok'. The Malays distrusted, resented and hated the Chinese, the highest achievers and the predominant ethnic group in Singapore. So it was a complex problem needing a multi-faceted remedy. This included active discrimination in favour of the Malays, to give them a statistically just proportion of everything from taxi licenses to prominent positions in government, notwithstanding that this might be – and, in the latter case demonstrably was – at the expense of better-qualified, more competent Chinese or Indians.

There was a baffling array of practical problems in the way of establishing racial harmony. The muezzin summoning the faithful to prayer at dawn (and dusk) was, we thought, a very pleasant, somehow comforting, sound – at a distance. But when the mosques installed an amplifying system, adjacent to high-rise apartment buildings, awakening infidel and faithful alike, the infidel majority strongly objected. Not only was their sleep disturbed. The value of their properties fell. There were times when Lee became depressed and exasperated by what he called "the low compression people" and "the blight" of their religion. Such strictures were almost invariably kept as private muttering, and behind the scenes he beavered away to establish racial harmony as a prerequisite to stability and progress.

Perhaps it's the same everywhere – that nothing is ever quite what it seems to be. Despite Lee's lucidity and notwithstanding the very cordial relations which my Australian colleague and I enjoyed with him, we could come away from a long discussion with him mumbling to each other, "What's he really driving at?" or even, "What the bloody hell is he up to now?" There was a measure of obscurantism, certainly ambivalence. Although as much as a sixth of Singapore was occupied by British bases from which Singapore derived its security and a fifth of its income, Lee could publicly, but never privately, maintain that Singapore was non-aligned. Although rectitude was taken to the point of prudishness – *Playboy* was banned and, to discourage his soldiers from drinking too much, they were required to pay the full retail price for beer in their messes – the Government nevertheless saw to it, indirectly, strictly behind the scenes, that Singapore's several thousand prostitutes were kept in hygienic condition and the libidinous expectations of American GIs, on 'R & R' leave from Vietnam, were amply provided for in upmarket premises. (As each new plane-load of GIs arrived, activities began with an ostensibly decorous tea dance at which the lads paired off with a girl and when, finally, they got to sleep, the girls sat out on their balconies in the tropical night air and, across the central swimming pool, swapped bedtime stories.)

Appropriately enough, perhaps, for so small a state so dependent on others, Singapore's foreign policy strongly resembled an all-risks insurance policy. All options were to be kept open for as long as possible. After Lee's official visit to Cambodia in 1968, his first engagement on his return was to play golf with Admiral Sharp, the United States Commander-in-Chief in the Pacific. The visits of the Australian and then the New Zealand Prime Ministers in that year were followed by a visit by the Vice-President of North Korea. Then the Foreign Minister of Singapore visited South Korea. Such nimble footwork mystified and, at times, irritated the more straightforward Malaysians and introspective Indonesians. Lee saw such reactions as clearly as anyone else. He said to me many times, wistfully, perhaps artfully, of the Malaysians, "They think I'm too clever by half … I have only to sneeze and they think I'm up to something."

There was a price to be paid for Lee's regime, most notably in the authoritarianism and curtailment of liberty. The expatriate members of the staff at the University of Singapore were aghast when a senior Cabinet minister, Toh Chin Chye, was concurrently appointed as their Vice-

Chancellor. Rank-and-file unionists, who had put Lee into power, could well have been at least puzzled when he tied wages to productivity. And young Chinese men must have thought their world was being turned upside down when, if they passed the fitness test, they were called up for two years of military service. The British had always thought the Singapore Chinese were 'unmilitary' and best left to make money while the more malleable Malays were recruited for the police force and army. Now here were the Chinese, mixed with all other ethnicities, undergoing military exercises with live ammunition, under the stern eye of Israeli military advisers. The press was brought to heel. The heavy doses of nation-building propaganda, on radio and television, were nauseating to Western ears.

But Singapore remained, in essence, an open society whose citizens might travel, transfer money and, in substantial degree, talk as they pleased. They were, moreover, exposed to the cosmopolitan influences of a great seaport, a centre of airways and other communications and of foreign investment and expertise. The leavening process was almost palpable, as was the mellowing process in Lee himself, as he gained in confidence with the success of his efforts. Local criticism of government policy was limited and related to peripheral issues. There was not the slightest sign that Singaporeans were in any way unwilling to pay Lee's price. On the contrary, they gave him the ultimate in the 'mandate of heaven', such as the ancient Emperors of China thought they had, when he topped off his clean electoral sweep in 1968 by responding to his appeal for contributions to a defence fund with gifts of money totalling over S$6 million. That his government was authoritarian by Western standards was irrelevant to Singaporeans, who saw no credible alternative policy and who, under his leadership, became better fed, housed, educated, paid, amused and motivated than ever before – or than any of their neighbours in South and South-east Asia.

II. FAREWELLING A GREAT EMPIRE

When Stamford Raffles established the East India Company's outpost in Singapore in 1819, he arranged for the several races – European, Chinese, Malay and Indian – to work together but live apart. That was the standard segregationist practice of Raffles' time and it remained the well-founded norm wherever the British went in their Empire.

> There were down-to-earth reasons why a British garrison, or a British community, should not live in the heart of a tropical town. Plagues and tropical diseases were little understood, women and children were less self-reliant then, the most broad-minded of colonels would hardly wish his soldiers to associate too easily with the bazaar whores.[21]

In Singapore, there were also formidable barriers of language, religion, diet and custom to separate the Chinese, Malays and Indians not only from the British but from each other. Even in our day in Singapore, the language laboratory at the Singapore Armed Forces Institute operated from 5 am, battering away at the linguistic barriers. And dietary and other differences persisted to such an extent that cooking for Singapore's armed forces created a chef's nightmare in having to provide for pork-free Muslims and Jews, beef-free Hindus, vegetarian Buddhists, meat-less Fridays for Roman Catholics and Muslim and kosher rites for the slaughtering of livestock.

And all this was despite the fact that, in the course of time and especially in Lee Kuan Yew's time, segregation had to a large extent disappeared. Of the four families neighbouring our home, four were Chinese, one Indian and one European. In the predominantly Malay kampongs (villages) of Singapore, Chinese lived cheek by jowl with – and profited from – Malays. In some respects segregation was never strictly observed. The earliest and most notable Hindu temple in Singapore (built originally in 1827 and later rebuilt on the same site), as well as a prominent old mosque, were in the heart of Chinatown, handy to the waterfront so that seafarers could pray before leaving. In a few cases of institutional social activity, segregation disappeared at a surprisingly early stage. The Singapore Cricket Club, with its playing field on the village green which formed the hub of the settlement which Raffles planned and which Lee's office overlooked, had been multiracial for more than a century.

Lee said, "There are now no more enclaves," and he was correct. But he was not counting the British bases. Both in law and in fact they were a

---

[21] James Morris, *Pax Britannica: The Climax of an Empire* (London: Faber and Faber, 1968), p. 131.

separate issue. Indeed, given the extent to which segregation was a thing of the past in Singapore and having in mind that Singapore and Britain had, in the new order of things, become partners in defence, it was extraordinary that the occupants of the British cantonments kept themselves so much apart from the rest of the community. In our five years there, British and Singaporean forces paraded together only once, and then it was only bandsmen participating in a massed bands rally. We often dined at the homes of senior British military officers but, apart from the Commander-in-Chief, whose list of Singaporean dinner guests was very short and obviously handed on from one incumbent to the next, only one British officer, Sir Rochford Hughes, originally a New Zealander, ever included local people. Shortly before leaving Singapore after an assignment of two and a half years, the General (a doctor) in charge of British Army medical affairs in Singapore and Malaysia told me he had never met a local doctor. Not even the padres wandered from the fold, notwithstanding that ten percent of Singaporeans were Christian.

It was the diplomats, of course, and not the soldiers, who were paid to enjoy sea slugs and civet cat soup ("The Chinese ... believe that practically everything is edible and may require killing first"[22]) and conversation with women like the wife of a minister of state who, after I had wrung the subject of her children dry, said, when I asked if she had seen a current film, "Oh, I never go to the movies." Nor can the British military people be blamed for being wary of their own compatriots in the business community when many of them failed to observe the unwritten rules (Air Marshal Sir John Grandy, the Commander-in-Chief, once remarked to me that a prominent local British businessman, probably the most prominent, had arrived for dinner "at thirteen minutes past eight – he's quite an impossible fellow") and were, anyhow, apt to reciprocate hospitality by inviting people to 'curry tiffin', a Sunday tribal rite where expatriates drank for several hours in the hottest part of the tropical day and then ate so ravenously that there was no escaping their conclusion that, "There's only one thing to do with a good curry and that's take it to bed" – sleep it off.

The British military establishment during our time in Singapore was a highly self-sufficient and disciplined world of its own, with a wide array of creature comforts and amenities – swimming pools, golf courses, churches (where, for instance, they practised, perhaps invented, Anglican Expeditious – singing only the first few verses of any hymn and somehow, it seemed, never allowing any sermon to exceed ten minutes so that elevenses were not unduly delayed, yacht clubs, cinemas (not subject to any censorship),

---

[22] D.B.Enright, *Memoirs of a Mendicant Professor* (London, Chatto and Windus, 1939), p. 78.

canteens (with duty-free liquor), radio stations, schools, medical and dental facilities and, for the top brass, pleasure craft carefully shown in the inventory as 'patrol launches'. And those facilities which the British Government did not provide, the Singaporean Chinese ensured were within easy walking distance of the gate. ("It's a funny thing about servicemen," observed a British military policeman as we drove past a rather sleazy-looking bar, "they have excellent bars on the base and beer is 50 cents a time. But no, they'd sooner come here – get away from the regimentation – and pay a dollar sixty for a beer plus lolly-water for the hostesses.")

The bases were so scrupulously well-ordered that every possible contingency was taken care of. The airport farewell for the Commander-in-Chief (Far East), to give Sir John Grandy his full designation, and his wife – we were told well in advance – was to be regarded as a military occasion and kissing, therefore, was out. A ceremonial occasion would be ordered in such a way that the written instructions declared, "The New Zealand High Commissioner is to arrive at 0913. It is imperative that this time be maintained." At all times and under all circumstances, every officer one rank or more above another was 'Sir' to those below him. Even visiting a high commissioner in hospital seemed to be covered by the rule book. A senior British officer would be too busy to come himself so he sent his aide with a volume of Kipling's verse on loan. Precisely right. They brought their seasons with them and, in a perpetually long hot summer, 80 miles from the equator, put on a magnificent Summer Ball – "Reception: 9 pm, Carriages: 3 am". (RAF Officers' Mess, Changi, 18 July 1969). In the end, they went back to "Shackleford Old Rectory, Eashing, Godalming, Surrey" (as a commander-in-chief did) or some equally charming address, notified in 'change of address' cards which rounded out an orderly life. The final step in departing etiquette was to leave Cookie, as the Chinese cook was invariably called, a fond testimonial, remembering that no one ever made Yorkshire pudding better than he did.

When the New Zealander Air Marshal Sir Rochford Hughes, got his 'K' in the New Year Honours of 1967, his mother and her sister, both widowed and in their eighties, living in Auckland, came to Singapore to stay at Air House, which was one down the scale from Command House, the residence of the Commander-in-Chief. The mother was inordinately proud of her son. The aunt was, too, but perhaps just a little bit jealous and anyhow determined not to be over-awed by it all. When someone admired her beautiful, long black lace dress, she replied matter-of-factly, "Yes, it is rather nice. I bought it in 1911." And when I sat next to her at dinner and remarked that Air House was a rather splendid place, with a garden of several acres, looking out on a golf course, she agreed hesitantly and, after pausing a moment or so, added, "But it's all rather a waste, you know. They could easily run a few chooks on this place … and a cow." And, of course, she was right.

But the British military establishment was not, by any means, a smug or blimpish world. At the top it was run by graduates of the Imperial Defence College, exceedingly lively-minded men whose range of interest and responsibility stretched from the Persian Gulf to Hong Kong and Fiji, with an eye also on Europe where their future would lie; whose accountability extended to five capitals with different expectations; and whose views kept closely aligned with those of the British Foreign Office. (The Commander-in-Chief had on his staff a 'political adviser', a senior Foreign Office man. It seemed to be an assignment given as the last job before retirement, a practice which led my feisty Australian colleague Bill Pritchett to remark, "Fancy winding up your diplomatic career by holding the po for an admiral!") It was a world schooled in hard and often bitter experience, including the experience of more widespread colonial administration than that of any other country; and a world immeasurably strengthened by the expectation that junior officers should speak their minds to their seniors ('Sir'). By his own account, General Carver, a commander-in-chief (Far East) in our time and eventually Lord Carver, Chief of the British Defence Staff in London, in his younger days often argued with Field Marshal Montgomery. And Carver became a brigadier at 29. It was a world remarkably tolerant of eccentricity within its own ranks and in which the human factor and the humorous aspect were never overlooked. In all, it was remarkably different from its intensely earnest and more rigidly hierarchical American counterpart. No country, I think, bettered the British in producing a military officer establishment, drawn from all quarters of society, then promoted on merit (although this had not always been so) with such a deep sense of leadership and duty – a sense shared by their wives – so much authorship and so little political ambition.

In the course of passing from British over-lordship to partnership in defence, the separate nature of the British military establishment in Singapore resulted in certain awkwardness, misunderstandings and irritations with the Government of Singapore. The Singaporean military people found the British professionalism daunting. The British admired Singapore's zestful determination to build up a serious fighting force in the shortest possible time. They envied Lee's ability to carry taxpayer opinion with him in suddenly embarking on massive defence expenditure. And they thought it was inspirational that he should appoint a wealthy banker, Lim Kim San, to be Minister of Defence in the socialist government of a commercial community. But the British found the Singaporeans woefully ignorant and full of 'theoretical intelligence' in military affairs, as, indeed, at staff level, they were. And only time and experience could alter that.

General Carver, when Commander-in-Chief, set up a series of five-nation Advisory Working Groups to consider practical problems arising in the wake of British withdrawal. I wondered at the time whether their work would ever have got off the ground if it had not been for the leavening influence of Australian and New Zealand. Listening from the sidelines to what our own military people reported, one could see all too easily that British professionalism was clashing with Singaporean ignorance in military affairs, and I reflected on how much smoother the transition might have been if only the people at the top had talked to each other a bit. It seemed to me inexcusable, for instance, that a commander-in-chief should have been in the job for three months before meeting Singapore's Secretary of Defence and longer still before he met Singapore's Minister of Defence, Goh Keng Swee, who, for part of that time, was Acting Prime Minister. It was inexcusable, too, that the British, who might reasonably have been expected to give Singapore a helping hand in putting together its own military establishment, should have largely priced themselves out of this role by making the ruling rate for the loan of a wing commander, for instance, £11,000 a year (including amortisation of his flying training costs), more than twice as much as Singapore paid its prime minister. (In February 1969, the amortisation of training costs was eliminated but the loan of a wing commander, at £6,500 a year, was still more than the Prime Minister's salary.)

The Singaporeans, mind you, were separatists, too. The Commander-in-Chief had no place, formal or otherwise, in Singapore's table of precedence, whereas the succession of Englishmen who in our time became President of Singapore's International Chamber of Commerce, representing the interests of expatriate firms, were openly given an unofficial place in that table of precedence, between Cabinet ministers and heads of departments. Only once in our five years was the Commander-in-Chief or other senior British military officers invited to a State banquet or similar occasion – the State banquet in honour of Princess Alexandra, which was part of Singapore's sesquicentennial celebrations. Senior British military officers were never invited (as the diplomatic corps was) to attend Singapore's rather spectacular National Day parade or receptions and suchlike at the Istana, the President's grand official residence (originally built, by convict labour brought from India, for the British Governor). Only very rarely did Lee or any of his Cabinet colleagues set foot on any of the British bases. No VIP visitor who arrived in or left Singapore at an RAF base was ever met or farewelled by a Singaporean.

Surprising although such separatism was, it was even more surprising that it worked so well. It was deeply rooted in the past, well understood and accepted by both sides. Separatism meant, moreover, that the British military presence could scarcely have been more discreet. Indeed, it was so discreet that any visitor to Singapore who kept to the main tourist attractions, as most of them did, saw absolutely nothing of the British bases. British (and Australian and New Zealand) servicemen rarely went into the city in uniform and their training areas were mainly in Malaysia. So Singapore could have its cake and eat it too. Important strategic bases were there all right but, when it suited, Singapore could claim to be non-aligned. It had also been an exceptionally good bargain for Singapore. For a long time it had been the British, in partnership with Australia and New Zealand, who had met almost the entire cost of Singapore's defence, both in lives and vast expenditure and, moreover, contributed a fifth of Singapore's income.

> British separatism had been part of the mystique of empire.
> … a few thousand white men ruled or worked among several million coloured people; throughout the dependent Empire, racial supremacy and imperial supremacy were synonymous. Racial separatism was employed by the British as an instrument of Government …[23]

Racial supremacy could become ugly, especially when there was a bit too much liquor about. James Hahn, a Korean, liked to tell of an attempt made in 1968 to hustle him and a friend from a ringside table at a crowded nightclub in Hong Kong. The white man glowered with complete assurance, "Don't you know who I am! I'm the Assistant Deputy Commissioner of Police!" To which James Hahn had the pleasure of retorting, "And fuck you. I'm South-east Asian Manager for Reuters!"

The Chinese never conceded they were racially inferior. They might allow the British their illusions but it was they, the Chinese, who belonged to the Kingdom of Heaven. And they had a point. They could consider what their civilisation had achieved when the British were still in coracles and woad. In reduced circumstances, the Chinese – in the main, it was the riffraff of the China coast – might flock to the protection and some sort of living in a British settlement such as Singapore, but when Kipling paid his first visit there, he was astonished at the extent to which the Chinese ran the colony: "England is, by the uninformed, supposed to own the island." For two generations after Singapore was founded and for almost a century after Penang was founded (1786), not a single British member of

---

[23] James Morris, *Pax Britannica* (London, Faber and Faber, 1968), p. 139.

the administration knew the Chinese language and when such a linguist, Pickering, was appointed in 1873, he found:

> We were styled in the Chinese copies of our own Government proclamations 'red-haired barbarians' ... In the courts, the judges, barristers and jury were all, by our own paid interpreters, spoken of as 'barbarians' or 'devils' and the police were distinguished by the flattering title of 'big dogs.'[24]

In 1875 Pickering was styled 'Protector of the Chinese', He spent his career in a losing battle to exert control over 'the Celestials'. He was obliged to work through their secret societies, obnoxious although he found them:

> The Chinese formed an imperium in imperio [a state within a state]. The innate feeling of superiority and racial separateness that characterised them in their relationships with foreigners, ignorance of their language and customs among the rest of the population and the fact that they regarded themselves as temporary residents with no loyalty to the place, seeking to make a fortune and return to their villages in China, were strong pre-disposing factors. But the main reason was that the powerful Chinese Secret Societies, which were blood brotherhoods, had enrolled a very large part of them and took upon themselves many of the normal functions of government in what amounted to an unmistakable although not necessarily unfriendly disregard of the official administration.[25]

In commerce, too, the Chinese had a knack of coming out on top. It was said, 'Englishmen have five dollar, make one dollar business. Chinese have one dollar, make five dollar business'.[26] The great British merchant houses enjoyed a privileged position in trade but "an accident of race conferred upon each Chinese businessman an acumen so acute, so ingenious and so resourceful that he was more than a match for any monopolist."[27] It was co-existence to the manifest advantage of both sides.

This then, was the background to Lee Kuan Yew's excellent rapport with the British. Sometimes he took it so far that I wondered if he was having me

---

[24] Quoted in R.N Jackson, *Pickering, Protector of Chinese* (London, Oxford University Press, 1965), pp. 18–19.

[25] ibid., p. 17.

[26] D. and J. Moore, *The First Hundred and Fifty Years of Singapore* (Singapore, Donald Moore Press, 1969), p. 233.

[27] ibid., p. 233.

on. In March 1970, he reflected in conversation, "I suppose we are all, in a way, prisoners of our youth ... When I was young, the battle raged about my home for three days and, in the end, the Indian soldiers shuffled by on their way to Changi jail. I don't blame them, shuffling. They were exhausted. They were defeated. They were mercenaries. But when the British came by, they tried to keep in step. There, in that gesture, there was pride, discipline, purpose. And I thought to myself, 'There is a people'." And he was deeply moved by the recollection. And so was I.

When he went to Britain to study at Cambridge after the war, his reaction must have been almost precisely the same as that of Han Suyin, a prolific, best-selling Eurasian author who first visited Britain in 1936 and wondered:

> Was this really England, whose mighty name had shaken our hearts in Asia, with terror and fear at her power? This narrow, grey, cold little island with rather dirty houses and gentle, kind people, harassed by the greyness and wetness of their island? Polite people, shy people and so many poor, so many poor, when I had thought the streets of London paved with gold ... I had come prepared to find a nation of supermen and superwomen, something like a perpetual vice-regal pageant; and I found a country of ordinary men and women ... with children pale and scrawny. The paucity and inferior quality of the cooking depressed me... And so I lost my fear of England and fell in love with it, precisely because it was such a sham, so poor and grey and wet and dirty ... and yet its people put up with all these discomforts. And it was in England that I knew myself as good as anyone else, liking and disliking individuals on their own. Even more quickly did I fall in love with the English language, that rich and inexhaustible treasure of words and music, feeling and thought ...[28]

For Lee (who first saw England war-torn while Han Suyin had seen it in the Great Depression) there was much else besides – beginning, perhaps, with Stamford Raffles, vigorous servant of a commercial company – and a pretty sordid one at that, by modern standards – but a self-taught scholar who left an astonishingly complete record of what he saw and did; a liberal and a visionary who could write:

> Let it still be the boast of Britain to write her name in characters of light; let her not be remembered as the tempest whose course was desolate but as the gale of spring reviving the slumbering seeds of

---

[28] Han Suyin, *A Mortal Flower* (London, Jonathan Cape, 1966), pp. 356–7.

the mind and calling them to life from the winter of ignorance and oppression. If the time shall come when her empire shall have passed away, these monuments will endure when her triumphs shall have become an empty name.[29]

Then, on top of Britain's historic ascendancy in commerce, technology, exploration and all the rest of it, the British had a gift for sleight of hand, one-up-manship, knowing when to look the other way. If things went well in the Malay states, Whitehall and the British advisers attached to the Sultans could smile and say, "Well, the advisers were there only to advise". In substantial degree, the economy of modern Malaysia – this was before the more recent discovery of oil – was based on their rubber industry, the world's greatest. And it had grown from the illegal act of an Englishman, Henry Wickham, in smuggling rubber tree seeds from Brazil in 1876. In 1851, another Englishman, Robert Fortune, had "travelled in disguise, pretending to be a Chinese from a distant province beyond the Great Wall [and] with prodigious difficulties" smuggled seeds and plants from China to establish the tea plantations of Darjeeling and Assam, whose trade shortly exceeded that of China.[30]

In all this, Lee could quietly admire the legerdemain, the adventurous spirit. And, in our time, when we picnicked with any Singaporean minister and his family – although few of them indulged in such light-hearted activity – we swam in a shark-proof enclosure by the shore. But, with the senior British military people it was always and often from a launch in the open sea. They declared gaily that the sharks were so well fed from the cast-off food thrown overboard by all the international shipping in these waters, they wouldn't bother with any of us. And after five years of swimming in this way, many dozens, perhaps hundreds of times, my wife and I and our children emerged unscathed to confirm the assumption.

But one day we learnt that it could be very different when swimming in the pool of a Chinese millionaire in Singapore. He lived behind high walls with broken glass embedded on top and high, unclimbable iron gates, locked at night, when guard-dogs were let out in the grounds. Late one afternoon we had been swimming – as we'd been invited to do at any time – at the pool belonging to Runme Shaw, a film magnate who lived across the

---

[29] Quoted in C.E. Wurtzburg, *Raffles of the Eastern Isles* (London, Hodder and Stoughton, 1954), p. 634. This extract is from a 10,000-word document originally written in 1819. The two sentences above have been put in reverse order to fit into the present context.

[30] George Woodcock, *The British in the Far East* (London, Weidenfeld and Nicholson, 1969), p. 87.

road from us. My son and I were dressed ahead of my wife and daughter, so began walking slowly home, expecting them to follow at any moment, but that day they tarried to use a hair dryer. Seeing my son and me leave, Runme's staff assumed we'd all left, closed and locked the gates and let out the three Alsatian guard dogs. As my wife and daughter emerged from the changing sheds the dogs savaged them viciously, bringing daughter Brendy, aged 11, to the ground. Runme's staff heard their screams and came running out to call off the dogs. My wife and Brendy were rushed to hospital, between them acquiring 54 stitches.

(Runme Shaw, who had been away from Singapore at the time, was profusely apologetic when he returned and wanted to compensate in any way he could. We declined any financial compensation, as he pressed us to accept but finally I said, "Well, you know what? How about giving Brendy a small poodle pup from your latest litter?" And so we acquired Puff (named after "Puff the Magic Dragon", a catchy song then current) who quickly became a much-loved member of the family who played endlessly with the children and especially excelled himself at hide-and-seek. And so dog-phobia in the family was averted. Puff so captivated visitors to our home that, after we'd returned to New Zealand and handed him over to our successors, I was walking down Lambton Quay one lunch hour when David Seath, a Cabinet minister, hailed me and reported delightedly, "I was in Singapore the other day and saw Puff!")

The Singaporeans, moreover, had not been obliged to struggle hard for self-government, as other colonies had. In this struggle, Nehru said he'd gone back and forth to prison nine times, like a shuttlecock. In Singapore, the transition from a British-governed to a self-governing colony seemed to proceed from the script for a jolly good farce in London's West End. Here was David Marshall, a Jew born in Singapore, with forbears from Iraq, of Persian extraction, becoming the first Chief Minister in a newly self-governing community which was predominantly Chinese with a substantial admixture of Malays, Indians and Pakistanis. When Marshall suggested that his elevated rank entitled him to a better office and the British demurred, he brought them to heel smartly by setting himself up in a broom cupboard under the stairs. This, he said, was where he would receive visitors from abroad. Well, that's how he told it. (He did well in his private law practice, married an English woman and they lived happily in their home by the sea at Changi Beach (now submerged under the reclamation for Singapore's splendid new airport), where they loved to have visitors, including children, for lunch on Sundays. On these occasions, he wore a straw hat with a badge proclaiming, 'If it moves, fondle it!' He apparently took this as something of a challenge for, although he couldn't have been happier than he was in his sixties when, after several daughters, he finally fathered a son, he went on to stray a bit when he was later appointed Singapore's Ambassador in Paris.)

(The New Zealand diplomat, Bryce Harland (1931–2004), used to recall an occasion in Singapore in 1956 when, as a third secretary on his first posting, the more senior members of the diplomatic staff in the office were away at SEATO meetings in Bangkok. He was so bored that he rang David Marshall, then Chief Minister, and Han Suyin (1917–), a Eurasian then living across the causeway in Johore Bahru and well on the way with her career as a prolific writer and influential Sinologist, and invited them to lunch at Raffles Hotel. "And," Bryce would grin triumphantly, "they both came.")

Then, too, as Lee would have it, the British quickly got the measure of the Malays. They were 'Nature's Gentlemen', a fun-loving, lovable people with whom it was possible to communicate because any fool could learn their language. But, once communication had been established, it was to find, "They can easily get their daily rice by working one day a week and they ask for no more. All fatigue is useless and harmful. Life is long – why hurry?"[31]

(Lee Kuan Yew once exclaimed incredulously to our Prime Minister, Keith (later Sir Keith) Holyoake, "You know, the Tunku (Abdul Rahman, then Prime Minister of Malaysia) only works two hours a day! Could you get by on that!") British imperial enterprise needed labour and the Malays were not about to fill that role. They contributed little to the development of the three main industries, rubber, tin and timber, and the marketing of these products, on which the comparative prosperity of Malaysia very largely depended, to Singapore's benefit, except armchair supervision and direction from government offices and board rooms. It was "the high compression people", as Lee called them, the British, and Indians, who did the work.

So the British enticed the Chinese, and to a lesser extent, Indians and Pakistanis, to become the secondary – the real – colonists of what became Singapore and Malaysia. The Chinese had traded in South-east Asia and mined tin in the Malaysian peninsula for centuries before the Europeans intruded, but it was under British patronage that the flood of migration occurred. It was to be confirmed as permanent settlement by the chaos which reigned in China in the 1930s and 1940s and by the Bamboo Curtain erected there in 1949. In masterminding this development, the British seriously disturbed the ecology, putting together two conflicting sets of values, each with much to commend it. Alongside the Malays, there came to live a roughly equivalent number of people who, by Malay standards, had an obscene capacity for work, vice and self-obfuscation, keeping themselves apart by their impossible language, abacuses and what passed for their religion. Singapore became an alien excrescence.

---

[31] Henri Fauconnier, *The Soul of Malaya* (London, Penguin, 1948), p. 59.

Lee Kuan Yew was far more at ease with the British than with the Malaysians, his neighbours and for two years, his compatriots. In January 1968, he observed to me that, by their precipitate military withdrawal, the British were cutting his throat. He soon came to acknowledge, however, that they were going about it like gentlemen. The following month, when the new British High Commissioner paid his introductory call, he did so with trepidation because, on top of everything which had just gone before, he was instructed to see whether, in the wake of British military withdrawal, Lee would consider £50 million was enough by way of 'mitigatory aid', as it was called. This was not a generous amount when the Maltese, as Lee knew, had received the same sum. In Malta, British military expenditure had accounted for about a third of the country's income, whereas in Singapore it had been only a fifth. But Malta had only a quarter of Singapore's population, a lower rate of unemployment and emigration outlets not open to Singapore. Moreover, the British offer to Lee was conditional on Singapore and Britain devising agreed ways to spend the money, whereas the Maltese – as the British by now had reason to regret – had simply been given the cash. There was the further condition that Singapore should keep its reserves in the sterling area. The Malaysians argued for months about the terms of mitigatory aid. On no count did Lee demur for a moment. In practice, however, Goh, as Minister of Finance, continued to salt away funds outside the sterling area – and Singapore thus reaped a fine harvest when the German mark was revalued. The British had no monopoly on sleight of hand. "It is a well known trick of oriental statecraft to pretend or let it be supposed that a policy, likely to cause trouble, is the work of a subordinate, who is represented as difficult to control."[32]

By and large, Lee concluded, the British gave Singapore a pretty fair deal. And he found the company of their politicians, dons, generals, diplomats, businessmen and journalists livelier, more articulate, more consistent, more disposed to listen and thus, in sum, more congenial, than those from any other country. Throughout my time in Singapore, he saw more of the British High Commissioner than of all other high commissioners and ambassadors put together. (That, however, is not saying as much as it might appear to. The Norwegian Ambassador had been there just on four years before he met the separatist Lee.) The only time protocol was ever disturbed was when Lee himself intervened to give the British most-favoured-nation treatment. British official visitors rated top priority.

When the New Zealand Minister of Defence visited Singapore in June 1969 his Singaporean counterpart, Lim Kim San, was obliged to rustle up the young majors to fill the dinner table because Lee had pre-empted

---

[32] Maurice Collis, *Siamese White* (London, Faber and Faber, 1965), p. 200.

the top brass for a simultaneous dinner in honour of Mr Ivor Richard. Ivor Richard? Parliamentary Secretary to the British Secretary of State for Defence. Sometimes Lee had trouble in taking his colleagues along. At the elegant banquet for Princess Alexandra in August 1969 he confided to me, "Goh and Toh [Chin Chye] are misbehaving. They think this 'playing Princess' business is rather silly and have slipped out the back for a quick one with the boys."

Was he chasing a will-o'-the-wisp? Not at all. In playing for time, he secured useful adjustment in British plans for military withdrawal. More importantly, he sold himself and his country in Britain, knocking politely but persistently for years at the doors of the Confederation of British Industry. At the same time he lured more impulsive investors, like the Japanese and Americans, to show what they could do with their money in Singapore. He persuaded British investors, who had, in recent years, shied away, to put their money down to such an extent that, by 1970, there was more new investment flowing into Singapore's manufacturing industry from Britain than from any other quarter.

Lee's rapport with the British served us well. I think he saw in New Zealand a country more like Britain than any other – a very long way behind in terms of significance, of course, but inheriting similar values. He once asked me if New Zealand's sense of values was set by the second and third sons of the British gentry – and he wasn't looking for an answer, he knew he was right. It was no coincidence that, of the last three expatriate heads of Government Department in Singapore, two were New Zealanders – N.V. Casey, Controller of Inland Revenue, who left in January 1970 and Bill Osten (the last of the Mohicans), Director of Telecommunications, who left in March of that year. Similarly, Singapore's principal defence and civil aviation adviser 1969–72 was a New Zealander, Air Marshal Sir Rochford Hughes. Nor was it any aberration which put Wellington on Lee's initial shortlist of places to establish diplomatic missions, whereas it was 12 years after Malaysia became independent before Wellington got on to their much longer list. Nor was it just good luck and good management which made the New Zealand Insurance Company, operating in Singapore since 1885, the biggest non-life insurance agency there.

Lee saw New Zealand as a steady, steadfast country (the Secretary of the Commonwealth Society in Singapore, C.K. Cheng, once said he liked New Zealanders "because they do not jump about") with a defence policy which had long been that of "a fledgling hawk" (Lee's term). He saw New Zealand, I think, as a country with some influence, although it might not be great, in London and Canberra and perhaps even in Washington. We were not, however, spared his critical appraisal, usually based on the irritating assumption – although he also applied it to himself – that everything in this world is capable of improvement. "Where would New Zealand be now," he once asked me, "if, instead of proceeding so cautiously after the war, you had forged ahead with immigration and industrialisation?" Or again, he once asked, "Why do you lose so many of your sparklers – Elworthy, Porritt, Hughes?"[33] In similar vein, Goh once remarked, "Aren't you just fiddling with tourism?"

Britain was comprehensible and so, too, was New Zealand in its small but useful way. But there were times when John (later Sir John) Gorton was Prime Minister of Australia, 1968–71, that he perplexed, irritated, indeed angered Lee Kuan Yew. When Gorton died, *The Times* (London) obituary was headed, "Larrikin Prime Minister who shook up Australian politics" (21 May 2002). 'Larrikin' is precisely the word Lee Kuan Yew would have used. In conversation not long after Gorton became Prime Minister, Lee was extremely critical of him for revealing publicly so much about Commonwealth defence. Seeking to staunch the flow of invective, I cut in to remark that Gorton was new to the job, feeling his way. Lee snapped, "OK, OK. But I wish he wouldn't do it in hi-fi and 3D!" On a subsequent occasion, he was lamenting uncertainties in Australian defence policy, then paused and said despondently, "I suppose all men are ambivalent. And some are quadrivalent – I think John Gorton is one of those!"

One day in March 1970, conversation about such difficulties led him back to another "prisoner of our youth" memory. Recalling the general who commanded Australian forces in Malaya and Singapore at the time of the Japanese invasion, Lee expostulated, "You [meaning New Zealand] would have shot a man like Bennett!" This was General Gordon Bennett who, without informing or consulting his British commanding officer, escaped in a sampan and made his way back to Australia through the Dutch East Indies (Indonesia). He was widely denounced for deserting his men who were interned by the Japanese and he was never again given a command in the field. (During our time in Singapore, the young discotheque set used the expression 'Gordon Bennett!' as a highly-charged, venomous expletive – although none of the young people I ever asked knew where the name came from.)

---

[33] Sam(uel) Charles Elworthy, Lord, 1911–93, born in New Zealand, Cambridge University, joined RAF 1936, Air Marshal, Chief of British Defence Staff 1967–71, returned to live in New Zealand in 1978.
Arthur Espie Porritt, Lord, 1900–94, born in New Zealand, Oxford University, physician, Governor-General of New Zealand 1967–72.
Rochford Hughes, Sir, 1914–1996, born and educated in New Zealand, joined RNZAF 1937, RAF 1938–69, Air Marshal; military and civil aviation adviser, to Singapore Government 1969–72, then returned to live in New Zealand.

Initially, New Zealand entered into defence arrangements in South-east Asia in the van of Empire – and we entered boldly, knowing our own mind, not waiting for the Australians to make up theirs. Between 1928 and 1936 New Zealand gave the British Government a million pounds sterling to help construct the naval base in Singapore. This was a lot of money in those days and it became an increasing burden as the Great Depression bit deeper into the New Zealand economy. When the British themselves vacillated, we nagged them to get on with the job. (Even Churchill vacillated for a time, when he was Chancellor of the Exchequor, questioning the wisdom and cost of arrangements centred on Singapore.) The Australians, instead, put their faith in 'National Self-Reliance' and expanded their own navy. (The successor slogan, in the 1960s, was 'Fortress Australia'.)

When I left Singapore in June 1970, the trend was for Lee Kuan Yew to adopt the equivalent of putting his faith in God and keeping his powder dry. He hoped that the Five Power Defence Arrangements (Australia, Britain, Malaysia, New Zealand, Singapore), would endure, but he was not placing complete reliance on it and in any event expected to contribute military strength to the alliance. Militarily, he was building up Singapore as a hornet's nest, "a poisonous shrimp", as he put it. Diplomatically, he was becoming more circumspect, even accepting that, on occasion, silence, on his part, had a place in the scheme of things. Personally, he was becoming more tolerant and assured. Economically, Singapore was thriving, to the advantage of adjacent states and others further away, including New Zealand. The future looked bright and so it proved to be.

III. LETTERS

In 1967, HMS *Valiant*, a nuclear-powered submarine, made an epic voyage underwater all the way from Scotland to Singapore where the British, Australian and New Zealand High Commissioners were invited to go on board. Half an hour down in a small submarine filled me with claustrophobic terror although I didn't report that aspect when telling the family what I'd been doing that day. My son, aged eight, was fired with ambition to go down in a submarine, too. So this was arranged. My letter of thanks followed:

New Zealand High Commission
13 Nassim Road
Singapore
7 April 1967

Dear Frank,

As a sequel to your kindness in arranging for Jamie and his two mates to see over a submarine, you may be interested in a conversation I had with my children yesterday:

Brendy (11): How long does it take for a baby to grow before it's born?
Me: Nine months.
Brendy: And a cat?
Me: One or two months – I'm not sure exactly.
Jamie (8):   Will you answer any question?
Me: I'll try.
Jamie: How far does a submarine's periscope go above the water?

Many thanks and kindest regards,
(Sgd) Jim

Vice Admiral Sir Frank Twiss KCB, DSC
Commander Far East Fleet
HM Naval Base
Singapore 27

Singapore at Sixes and Sevens

> The Chartered Bank
> Tanglin Branch
> 356 Orchard Road
> Singapore 9
> 19 December 1968

Dear Mr Weir,
Savings & Disney (Donald Duck) Accounts
We thank you for your cover letter dated 9th December and appreciate the difficulty with which you are faced in endeavouring to explain to your young son how it is possible for a larger sum of money on deposit to earn less interest than a smaller sum under identical conditions [as he had noted in his sister's account].

It is not often that 'Donald Duck' makes mistakes when calculating interest on savings accounts but as the saying goes 'To err is human' it would appear that even Donald Duck is human at times after all, for the difference in the interest credited was due to a calculation error in the interest for May 1968 with a resultant short credit of 16 cents. This however has since been rectified and a credit of 16 cents passed to your son's account.

We had considered just crediting your son's account with an extra 16 cents to compensate him for the embarrassment suffered, but as this may have had further repercussions on your daughter, we have therefore credited both accounts with an extra 16 cents.

Interest for the current half year has now been credited, and if you will be good enough to forward the relative passbooks, we will bring them up to date.
Yours faithfully,

[Signature indecipherable]
Manager

J.H. Weir Esq
High Commissioner
New Zealand High Commission
13 Nassim Rd
Singapore 10

Wood End House
Wickham
Nr Fareham
Hants PO 17 6J2
United Kingdom
Jan 31 2002

Dear Jim,

It's good to hear a voice from the past and from a distant land remembering my Michael so kindly.

We had good times then in Singapore (except when Mollie was bitten by Runme's guard dogs) and I am sorry to hear of her death. So indeed you know how hard it is to be left. I find great sympathy in those who have been bereaved and our children have been wonderful.

I hope you yourself are keeping well and have family and friends nearby.

Thank you so much for writing.

Yours affectionately
(Sgd) Edith [Carver]

The Times (London) obituary of II December 2001 said of Field Marshal Lord Carver, 1915–2001, Commander-in-Chief (Far East) in our time and subsequently Chief of British Defence Staff, "Mike Carver was unquestionably the most cerebral British officer of the post-war era – and, it could be argued, of all three Services. Had there been a third world war in the 1970s, he might well have emerged from the struggle as a Montgomery or even a Wellington. He had the military abilities and characteristics of both men, with greater tact than the former and none of the political ambition of the latter. Happily, no such war occurred, and Field Marshal Lord Carver fought his greatest battles in the jungles of Whitehall, developing and implementing Britain's post-imperial defence policy."

Singapore at Sixes and Sevens

Drifting out of the first session of the Five Power Defence Conference in Canberra, 19–20 June 1969, George (later Sir George) Laking, (Secretary of Foreign Affairs 1967–72) and I encountered Sir Peter Hill-Norton, Commander-in-Chief (Far East). After greeting him probably with nothing more than, "G'day, how are you?" we received the totally unexpected but certainly memorable reply, "I feel like a maiden who's just been deflowered. I've lost my fucking hat!"

He subsequently became British Chief of Defence Staff with the rank of Admiral of the Fleet and the title Lord. Noting in *The Times* (London) that he had died, aged 89, and that his widow was now frail, I wrote a note of condolence to his son, also an admiral, to whom I felt free to tell the little story of his father's lost hat. He replied from another of those charming addresses.

The Barns
Newton Valence
Alton
Hampshire GU34 3RB
21 August 2004

Dear Mr Weir,

Thank you very much for your kind words about my father's death.

Fate dealt him a cruel blow some time ago when he became partially sighted. Everything he did was more difficult and he not only lost his independence but also his capacity to remain involved in so many things in which he was interested.

He managed his disability brilliantly, never complained, and used much ingenuity to get round the problems it created. Then my mother was taken seriously ill early last year and he devoted his full energy and attention to her support and well being. [They were married for 68 years.] Quite superhuman in his efforts, he got her home and they had many months of life together there.

In all he rather neglected – or rather he stoically ignored – his own health, which deteriorated. And sadly, while they were away on holiday to recover from a bad winter of illness, his heart failed.

He leaves a huge gap in our family. But he was himself to the end – proud, uncompromising and devoted to his wife.

Very much enjoyed your happy story – typical Hill-Norton response. One of his best friends was Terry Herrick from Masterton. You may know him.

All best wishes

(Sgd) Nick H-N.

I didn't, in fact, know Herrick (another RN admiral) but came across his obituary in *The Dominion Post* (Wellington) on 7 May 2009 and sent a copy to Nick Hill-Norton who promptly sent me the obituary which had appeared in *The Times* (London). (Swapping obituaries … Old men do strange things.) Without doubt, the local obituary, written by Hank Schouten, was far better. It concluded: "He [Terry Herrick] loved New Zealand and always regarded himself as a Kiwi, but had the manner of a British officer, complete with stiff upper lip. He was unflappable, always enjoyed good company and adored his offspring." Born a New Zealander and retiring here, he was 97 when he died.

After leaving Singapore in June 1970, I didn't meet Lee Kuan Yew again but in 2004 sent him the original of a cartoon by Illingworth, published in the *Daily Mail* (London) in January 1968. It playfully showed Lee as a dapper young schoolmaster giving the British Prime Minister, Harold Wilson, a lesson on world strategy, with Denis Healey, the British Minister of Defence saying to other Cabinet colleagues, "I wonder if Lee Kuan Yew would stay here if we gave him the navy and half the air force …" (As the cartoon made no reference to New Zealand I decided it really belonged to Singapore and, in particular, Lee Kuan Yew.)

His acknowledgement read:

Minister Mentor
Singapore
13 October 2004

Dear Jim Weir,
Thank you for your letter 29 September sending me a cartoon which you acquired when you were High Commissioner in Singapore.

It appears to be from the *Daily Mail*. How did you come to get it? Anyway many thanks and all the best to you.

I have not been to New Zealand for a few years. I remember all New Zealand's High Commissioners in Singapore of the 1960s to 1980s with great affection.
With all best wishes,
Yours sincerely

(Sgd) Lee Kuan Yew

Wondering About and Wandering in Burma[34]

1. TOO GOOD A COUNTRY TO RUIN COMPLETELY – BUT THEY'RE TRYING

A GENEROUS ROUND of hospitality organised for delegates at the Colombo Plan Conference in Rangoon, from 21 November to 8 December 1967, included a reception hosted by the mayor of the city. This prompted Alex Owen, a New Zealander who had lived in Rangoon for three years (working as a Colombo Plan expert in trade training), to say he hadn't realised there was a Mayor of Rangoon. The Burmese Secretary of Education, who was standing with us, added, "And neither did I." Whoever it was, he was welcome to his crowded hour. It was a splendid reception, with Burmese dancing girls, jugglers and tit-bits.

And nothing could have been more splendidly arranged than the dinner hosted by the President, General Ne Win, with all the heartiness and aplomb of a good old-fashioned British Governor-General. The dinner was held on the lawn in front of the enormous and incongruously English palace, which had been Government House in the days when Burma had been a British colony. Nor could anything have been better organised than the post-conference tour of Mandalay and Pagan. We stayed overnight in Mandalay where staff from the university acted as exceedingly friendly, attentive, and well-informed guides. In Mandalay, those of us who wished to do so were organised to get up early and climb a very steep hill, most of the way by a long flight of steps, to reach a pagoda on top of the hill, in time to see "the dawn come up like thunder", as Kipling had promised it would.

---

[34] Burma was renamed Myanmar in 1989 but Burma has continued to be the preferred usage in British news media.

Such hospitality and good fellowship had become unusual in Burma. This was the first international conference to be held there for many years. The most recent, someone said, was a gathering of Buddhists in the early 1950s. The conference was held in an air-conditioned hotel – the only one in Rangoon – beside Inya Lake which was a pleasant sight after dark when you couldn't see how dirty it was. This was on the outskirts of the city, insulated, as it were, from the mainstream of Burmese life. We made occasional forays into the city, as well as two excursions into the countryside, one being the post-conference tour. Then there were casual conversations with members of the diplomatic corps resident in Rangoon and with Burmese officials – mainly officials associated with the conference. In such ways, one began to see other aspects of Burma which lay behind the bonhomie and generous hospitality.

One could see immediately that, whereas in Singapore about 95 percent of the local men wore Western garb in one form or another – even if, in many cases, the working garb was not more (and often less) than a shirt and shorts – in Burma and notably in Rangoon, the capital and main port, 95 percent of the men and all the women wore the traditional local form of the sarong. It seemed a sign that Burma was resisting Westernisation.

In fact, it was far more than that. Burma was becoming a hermit state. Then the evidence mounted. As a rule they were doing their utmost to keep foreign journalists out of the country. An exception was made for the Colombo Plan Conference but only for government agencies such as USIS, the BBC and the ABC. Ordinary tourists, in the normal course of events, could get a visa to enter Burma for only 24 hours, which allowed them to stay overnight, with a quick look around Rangoon. No one could enter Burma by any land frontier. The Russian-built hotel where we stayed had several hundred rooms but it usually had only about half a dozen guests. Outside Rangoon, we saw not a single white face. And our white faces were of great interest to the local people who, in Mandalay and elsewhere, gathered to look at us while we looked at temples and bazaars.

Almost all the many businessmen who had once lived in Rangoon and elsewhere in Burma had now left. (The New Zealand Insurance Company once had an office in Rangoon.) A few stray businessmen remained, still trying to get some compensation for the nationalisation of their businesses. Nearly all the European missionaries had gone. Only those living in Burma before Independence (January 1948) were allowed to stay on. One was a New Zealander, a Roman Catholic priest stationed near the border with China. The only other New Zealander resident in Burma was Alex Owen, the Colombo Plan expert.

Squeezing out the Europeans seemed to have taken priority but other 'outsiders' were also being dealt with in a similar way. This applied most notably to those of Indian, Pakistani and Chinese extraction and notwithstanding that most of their families had lived in Burma for many generations. On 2 December 1967 an item in the Burmese press reported a special flight had left the previous day to take 64 resident Chinese back to China because the regular weekly flights to that country could not cope with the numbers wishing to leave. Another report, on 3 December, recorded the sailing the previous day of a ship taking 1,100 Indians to India. The report added that this was this ship's 89th trip, taking 'repatriates' to India since July 1964. A government publication, *A Handbook on Burma*, given to all conference delegates, stated: "The number of foreigners who have left Burma up to 30 June, 1966 totalled 146,000 Indians, 13,855 Pakistanis, 2,934 Chinese and 5,786 other nationals." In the case of the Indians, Pakistanis and Chinese, most of these 'foreigners' would have been born in Burma, in families which had lived there for generations. The blunt facts of ethnic cleansing were stated, it seemed, almost with pride.

Burma had become a country for the Burmese. And many would have said they were welcome to it, as it had deteriorated so much. As in other countries in South-east Asia, the Indians, Pakistanis, Chinese and Europeans had provided the backbone of commerce and had also been prominent in the professions. Burma was much the poorer for their departure, as could be judged, for instance, by the number of shops hoarded up, the little there was to buy in the shops which remained open and the indifference of the Burmese shopkeepers who were now employees of the state and running the shops taken from the 'foreigners' when the shops were nationalised. The British and American embassies ran their own commissaries, obliged to stock even such basic items as toothpaste. The wives of diplomats went to Bangkok to shop. The Pakistani Ambassador, whom I had known of old, said that when the diplomats in Rangoon got together, "they always talk about rations".. Although Burma was rich in gems, jewellery was cheaper and better in Bangkok or Singapore, so the diplomatic wives in Rangoon said.

There was scarcely a building in Rangoon that did not need a coat of paint. The few exceptions included the town hall, which had been done up as a venue for a Colombo Plan conference function, the main pagodas, which remained faithfully gilded, and diplomatic missions. Most of the pavements in central Rangoon were broken. The Pakistani Ambassador did not exaggerate much, if at all, when he remarked scathingly that the trade training school, which New Zealand had sponsored under the Colombo Plan, was the only new building completed in Rangoon in the past two years.

Rangoon was sad, run-down, regressive – certainly by comparison with Singapore or Bangkok, where new construction and other activities were a constant source of astonishment, justifying Lee Kuan Yew's most recent impish comment that the pace of change in Asia was now several times the pace in Europe. In some respects, Rangoon nevertheless remained a pleasant city – compared, for instance, with Calcutta where one would be accosted by an appalling variety of beggars, touts and pimps and see hundreds, if not thousands of people sleeping in the streets. There was none of that in Rangoon.

Professor Speight, of the Australian National University and a 'special adviser' to the Australian delegation at the Colombo Plan Conference – his first job, in the pre-war period, had been with the University of Rangoon – said Rangoon reminded him of Moscow in 1924. To the Singapore Minister of Law, Eddie Barker, it was like Singapore during the Japanese occupation. Such thoughts were prompted not simply by the dilapidated appearance of the place, the scarcity of consumer goods or the dourness of a television-less capital where the brightest nightlife was confined to what purported, expensively, to be nightclubs in the two main hotels. On top of all that, one did not go far before coming across the ugliness of an introspective and autocratic society.

Even during the fortnight of our conference, for instance, there were several cases reported in the Burmese press indicating how severe the sentences could be for those caught infringing government regulations. One case concerned two Canadian lads of about 20 who had been brought to trial for peddling a handful of cheap watches while visiting Rangoon on a 24-hour visa, en route from Bangkok to Calcutta. The Canadians attending the conference said the lads had been in jail for four and a half months before the Canadian authorities had been informed they were there. The British Embassy, which acted for the Canadians in the absence of a resident Canadian mission in Rangoon, had not been informed either. Letters from the lads had not got through. The Canadians attending the conference arranged to visit the lads in jail – they were also, by now, being visited by the British – and said they had suffered badly from dysentery and had the appearance of prisoners-of-war emerging from Changi jail at the end of World War II. At their trial, the two young Canadians had been sentenced to nine months "rigorous detention", as well as being heavily fined. The fines were paid immediately by their parents.

Then, at a reception given by the Malaysian Ambassador, an old colleague, he introduced me to and left me talking with a man by the name of Raschid (this spelling may not be right). He would have been in his early thirties and was formerly a lecturer in architecture at the University of Rangoon, a fourth generation Burmese, of Indian extraction, married and with three children. His father had been a Cabinet minister for eight years but after the military coup under General Ne Win, his father had been arrested, although never brought to trial. He was being detained indefinitely. He was, declared the son vehemently, in a "concentration camp". The family was not allowed to visit him although – a little strangely, perhaps – he was allowed out to attend funerals of members of the family.

Moreover, the son, thinking to leave Burma for a while but fully expecting to return from time to time, applied for and was accepted to a position at a university in Pakistan. He resigned from the University of Rangoon and made preparations for departure, but then discovered that the Burmese authorities would not issue him with a Burmese passport, only a certificate of identity which meant he could leave Burma but not return. He refused to accept such conditions. He had too many close ties with Burma and thought of himself as Burmese, born and bred. He couldn't get his old job back – it had been filled by an ethnic Burmese. Nor could he get any other job. He had been unemployed for over a year.

Then again, Alex Owen, the New Zealander, said the Burmese authorities made it very clear that they didn't want Colombo Plan experts – regarded as virtually employees of the Burmese Government – fraternising with resident diplomats. Burmese officials had to get permission before any such fraternisation. Only rarely, said the Pakistani Ambassador, could he get the Minister or Secretary of Foreign Affairs to dinner – and certainly no other Burmese. These others, said the British Ambassador, would prevaricate over invitations to dinner and then, at the last minute, excuse themselves. If invited to a reception, they would neither reply nor attend, although they did during the conference.

By all accounts, the advent of the military regime had prompted many Western-educated, liberal-minded, full-blooded Burmese, formerly in senior positions in the civil service or the universities, to quit the country and take jobs in international secretariats or universities abroad. This had skimmed off many of Burma's ablest people in their prime.

Burma, moreover, was seriously troubled by a major problem of insurgency. The general assessment was that the Government controlled about two-thirds of the country by day and less by night. This included, as in Vietnam at that time, government control of all the main centres of population, although some 85 percent of the Burmese people lived in small villages. We were heavily guarded everywhere we went, outside the main centres. Similarly, diplomats resident in Rangoon were severely restricted in where they might go, by road or rail, outside the main centres of population. And such restrictions must have given these diplomats – and more especially, perhaps, their wives – added incentive to go shopping, or whatever, in Bangkok or Singapore.

The number of insurgents was reckoned to be somewhere between 15–20,000. Of these, perhaps 1,200–1,500 were communists, followers of

Mao-Tse-tung. Other insurgents were against the Government for a wide variety of reasons. In fact, some were thought to be bandits of a kind existing in Burma for centuries. Anyhow, the insurgents were obviously creating a great deal of havoc in the countryside. Even within recent weeks, trains had been derailed and godowns (warehouses) burnt down within 50 miles of Rangoon. The British Ambassador thought that, in present circumstances, Burma needed a strong, firm government, especially to deal with the insurgency. He added that Ne Win's government was at least trying hard to wipe out corruption, which was more than could be said for their civilian predecessors or many of their counterparts in other countries.

Insurgency was only one factor contributing to a drastic decline in the Burmese economy over a period of many years. Other factors included the Government's pursuit of ideological objectives in a simplistic, doctrinaire fashion – the Burmese Way to Socialism – a slogan repeated so often and to explain so many things that outsiders had come to regard it as a bit of a joke. Then there had been the expulsion of 'the exploiters': the Indians, Pakistanis and Chinese, as well as the Europeans, most notably the British, all of whom had provided the backbone of commerce. Then again there had been bad harvests caused by floods, droughts and pests. Before World War II, Burma had been the world's biggest exporter of rice. Seven and a half million tons of rice were produced annually and three million tons of it were exported. In 1965–6, rice production was down to 6.5 million tons and exports, at 1.1 million tons, were about a third of the pre-war level.

The decline, moreover, continued. Between 1965 and 1966, the output of rice, the pivot of the economy, declined 18 percent. In that period exports of all kinds declined by about 24 percent. Some of the statistics, mind you, had to be taken with a pinch of salt. It was a safe bet, for instance, that gems, in which Burma was rich, were smuggled across the border to Thailand. Again, how could rice or other rural production be reliably calculated, let alone gathered systematically, in the two-thirds of the country that was held by the insurgents?

Despite so much that could be criticised, however, I was left with the very firm impression that Burma was too good a country for any government to ruin completely, although one might have added cynically that the present government was trying hard. But, looking at the bright side, there was a fertile soil – any gardener would drool over that Irrawaddy River silt – capable of producing far more food than the Burmese needed and far more than it had pre-war, given the introduction of fertilisers, modern pesticides and new strains of rice of higher yield. Even in its reduced and dejected circumstances, there was nowhere near the pressure of population on resources as there was in India. There were indications, too, that Burma was rich in minerals: silver, lead, gold, tin, tungsten, copper, precious stones, limestone, zinc and antimony. If only Burma could get organised, it surely had the resources and basic infrastructure to move ahead, not backwards as it was now doing.

Well, that's what one wished, of course, although no one could have hoped for snappy changes. Burmese methods, one suspected, were those of gradualism and ambivalence with a good dash of obscurantism thrown in for good measure. But clearly the Burmese were not an indolent people; no country of rice growers could ever be. Nor were they an unthinking, compliant, people. The insurgency was proof of that. A news report of 3 December 1967, in the (English language) *Working People's Daily*, said that 1,889 books, including 214 translations, had been published in Burma in 1966. Undoubtedly, all of these books would have been anodyne. But it indicated that the people were readers who presumably thought about what they were reading, and did not always agree with it.

Then again, the extreme and introspective nationalism and the ruthlessness of the military junta seemed at odds with the charm, good humour and decency so evident in so many Burmese – perhaps, in some degree, reflecting the Buddhism of centuries – evident even in Ne Win when he relaxed. And evident, too, even in such a victim of the military regime as Raschid, who remained confident that Burma would find its way out of the mess it was in, although no doubt he was thinking that this would take far longer than would occur to Westerners who expected their governments to get them out of any mess before the next election. But, in the end, surely Burma would come right and, in the meantime, was well worth helping.

Well, all that's rather by the way, picked up over drinks while attending a conference. Which is not an unusual way for a love affair to begin. As mine did with Burma.

11. "EVERYBODY DOESN'T LIKE OUR GOVERNMENT."

When I first went to Burma in 1967, to attend a Colombo Plan Conference, I'd been High Commissioner in Singapore.

When I went back to Burma, in February, 1975, it was to present credentials as the first New Zealand Ambassador to that country. By then, after a couple of years at headquarters in Wellington, I was High Commissioner in Kuala Lumpur and now caught up in a rather excited flurry of cross-accreditation to extend the web of New Zealand representation abroad. Many other countries were also engaged in this business of cross-accreditation.

Some months before going to Rangoon in 1975, I had heard that the Swiss Ambassador, resident in Bangkok, had been obliged to go to Rangoon three times before finally getting to see the President and present credentials as Ambassador to Burma, as well as Thailand. It was a warning to proceed warily. So, as soon as I received word from Wellington that the necessary approvals had been given and the assurance from our High Commission in London that my credentials – which, in those days, were signed by the Queen – were in order, I wrote to the Burmese Chief of Protocol on 20 December 1974 to inquire whether it would be convenient to present credentials during the first fortnight in February. This seemed reasonable enough: to give the Burmese more than a month's notice of my proposed visit and a fortnight from which they could pick a date. Not expecting a quick or clear-cut reply from the Burmese, I sent a copy of my letter to the British Ambassador in Rangoon (who happened to be an old friend), so that, if need be, I could call on his help. He replied immediately, in fine Foreign Office style: "… this is exactly the right way to go about your business".

This would have been comforting had there been the slightest sign that the Burmese agreed. The days and weeks went by. Absolute silence from the Burmese. By 25 January, less than a week away from the nominated "first fortnight in February", my patience ran out and I asked the British Ambassador to prod. His reply, after he had checked with the Burmese Chief of Protocol, was reassuring but still indefinite. This coincided with a rather puzzling letter from the Chief of Protocol: "… the first fortnight in February will be convenient for the President … but I will have to confirm it in a few days time. As soon as I hear from the President's office, intimation will be sent by cable via our mission in Kuala Lumpur."

By now it was 30 January. The Burmese Embassy in Kuala Lumpur had heard nothing further. So, what to do? Rely on the general assurances? Or stay put and make sure? Opting for 'boldness, be my friend', I asked the British Ambassador to let the Burmese Chief of Protocol know that I would be arriving on the evening of 5 February and our Third Secretary, Christine Rowe, would arrive a couple of days in advance to help with arrangements (and we also had in mind that she would sort out some Colombo Plan problems).

There was another prompt reply from the British Ambassador, inviting my wife and me to dinner – first things first – and saying the Burmese would put two cars at our disposal. (We made do with one.) All very welcoming and reassuring. But there was still no definite answer to the basic question of whether a date to present credentials had been, or could be, set. Was I going to follow in the footsteps of the Swiss Ambassador? The journey began to take on some of the nervous anxiety of a military campaign. Chris Rowe went ahead to reconnoitre. My wife, having been regaled with travellers' tales about all sorts of things which Burma did not have, set herself up as quartermaster and packed a suitcase full of food.

But the longer one lives in the East, the less mysterious it becomes (and, conversely, the more one comes to see how mysterious the West must seem to them). Before we were off the tarmac at Rangoon airport, the Burmese Chief of Protocol observed that they had had some bad experiences with cross-accredited Ambassadors-designate: they had been given a firm date to present credentials before they arrived in Rangoon and then they failed to turn up. The President had, therefore, decreed that no firm date was to be fixed until an Ambassador-designate actually arrived. I murmured that this was only fair and reasonable. So now, beamed the Chief of Protocol, he could begin to get a firm date for me. In short, having by my arrival proved my existence, we were, triumphantly, at square one.

Before he left us that evening, the Chief of Protocol also told me the cautionary tale of "a certain European Ambassador" (presumably the Swiss) who, on arrival in Rangoon, had too vehemently expressed his impatience in waiting for a date to present credentials. So, he had been made to wait even longer than necessary. Whether the Chief of Protocol was already sizing me up to judge whether I met the required standards of patience and affability, was impossible to say. But, if so, I appeared to be passing the test. We arranged that evening, a Wednesday, that I should call on him and then the Foreign Minister, the next day. And, he added, the tentative date for presenting credentials was Friday or Saturday at 9 am. What could be more expeditious? I purred while the Chief of Protocol, a charmingly timid little brown rabbit of a man, faded into the night, murmuring, "We'll let you know, we'll let you know."

This became a refrain. When I called on the Chief of Protocol next day, the Foreign Minister had become "unfortunately not available". As to when I might see him, the Chief of Protocol could only murmur, "We'll let you know." It was, in fact, the next day. But the President was still proving elusive. As the days went by, the tentative date to present credentials slipped from "Friday or Saturday" to "Saturday or Monday" to "Monday or Tuesday, we'll let you know". My time was beginning to run out. The presentation could not be on the Wednesday because this was to be a public holiday, a fact we had not known before arriving in Rangoon, and I was due to leave early on Friday morning to be back in Kuala Lumpur for a visit by the Leader of the Opposition, Mr Muldoon.

In short, I had only one day in hand. I had a growing sense of fellow-feeling with the Swiss Ambassador in Bangkok, a man I would never meet. I filled in time by calling on my diplomatic colleagues who were good enough to receive me at short notice when it was impossible to arrange an orderly programme of such calls in advance, in case there should be a sudden summons from the Burmese. And the more often the Chief of Protocol murmured, "We'll let you know," the more often I found myself exclaiming, "They've got me hog-tied!" Then, late on Saturday evening, there was a message to say the President would receive me at 9 am on Tuesday. This was confirmed by letter received on Monday.

This letter, enclosing 'the programme', contained more of the voids which occurred in Burmese correspondence and conversation. It was specific on the minimal number of points: the Chief of Protocol would call for me at 8.30 am and we would arrive at the President's place at 9 am. There was no indication of what I was expected to wear, whether there were to be speeches, a guard of honour to inspect or any expectation, as in Kuala Lumpur, of measured paces, bowing, backing away from (not turning one's back on) and while seated, not crossing legs in front of The Presence, who took leave of whom, when, and on what cue. As it turned out, none of this needed to be recorded. Apart form the fact that I wore a lounge suit, as the Chief of Protocol told me to, and apart, too, from the well-guarded entrance to the President's house – and it was a house rather than a mansion and certainly not a palace – there was scarcely any more formality than if I'd been calling on my own grandfather.

We arrived precisely on time, to be met at the portico by a grey-haired man I assumed was the Burmese equivalent of a Comptroller of the Household. There being no introduction, I thought of him as the Grey Rabbit. The Chief of Protocol brought up the rear. In ceremonial dress, he now looked more than ever like a Brown Rabbit with one ear cocked. The Comptroller immediately ushered me into the entrance hall where the President came forward to greet me warmly. He ushered me into a large room overlooking Inya Lake, a splendid sight with the early morning mist and the distance not allowing us to see how dirty it was.

We sat in easy chairs at a long coffee table, every square inch of which was covered with plates of food. The Brown and Grey Rabbits poured coffee. While listening to the President begin to open the conversation, I was scarcely conscious of what the Rabbits were doing until the President suddenly interrupted himself to bark loudly at the Brown Rabbit, "You're putting too much milk in his coffee!" I assured them both that this wasn't so (although it was). The Grey Rabbit passed me a plate of delicately-cut cucumber sandwiches. I reached to take one when the President barked again, to no one in particular, "People eat too much!" I nevertheless took a sandwich. The two Rabbits were not about to be so defiant. They sat together at the other end of the long table, ate nothing, said nothing and neither did they smoke, just as the Chief of Protocol had cautioned me not to do in The Presence.

I was beginning to wonder whether 9 am was much too early to be calling on an elderly gentleman who had recently married a much younger woman. Then, in an attempt to smoothe things over, I remarked that Burmese coffee tasted much better than Malaysian coffee. The President smiled. "Of course it is. They ruin theirs with chicory." But he was not about to be diverted so easily. With a deadly glance at the Brown Rabbit, he asked whether I was quite sure there wasn't too much milk in my coffee. "We can easily get another cup. It *is* too much, you know. Milk has too much fat in it. Bad for the heart." (The British had warned me he was becoming "a dreadful hypochondriac".) I assured him it was fine: he must expect a representative of New Zealand to promote the dairying industry. He chuckled at this and it led him away to the dairy farm he had been to on his visit to New Zealand in 1974. He ended his brief account of the New Zealand dairy farm by saying, "Your farmers work very hard." I added, "And so do their families; the farmer's wife, his children." Unwittingly, I had struck a responsive chord. "I come from a farming family, too," and he was away, at a gallop, for over an hour.

First, however, he spoke very appreciatively of the kindness extended to him during his visit to New Zealand, especially by the Governor-General, Sir Bernard Fergusson, an old Burma hand, with whom he had stayed in Wellington. And he paid a fine tribute to the Prime Minister, Mr Kirk, who had died unexpectedly, very soon after the President had been to New Zealand. It was the tribute of an older man, a soldier, brisk but with genuine feeling. He recalled and pronounced the names of New Zealand people and places unerringly. He seemed a little puzzled to have been taken to see a stud farm in New Zealand, as he had banned horse-racing in Burma 11 years ago. Gambling, he declared, led men to squander money, creating social problems, breeding crime. "I wasn't going to have a mafia here."

With Brigadier Les Hunt and Bert McGregor when the Netherlands delegate walked out of the Economic Commission for Asia and the Far East, Lapstone, Australia, 1948.

Bangkok, 1948–9, showing little traffic on the main street. Our hotel is on the right.

At the United Nations, 1949, with Arnold Reedy, Bill Sutch and Jim Webster.

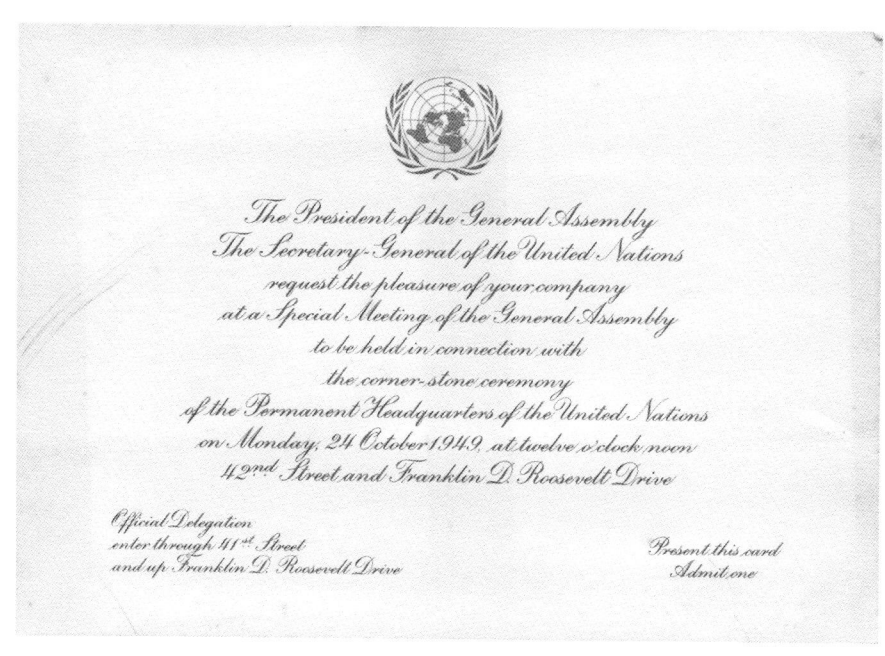

Invitation to the Cornerstone Ceremony of the permanent headquarters of the United Nations.

*Sir Carl and Lady Berendsen, 1950.
(Photograph courtesy of their grandson, Carl Berendsen.)*

*As acting High Commissioner, laying wreaths with the Prime Minister of Australia,
R.G. (later Sir Robert) Menzies, Anzac Day, 1957. (Official Australian photograph.)*

Talking to the press on arrival in Singapore, 1966, with my wife and two of our children, Brendy and Jamie.

First encounter with Prime Minister, Lee Kuan Yew of Singapore, 1966. (Some wag captioned this, "First to the left, then to the right, swing your partner through the night.") (Official Singapore photograph.)

With my wife in Singapore, 1970.

Drinking coconut milk, Borneo, 1975.

Alister (later Sir Alister) and Doris McIntosh, 1970.
(Photograph courtesy of their son, Jim McIntosh.)

Presenting credentials to President Ne Win of Burma, 1975. (Official Burmese photograph.)

Rome, 1981.

Caricature drawn by a multi-talented young friend, Guy Horrocks, to mark my 85th birthday.

For the most part, he talked of the land: for instance, of how his mother used to plant six seeds of corn a day when it was not the planting season. The young plants needed daily care but it meant they had corn on the cob when the market price was high. Then she did not plant corn at the 'right' time but could buy it in the market when the price was low. We talked – well, he did most of the talking – about other tropical vegetables and fruit, the different varieties and some of the curious manifestations, including how, for instance, the papaya (pawpaw) grew from seed to ripe fruit in the same period as human gestation. At times, he spoke philosophically and frankly: "Our people are lazy. Nothing has been done to our tea estates for 15 years." There was no use trying to stop people from growing opium, he declared, unless you gave them another source of income that was just as lucrative.

I wondered later whether his ministers had begun to humour the old boy by telling him what they thought he wanted to hear. He gave me a far more optimistic assessment of the current rice crop than the Minister of Agriculture. Ne Win went on to say that recent floods in rice-growing areas had prompted him to experiment with rice-growing in his own garden. And it was astonishing, he could report, what a difference it made if you struck it right, in planting-out from nursery to paddy field. He had planted-out 25, 28 and 31 days after sowing the seed and the plants in the middle bracket had done 40 percent better than the others. Was that a coincidence, I asked, or could there be some scientific explanation? Ne grinned and said (without answering my question), "It's like marriage. A woman of 25 will give you much better results than one of 40." And perhaps the President and I reached our closest accord in agreeing that by far the best fertilizer for the land was cow manure.[35]

I came away thinking, "Well, after a faltering start, that was pleasant, and thoroughly inconsequential." We had not touched on China or internal security. The only reference to Burma's neighbours had been scant, although sufficient to establish Ne Win's traditional Burmese sense of superiority. The only individual neighbour he spoke of with any warmth was the Prime Minister of Malaysia, Tun Razak. My colleagues in the diplomatic corps assured me that, if I had raised such bigger issues as China or internal security, Ne Win would have clammed up. My Malaysian colleague, who had presented his credentials six weeks previously, had, on instructions from Tun Razak himself, used the occasion to suggest that Burma, like Malaysia, could benefit from joint enterprises with foreign companies. He was sternly rebuked.

---

[35] When I went to Rome in 1980 I found the Italians declared sheep manure was best. It produced amazingly good results with tomatoes if buried with the occasional cat killed outside our house by a passing car.

Had I found the real Ne Win, reflecting the real Burma in his preoccupation with the good earth and what, with care, it could produce; in his paternalistic concern to preserve decent, traditional standards of behaviour; in his view of the world, both introspective and, one sensed, deeply religious? ("They really believe," said the American Ambassador.) Up to a point, that was so. He was remarkably easy to talk to, a grandfatherly man, amiable, courteous, good-humoured, humane. It was difficult, almost impossible, to believe that this man presided over a country in which the current numbers game among the expatriates was to consider how many workers had been squashed to death by army tanks rolling over them to quell riots last June. And how many students had been bayoneted to death to end riots last December? There was an ambivalence in all this which reminded me of Lee Kuan Yew's remark: "All men are ambivalent," to which he added a rider, "and some, I think, are quadrivalent." Was Ne Win one of them?

I wondered whether the fire in Ne Win's belly was subsiding. At 64, he was old by the standards of tropical Asia where the retirement age was usually 55, having regard to both life expectancy and expectations of life. There were signs of an increasing inclination to delegate ("I've got a prime minister to look after the detail now"), an old man's inclination to look back happily on his earlier life rather than remain involved in the resolution of current problems, especially, perhaps, when the riots of the previous June and December had been such a stinging rebuke. But the ministers and senior officials to whom I talked all regarded him with awe and seemed to assume he was more or less a permanent fixture. The diplomats in Rangoon thought he was likely to carry on for many years yet. He was, said the British Ambassador, apt to cite Tito of Yugoslavia, then in his eighties. Some of the diplomats added the proviso that much could depend on how the economy fared. If it worsened and triggered further disturbance which could only be put down by force, Ne Win might opt to resign or be toppled.

So how was the economy faring? Taxi drivers elsewhere in the world being chatty folk and often a good guide to what was going on, I picked the brains of the local equivalent, the man who operated the trishaw based outside the Strand Hotel where we were staying. He came to my notice when I went out to get a breath of the balmy night air and he asked if I'd sell him foreign currency: "Very good rate, Sir." I asked what he would do with it. He was chatty, all right. He would sell it, he said, to his mates on Burma's Five Star Shipping Line and they would buy transistors and suchlike in Penang and Singapore and sell them for a tidy profit back in Burma. This was confirmed in *The Far Eastern Economic Review* which reported on 28 February 1975 that a growing number of Burmese youths, including university graduates, were "scrambling" for jobs on foreign-owned, ocean-going ships, lured mainly by what, by Burmese standards, was the handsome remuneration. An even stronger lure was the right of Burmese sailors serving abroad to use half their foreign exchange earnings to buy foreign-made goods, including cars, which they could bring home, ostensibly for personal use. There were, said the report, 3,000 Burmese youths serving with foreign shipping lines. One could be confident that they engaged in smuggling, too.

Burma's legal trade with Thailand was running at US$500,000 a year, said the American Ambassador, but the illegal trade was probably US$150 million a year. At best, that could only be a rough approximation. The *Asia* magazine of December 1974 declared, "supplying the black market [in Burma] is a smuggling industry of extraordinary scope and insouciance. 'You want a herd of elephants?' asks a Rangoon taxi-driver. It's possible to get them from Thailand … A loaf of French bread? A certain airline's crew handles that, fresh from Bangkok."

The border with Thailand, extending for the better part of 2,000 miles, and Burma's coast, of similar lengths, were far beyond Burma's capacity to monitor while they tried to grapple with a dozen different kinds of insurgency. For many Burmese, the risks of smuggling were worth taking when the official exchange rate was pegged at an artificially high level – at least three times its real value, so expatriates said. "Most of the imported goods you see in shops in Rangoon are smuggled in from Thailand, in exchange for gems and rice," said the Thai Ambassador. "We've offered the Burmese a barter agreement, such as we have with India, but they don't seem to be interested; they're apparently content with things as they are. We regard our relations with Burma as good."

All the ambassadors were quick to say what was wrong with Burma. It was once a prosperous country, said the British Ambassador, but it was the outsiders who had made it so, and the Burmese kicked them out. Burma remained more richly endowed with mineral resources than any other country in the region, "You name it, they've got it," but, in every case, mineral production was less than 30 percent of 1939.

The Burmese, of course, saw it quite differently. The British had taken over their country by force, ousted the monarchy and established a new capital so grandly British in form that it would not have been surprising to turn the next corner and come across the pigeons in Trafalgar Square, though, in fact, nowadays, you only came across more crows and dilapidation. And, with themselves at the helm, the British brought in Indians to administer Burma and, worse, to administer it as part of India until as recently as 1937. And they had brought in Indians and Chinese to run commerce and industry. It was easy to see that, in its heyday, Rangoon had been the Garden City of the East, as it had been called; a prosperous, pleasant place. But it was also easy to see how galling all this must have been to the Burmese who, until subdued by the British, had been accustomed to lording it over their neighbours.

When given back control of their own country, the Burmese reacted violently: left the Commonwealth, ousted the interlopers, and progressively nationalised all commerce and industry. And, because know-how had been ousted with the interlopers, nationalisation had, to a large extent come to mean, as our Burmese driver laughingly said, "It's been taken over by the Government so it doesn't work any more". (The only compromise in the programme of nationalisation had been in offshore oil exploration and extraction. The British and Americans thought this would remain the only exception, being largely out of sight, and not a forerunner of further compromise, in the extraction of other resources, even of on-shore oil for instance.)

The exodus of the outsiders had continued since my visit to Burma in 1967. The Indian community had once numbered 550,000, said the Indian chargé. It was now down to 200,000. A further 5,000 left every year but this was offset by births. The Indians who remained were, for the most part, farmers. Unlike the Chinese, they had rarely married Burmese. All the Indians wanted to go home to India to die. The Burmese squeeze on the Indian community had ceased being the irritant it had once been in relations between the two countries. Indeed, when the Indian Foreign Minister had recently visited Rangoon, the subject had not even been mentioned. The Chinese who had migrated to Burma were mainly men, many of whom had married Burmese women and been assimilated far more than the Indian community. Several members of the Cabinet, the Indian chargé added, were of Chinese-Burmese extraction. So, too, was Ne Win. (Rangoon, I discovered, had a prominent but subdued-looking Chinatown.)

Rangoon invited you to reconsider your sense of values. Why shouldn't the bar in the leading hotel run out of soda, decline to serve beer (although it was available when you dined in the next room), and provide a haven for rats and cockroaches who staged a kind of floor show to watch while you had a drink before dinner? Was it really essential for the water to run hot in the bathroom more than once a week? What was television? Why should there be a news-stand in any hotel or at the airport? Why have books in English available for sale at all? … The expatriates were quick to rattle off the list of all the deficiencies: the shortage of houses to lease – houses, like land, were still privately owned; the shortage (usually the complete absence) of such ordinary commodities as toothpaste, nails or house paint. (But we were able to buy some stunningly good watercolour paintings in the modern style.)

Wondering About and Wandering in Burma

By the time I got to the American Ambassador, an old hand in the area, the complaints were becoming rather a bore. So I put it to him that, despite all the deficiencies, it was nevertheless my impression that Rangoon was in slightly better shape than when I'd encountered it in 1967. The streets and sidewalks, the grass verges and the public gardens were in better order. There were more cars about and fewer of them had broken down. There was a little more new construction under way, more tourists. The Burmese were friendly, quick to smile; there was none of the sullenness one encountered in Saigon. I'd encountered a young New Zealander, working on an oil exploration ship in the area, who'd described Rangoon as "paradise compared with Dacca" (although he couldn't wait to get back to his real Eden, Bangkok, and I'd had no need to ask why). In other words, if one judged Burma as one might expect the Burmese to judge it, were things really as bad as the riots of the previous June and December suggested? Wasn't there a certain level of content?

He agreed. The Burmese level of expectation was not high. The sense of contentment was even more apparent in the countryside and small towns. He thought the contentment stemmed mainly from deep religious beliefs. In part, too, the Burmese were content because they didn't know any other country to compare with Burma. Remarkably few Burmese were allowed, or could afford, to travel abroad, even to Bangkok, a completely different world less than an hour's flight away. No Burmese naval ship had been to any foreign port, and no foreign warship had visited Burma since 1963. There were more tourists in Burma but the number was still small: 17,000 a year, compared with a million a year in Malaysia, and that excluded the considerable number going across the causeway from Singapore. Most of them came on organised tours, 'doing' Rangoon, Mandalay and Pagan on the standard seven-day visa and having minimal contact with the Burmese. All news was severely controlled and, at least in the English-language press, presented in a manner that was excruciatingly dull, avoiding any suggestion of controversy or trouble. And there was no television.

On the other hand, said the American Ambassador, the older generation of people in Burma remembered the better days and the young folk were surely aware, however vaguely, of the good things which Burma might have.

However much the outsiders might criticise Burma, it struck me that the severest critics of all were the Burmese themselves. The Burmese Ambassador in Kuala Lumpur remarked to a group of us at a social gathering around that time, "My government believes that the best place for oil is where it is – underground. How stupid can you get!" The President himself had said to me, "Our people are lazy. Nothing has been done to our tea estates for 15 years." The Minister of Education was entirely frank with me in saying that their educational system needed a thorough overhaul, to get it away from arts and pure science, in which they had a ridiculous excess of graduates, and move into more practical areas that were more in keeping with Burma's level of development.

In the hotel dining room one evening, my wife remarked to the waiter, "There seems to be something wrong with this pepperpot. It's not working properly." He replied instantly, with a grin, "Yes, it's Burmese." When we visited the Shwe Dagon Pagoda in Rangoon, the largest and most revered in Burma, a lad came up and asked if he might talk with us, to practise his English. In the course of conversation he observed with a grin, "Everybody doesn't like our government." The Burmese had this admirable capacity to laugh at themselves. And there was evidence, too, of an even more admirable resilience. The former Chief Justice and the former Foreign Minister, whom we met at the British Ambassador's dinner, were bubbling over with good humour. It required others to tell us that Ne Win had clapped them both in jail for six years, along with several thousand others who had been in office when he staged his military coup.

The 'Burmese Way to Socialism' began with the incontestable assertion, 'This land is our land'. It was a land where most people lived close to the good earth and a good God, from one harvest and one baby to the next, with confidence in the next life. There was a great deal to commend in this simple life and Ne Win aimed to conserve it. As he saw it, economic development was to be pursued in a moral, social and cultural context. Not for him the side-effects of 'progress', evident in, say, Bangkok, with its incorrigible hedonism, traffic snarls and corruption.

It was not Ne Win's intention to deny that economic development could be beneficial and certainly not to preside over a declining economy. Well, what went wrong? He pursued the Burmese Way to Socialism with about as much finesse or thought of compromise as his Burmese forbears had shown in sacking Ayuthia, the ancient Thai capital. He brooked no opposition, either from outsiders, who included people who had lived in Burma for many generations, or his own Burmese countrymen. He played it by the book: a book which counselled that government, like war, was not for the squeamish. There developed strains of paranoia and mindless xenophobia. Added to all this, he inherited a more complex problem of insurgency than existed in any other country.

In fact, there had been a little compromise in recent years. Tourists were now more welcome, although restricted to the capacity of a few hundred hotel rooms at any place in the country, and visas now allowed people to stay in Burma for seven days, instead of 24 hours which had previously been the norm. Again, Burma now submitted itself to the inquisitional requirements of Asian Development and World Bank loans. Ne Win had begun to travel more abroad than had previously been his custom, and Burmese officials were allowed to fraternise with Westerners far more freely than when I was there in 1967. Yes, adjustments were being made. But the evidence of change was barely perceptible.

And what of Burma's relations with China, its most important neighbour? It had long been said, 'When China spits, Burma swims'. What did that mean? China had been spitting at Burma a lot in recent years: providing arms, training and personnel to the so-called White Flag Communist insurgents. Yet, ostensibly, Burma had reasonably good relations with China. Did the two countries somehow keep relations between governments separate from relations between political parties? "Of course," said the American Ambassador.

* * * * *

Wherever you go, there's a New Zealand connection.

During this visit to Rangoon, the Deputy Prime Minister told me that a man named Douglas Blake, an Anglo-Burmese who had once been second-in-command to General Ne Win, was now living in New Zealand.

And, as I was leaving the Minister of Agriculture after chatting with him for about an hour, I was surprised when he said, "And how's my good friend, Frank Childs?"[36] The Minister seemed to assume that all New Zealanders would know each other. In this case, he was right. Like most Cabinet ministers in Rangoon, the Minister had been a military man – although, in their new roles, they all wore mufti – and had been on the same course as Colonel Childs at the Queenscliff Staff College in Australia.

But perhaps the most surprising New Zealand connection came to light when we went some 25 miles out of Rangoon to visit the immaculately kept Commonwealth War Graves Cemetery where seven New Zealand airmen were buried. The curator, a lively Burmese man of about 30, asked where we came from and, when I told him, his eyes lit up. "Oh," he said, "I've got a New Zealand stepfather." He was Francis Eric Dewar, a missionary who had spent many years in Burma and in 1975, at age 66, was living in Chiang Mai, northern Thailand.

(When Sir Bernard Fergusson, as Governor-General of New Zealand, visited the Commonwealth War Graves Cemetery at Kranji, in Singapore, in 1966, he asked the man in charge, a Mr Tan, who was in the job for many years, whether he could find the burial plot of an old friend, a naval man who had been killed in action in Singapore waters during World War II. Mr Tan replied instantly, "Oh, yes. Three rows up and 17 graves in," – or whatever the specifics were. He knew them all by heart.)

[36] Colonel Frank Childs, 1923–78.

III. A ROUGH ROAD TO NIRVANA

From 18 February to 2 March 1976, I paid another visit to Burma. And it all went well, although according to a Burmese kind of schedule. Until I arrived, they assumed I might not. Although I had given more than a month's notice of the visit, together with a list of the ministers and officials I wished to see and places I wished to visit, I found on arrival that absolutely nothing had been arranged except, said the British Second Secretary who met me, a car which, at his increasingly frantic insistence, had been put at my disposal only just in time to meet the plane. (This was a Burmese Government car but we paid for the hire of it; there were no car rental firms in Burma.) Otherwise, the only thing the British Second Secretary had to report was that the Burmese had turned down my bid to go to Myitkyina, "but, of course, no one is ever allowed to go there".

But I'd been learning that, if you kept smiling along with them but remained quietly persistent, the Burmese came good. By next day, I had appointments to see three ministers, an invitation to dine with one of them; and the visit to Myitkyina was approved. And, when I called on these ministers, there was never a moment's waiting in anyone's anteroom. I was received with the utmost cordiality and, in the arrangements made for the visits outside Rangoon, the Burmese could not have been kinder or more attentive to every detail. (All this, of course, was attributable to New Zealand's good reputation. All I had to do was be congenial.)

I was beginning to feel a little peeved that I was again failing to see the Foreign Minister until my colleagues in the diplomatic corps, resident in Rangoon, asked about my programme and it then became clear that I seemed to be getting preferential treatment. None of my colleagues had ever been allowed to go to Myitkyina. And the Australian Ambassador said, with admirable directness, "Christ! How did you get to see the Prime Minister? I've been here for ten months, trying to see him and I've decided to make just one more bid and, if the bastard won't see me, then to hell with him!"

Ministers kept their distance from the diplomats in Rangoon. The Foreign Minister appeared dutifully at National Day receptions but otherwise ministers rarely attended diplomatic functions except to honour a cabinet minister visiting from another country. Burmese officials required clearance to attend any diplomatic function and, while this was usually granted, it took time and was irksome. When I asked the British Ambassador how often he saw Ne Win, he replied, "Almost never." An ambassador would see him to present credentials and then, eventually, to say farewell, but otherwise only to shake hands a couple of times a year, at a function celebrating Burma's independence or on the occasion of a visit by another head of state but, at such times, there was rarely any opportunity to converse.

The British Ambassador leaned back in his chair, grinned impishly and reflected that Ne Win was becoming more and more like Henry VIII. His dissolution of foreign and private enterprise corresponded with Henry's handling of the monasteries. And neither henchmen nor wives knew how long they would last. On Christmas Eve, Ne Win had been disturbed by the sounds of revelry, including very loud, modern Western music, drifting to his home from across the lake. He drove around to the source of this revelry, the Inya Lake Hotel, strode in tempestuously, kneed a bandsman hard in the groin and, when he fell, kicked him. Then he ripped off the top of the dress of one of the revelers – his wife of some two years. They had already fallen out, mainly, it seemed, because her sister had been caught in a smuggling enterprise and Ne Win had refused to protect her. Never mind. He now had a new wife and a new Minister of Trade whose portfolio included the Tourist Corporation which was supposed to keep decorous standards of behaviour at the Inya Lake Hotel. And, since Christmas Eve, following Mae Tse-tung's example, Ne Win had been orchestrating a cultural revolution – Burmese-style of course – which meant, like the Burmese Way to Socialism, that people weren't taking it too seriously.

Around the middle of 1975, Ne Win recalled 19 Burmese Ambassadors, most of them former generals. Only three of them had so far been given new assignments. I called on one of the unlucky ones, who had become a good friend of mine when Ambassador in Kuala Lumpur. He was now growing orchids commercially in the grounds of his home and had been waiting, for seven months, to know whether he would get another assignment and, if so, when. But he was still smiling. So, too, was the former Ambassador to London and Scandinavia who seemed to epitomise the finely-tempered steel you could come across in Burma. Lord Mountbatten, he said, had been kind enough to send a note to his uncle, King Carl Gustav of Sweden, introducing him as "the youngest battalion commander I ever had". He had been a colonel, on active service, at 22.

Ne Win's court was in no way scintillating but his performance was, in its fashion, adroit. He scratched the army's back and they scratched his. Almost all the ministers and deputy ministers were army men (in mufti). So, too, was the Chief of Police. Ne Win depended on them and the army to carry out his wishes – on occasion, ruthlessly – to suppress disorder. (Following peaceful demonstrations in June, 1975, students had been sentenced to terms of imprisonment of up to nine years and industrial workers up to 16. The jails had overflowed with some 20,000 new inmates, many of whom had to be moved to detention centres outside Rangoon.)

In return, the military establishment enjoyed preferential treatment in the allocation of housing and access to medical facilities and consumer goods. It was therefore cushioned from the effects of a declining economy. Ne Win kept the Generals guessing, not only by moving them around and letting them cool their heels from time to time, but also by talking over their heads to the sergeants: "Well, hello, Sergeant. It's good to see you again. It's been a long time since we were in that campaign together … Any problems? Well, if you ever have any problems, you've only got to let me know." With ploys like that, the diplomats reckoned, it was extremely unlikely that any military plot to overthrow him could ever succeed.

But Burma had become 'Frightened Rabbit Country'. For every one of my ministerial appointments, including the dinner, I was telephoned at least three times, in a crescendo of anxiety (from 7 am onwards when I was to call on the Prime Minister) that I might somehow forget to appear. And the reminder calls came not just from the Minister's private secretary but also from his permanent head and the Chief of Protocol. Moreover, civil servants hesitated to give answers to what seemed entirely straightforward questions and, in the Foreign Ministry, declined to discuss the simplest issue of foreign policy without first clearing it with the Minister. Not did it stop there. When I asked the Prime Minister how Burma viewed ASEAN these days – Burma having for some time having been in two minds about joining – he replied hesitantly (but still smiling), "I'm not qualified to answer your question."

A curious example of Frightened Rabbit Country occurred one evening at the Inya Lake Hotel where there was to be a showing of documentary films on Burma for participants in the current Gems Emporium, an annual international auction of jade and other gems: the Burmese equivalent, you could say, of New Zealand's yearling sales. We asked the men in charge of the film evening whether my wife and I might also attend. That was obviously impossible, he pointed out, because we did not have badges to say we were registered participants at the Gems Emporium. That was undeniable but as there was no sign that they were going to be short of seating, and the man's English being limited, I appealed to the receptionist at the hotel desk. She spoke to the man and he agreed to refer the matter to higher authority. He went away, returned about ten minutes later, and let us in. There was no charge. In fact, they were the dullest films imaginable and it was tempting to think that the participants in the Gems Emporium had been forewarned of this. In a room with seating for about 300 people, there was only one other person present.

When you talked to members of the Establishment in Burma, you could readily be led to believe that all was well. The Western materialists in the diplomatic corps, however, although agreeing that Burma's international relations were in fair shape, told you the very opposite of what the Burmese

Establishment said about almost everything else. The Western Materialists were most adamant about the Burmese economy. It was, they declared, in dire shape. And this was lent credence when we were in Myitkyina and met Father Rillstone, the only permanent New Zealand resident of Burma (he had been a missionary there since 1940) and I asked him how he found material conditions in Burma. He replied, with feeling, "They get worse by the day."

But when I talked to ambassadors of countries whose circumstances and standards were more akin to Burma's, I got a rather different slant. As the Indonesian, Indian, Sri Lankan and Bangladeshi Ambassadors saw it, Burma wasn't doing too badly. (And, for the people of Indo-China – Cambodia, Laos and Vietnam – long involved, in bitter strife, there must have been much to envy in Burma.) True, they readily admitted, there was mismanagement in Burma and the Government was far too doctrinaire. But, said the Ambassador of Bangladesh, Ne Win was entitled to say to him, as he had recently, "No one is starving in *this* country." Moreover, said the Ambassador, everyone in Burma had footwear; rice was reasonably plentiful and although inflation had been around 40 percent in 1975, this was light compared with the several hundred percent recorded in Indonesia in Sukarno's day.

Moreover, said the Indian Ambassador, it was misleading to judge Burma by the official statistics. Figures of income, for instance, suggested that wages had been frozen at an unrealistically low level in relation to the rising cost of living but this ignored two basic facts which the statistics did not take into account. First, anyone who was in a position to do so was 'fiddling' – engaged in the black market or corruption of some kind. Secondly, 80 percent of the Burmese lived in rural areas and, to a large extent, were not part of the cash economy: they grew their own fruit and vegetables, often their own rice, raised their own chickens and so on. The Indian Ambassador questioned whether the standard of living in Burma had fallen at all since independence in 1947, although he conceded that this level was below that of 1939. The elderly Sri Lankan Ambassador, who had first visited Burma more than 20 years previously, said much the same thing. And "How do you measure the standard of living?" reflected the Indonesian Ambassador. It depended on you sense of values. Westerners, led by the Americans, worshipped the dollar and technological advance; Russia and China worshipped the masses; but Burma differed from every other country – Buddhism provided their sense of values and dictated that man was supreme.

This train of thought was elaborated by the German wife of a Burmese doctor. She had lived in Burma for 21 years (and was, her husband said, with great affection, "the most senior expatriate wife in the country!"). Burma was not ruled by the Government at all, she maintained, except in peripheral ways; it was ruled by Buddhism; to the Burmese, the important, enduring thing was their faith; it was not so much a formal religion as a way of life, enjoining its adherents to work their way to Nirvana, equivalent to the Christian concept of heaven. Although maintaining the detachment of a German passport and Christianity,[37] she said she found the Western world increasingly neglectful of human relations, increasingly confused about its sense of values, increasingly neurotic. By contrast, she laughed, no psychiatrist could ever make a living in Burma. In their daily lives, the Burmese kept their eyes on the symbolic pagoda. Wherever you went there was a pagoda in sight and often there were dozens and sometimes hundreds. Moreover, there was symbolic significance in the fact that the pagoda had always been built of bricks and mortar – permanent materials – whereas even the kings had dwellings of timber.[38] In 2,500 years there had been six Buddhist Synods and the only two in Christian times (1871 and 1954) had been in Burma. In Mandalay we saw 729 large white marble tablets on each of which was inscribed the definitive text of the Buddhist scriptures, as determined by the Synod of 1871.

We felt closest to the Buddhist sense of values in the rural areas and most of all at Myitkyina, 'the place by the big river', a town of 70,000 people at the head of the railway, overlooking the upper reaches of the Irrawaddy and itself overlooked by the hills of China, 40 miles away: ("In the old days," said the New Zealand missionary, Father Rillstone,[39] "you could wander in and out of China without realising you had crossed the border.") In the streets of the town, the rain trees met overhead and the wayside was carpeted

---

[37] Ten percent of Burmese were Christian. We found the century-old Anglican Cathedral in Rangoon remarkably well cared for, the sign "Church of England" now reading "Church of Burma", and the (Burmese) archbishop in full regalia, with bare feet.

[38] The Palace at Mandalay consisted of 49 elaborately-carved timber 'pavilions', one for each wife of the second-to-last king, within a high-walled compound, a mile and a furlong square, surrounded by a wide moat. The buildings were destroyed by Allied bombing during World War II, the palace having been taken over as a Japanese regional headquarters. The only pavilion to survive was the one in which the second to last King died. Considered, therefore, to be of ill omen, it had been removed from the compound and made into a monastery, in accordance with the Burmese dictum, 'If you have anything useless, give it to the monks.' The carving on this building was probably finer than anything of its kind in the world.

[39] This was Father Tom Rillstone, a missionary in northern Burma among the Kachin people for 36 years. Ordained in 1939, and assigned to Burma in 1940, he was interned by the Japanese in 1940 and, along with other missionaries, "spent three hungry years in a leper asylum in Mandalay," according to an obituary in *The Evening Post* of 9 July 1981. He returned to New Zealand in 1977 and died in Invercargill in 1981, aged 68.

with ageratum, growing wild and in full bloom, a pale bluish-mauve colour which the Chinese called "sky after rain".

The weather was like Wellington's on a hot summer day, the nights similarly cool. For a brief weekend, we followed Burmese ways, rising at dawn, bathing with a dipper, swimming in the Irrawaddy (so cold, in these upper reaches, that germs could scarcely have survived, supposing that an injection against bubonic plague had not taken), drinking the sun down (probably a custom introduced by the British rather than being a Burmese tradition) and dining in a leisurely fashion in time to bed down by ten o'clock when the electricity stopped functioning.

In between appointments, we passed the time of day with our Burmese hosts who had come from Rangoon, where they worked in the Ministry of Education, and from the local Kachin State Peoples' Council. And what charming people they all were with such an engaging ability to laugh at the Burmese Way to Socialism, at the Government: not something you'd expect from people who lived under an iron-fisted military junta. It took my breath away one evening when Father Rillstone remarked that the insurgents let the missionaries come and go freely – nothing in Burma troubled him except the Government. All the Burmese laughed heartily. They talked of their families (none had fewer than seven children) and Burmese traditions and customs. For centuries before the British had introduced modern schooling, it had been the practice for all boys to get at least a rudimentary education by entering the monkhood for a time, the monasteries being centres of learning.

It was compulsory in Burma, they said, to register births and deaths, as matters of concern to the State, but marriage was considered the private concern of a man and a woman and not registerable at all.[40] In fact, there was no Buddhist or state marriage ceremony in Burma. The occasion need not necessarily be announced, although it usually was, by a celebration of some kind. Similarly, there was no restriction on the number of wives a man might have although practicality and convention had come to make Burma, in effect, a monogamous society. After marriage, women kept their maiden names, and to a large extent, controlled the purse strings. The conversation about all these things was constantly punctuated with much laughter, some ribald.

The 'open sesame' for us in going to Myitkyina had been the New Zealand Government's gift of equipment to the local Trade Training Centre, a Colombo Plan project supervised by New Zealander Alex Owen.

---

[40] This probably accounts for uncertainty about how often Ne Win had married. One British newspaper, *The Independent*, said, in its obituary of 6 December, 2002, that Ne Win had married twice but the *Guardian* obituary of the same date said "he was thought to have married five times … twice to the same woman".

We found this equipment in wonderfully good order and greatly valued. The project had, in fact, been discussed by Ne Win during his visit to New Zealand in 1974 and had his wholehearted backing. So, when our visit to Myitkyina happened to coincide with that of the Commissioner of Police from Rangoon, he didn't stand a chance of being allocated the better of two Government Rest Houses. We won handsomely with Irrawaddy Villa, a charming although neglected relic of British days.

We assumed the cook must be of similar vintage, and undoubtedly Chinese, such a splendid succession of meals did he produce. He was never in sight so, just before we left, we asked to meet him, to thank him. He turned out to be a young Burmese of about 30. The Director-General of Technical, Vocational and Agricultural Education, who came from Rangoon for the weekend, had recruited students from the local agricultural college to attend to household tasks, including waiting on tables. The bathroom fittings (made by Shanks) had long since ceased to function but an old Gurkha retainer had been found to heat water over an open fire and bring it to us in buckets twice a day. When we went for a stroll or swam in the Irrawaddy, there were always five soldiers to guard us, their rifles held at the ready, grenades clipped to their belts. When we went further afield, by car, we were preceded by a whole truckload of soldiers.

Burma Airlines, we found on this journey, operated with rather startling insouciance and by indicative scheduling. When we went from Pagan to Mandalay, a half-hour flight, we were seven hours late in leaving. Next day, going from Mandalay to Myitkyina, we were two hours early. The airline's international operations, which extended to Bangkok, Kathmandu and Hong Kong, were run with one Viscount and the domestic routes mainly with Fokker Friendships. When the larger planes were being serviced, the Fokkers replaced them and the regular Fokker runs were suspended. Other things were unusual, too. When a Burma Airlines plane took off or landed, the air hostess didn't strap herself into a seat like everyone else. She stood in the aisle, holding onto the luggage rack. And, the door to the cockpit being invariably unshuttable, it would swing to and fro, allowing us to see (on the long flight back from Myitkyina to Rangoon, with stops at Mahmo, Lashio and Mandalay), that the pilot had learnt from experience that the time he needed a cigarette most was to ease the tension of take-off and landing.

IV. GOODBYE AND GOOD LUCK

I paid a farewell visit to Rangoon between 19 and 26 October 1976. When I arrived, around noon, it was to find, as usual, that none of the appointments, requested a month before, had been arranged. But, again in accordance with usual practice, every one of those appointments, as well as a ministerial dinner, had been set up before the day was out. And, again as usual, when I went on my rounds, there was never a moment's waiting in anyone's anteroom. This encouraged the belief that, if the Burmese could be so efficient in these small things, then perhaps one day, they could do better in other things, like running the country, or even in cooking food at the Strand Hotel.

After I'd been in Rangoon in late February and early March, various predictable things had happened. General Tin Oo, who had long been regarded as one of Ne Win's likely successors, had been ousted, on corruption charges, although it was said he had probably been framed because he'd become too popular. Then a group of young army captains had organised a coup to put Tin Oo in Ne Win's place. The captains failed, of course. ("Very sloppy planning," the American Ambassador declared. "Kindergarten stuff," sniffed the British.)

Predictably, too, Ne Win had found a new friend, Rose June Bellamy, the daughter of an Australian bookmaker and a Burmese 'princess'.. The ambassadors in Rangoon were eager to tell me all the details. She was a comely woman in her mid-forties who had already discarded two husbands, one a World Health Organisation official, the other an Italian count, and she lived in Switzerland. So, during the year, Ne Win had been to Switzerland twice, each time for two months, 'for medical treatment'. ("Nothing much wrong with him," snorted the British Ambassador.) And, with absences like that, it was little wonder that Tin Oo and the captains had been busy.

Predictably, too, the security situation in Burma remained much the same although the army was continuing to clobber the insurgents as hard as it could. Again predictably, Burma had given up any interest in joining the regional organisation ASEAN.

On the other hand, various rather unexpected things had happened. Most notably, there seemed to be a small but definite improvement in the economy. I was alerted to this in noting that, when the Strand Hotel enforced their ban on serving beer in the bar, to keep out the Burmese riff-raff, they now came in and drank whisky instead. Certainly, the diplomats all said, the pragmatists in Rangoon were having a much greater say in managing the economic affairs of Burma. The tax system had been restructured, incentive pay rates introduced and so on. And the Government was paying more realistic prices to farmers for rice and other crops. In addition, the 1975–6 harvest had been bountiful and the harvest just beginning to come in promised to be just as good. But there were no indications that the Government was prepared to compromise with its 'socialist' principles, for instance by inviting in foreign capital, management or enterprise in any form, except in an advisory role under aid.

Although it was predictable that a coup would fail, it was nevertheless unexpected that the young captains had been able to plot for about four months without being discovered. This indicated a greater degree of disenchantment with Ne Win, and especially with his economic policies, than any outside observer had thought possible. That such a degree of disenchantment should have existed in the army was especially surprising. All this was coming to light in the current trial of the young captains.

It was probably coincidental but I wondered whether there was additional, if minor, evidence of declining respect for Ne Win when the driver turned up ten minutes late to take me to see the President. The Chief of Protocol, who was to accompany me, became increasingly agitated. The driver, all smiles, offered no explanation or apology for his late arrival and quickly made up for it, on the way, by ignoring a few red traffic lights – not especially hazardous in Rangoon's sparse traffic. (The lads played soccer in the main streets during what, in other parts of the world, would be the rush hour.) The driver, incidentally, was of Shan–Chinese extraction. He talked (in English) incessantly and very quickly and apparently tried to make up for the unintelligibility of most of what he was saying by gesticulating, with both hands, as we went along. The steering wheel was similarly unattended as he made obeisance to every pagoda we passed – and there were many.

After the call on the President, it struck me that the driver had done better than I had. From somewhere in the nether regions of the President's establishment, he had picked up the news that the heads of seven 'dignitaries' were about to topple. So far as I know, however, there was no subsequent confirmation of this. Perhaps, although, it confirmed that Ne Win himself was a prime source of such rumours which abounded in Rangoon, as one way of keeping lesser 'dignitaries' in their place.

The President was more closely guarded than when I presented credentials in February 1975. But I was not frisked, on arrival, as the British Ambassador thought I might be. The President received me in his office, a modest room (about Second Secretary standard, according to the New Zealand Overseas Accommodation Board's guidelines) and originally, no doubt, one of the lesser bedrooms in some British business executive's home by the edge of Inya Lake. I was seated in an upright chair, immediately in front of the President's desk, opposite him and flanked by a young colonel whose job it was to agree with the President and presumably to restrain me if the need arose.

Contrary to Burmese custom, I was offered nothing to eat or drink and I had, of course, been warned not to smoke. I thought there had been a noticeable decline in Ne Win's physical condition and mental alertness since I'd met him over 18 months ago. He now seemed a little stooped, as the French Ambassador had also noticed when he paid a farewell call about three months earlier. He spoke a little more slowly, perceptibly groping for the facts, as he hadn't at all when I'd presented credentials.

Indeed, I wondered whether he'd suffered a mild stroke. But I could find no confirmation of anything of this kind among the resident diplomats, although most of them had not seen him since March. Undoubtedly he had become a confirmed hypochondriac and more reclusive. In the hour or so I spent with him, he was, as before, entirely congenial, an amiable, grandfatherly man. He again recalled his visit to New Zealand with great pleasure and again asked me to convey his greetings to the Governor-General, Sir Bernard Fergusson.

He talked mainly about China. He had probably been there and seen Mao Tse-tung more often (from 1955 onwards, he observed) than any other outsider. He took pride in having long predicted the course of events after Mao's death. It would take a long time to settle down, he thought, before anyone could be certain that the new leadership and its policies were firm. As he talked, it struck me that he had as good a knowledge of Chinese politics and politicians as Lee Kuan Yew did of Britain. He similarly claimed to know much of the inside story: of how, for instance, the Party, including Chou En Lai, had made it a condition of Mao's marriage to Chiang Chin Ching that she stay in the kitchen and, when she didn't, she had her knife into Chou En Lai's wife, among others. He seemed extraordinarily well informed about the various purges in Chinese leadership over the years. I suggested he should write his memoirs. He agreed but said they couldn't be published for five to ten years after his death, otherwise relations among states, and not only Burma's relations with others, would be compromised.

When we got on to the local scene, I expressed regret that no oil had been found offshore. "It's a trick," he retorted, laughingly. "I know it's there. They can plug it up if they like but they can't take it away. I want to see the records of their exploration, not just week by week, but foot by foot …"

When we turned to the harvest, he was at his best, a countryman at heart. It was difficult, then, as it had been before, to recognise him as a pretty ruthless military dictator. Throughout the conversation, he was, indeed, more philosophical than would be expected of a man who ran his kind of regime. At one point, I remarked that communist states tended to become bourgeois. He mused, "What does 'bourgeois' mean? Words sometimes change or lose their meaning. Does 'proletariat' have meaning any more?" It wasn't a word used in New Zealand now, I said, and blue- and white-collar workers earned much the same. "Ah, yes," he said, "but they are different, have different capacities, complement each other, just as a man needs a woman. Despite Women's Lib, a woman still needs a man's help to have a child." He went on to observe that in Burmese society women had always enjoyed a more honoured place than in the West. Nevertheless, he went on, "and I warn you," he added graciously, "that this is rather crude. We have a saying in Burma that a man shoots straighter than a woman, even in pissing."

* * * * *

I concluded my association with Burma by echoing the valedictory remarks of a former British Ambassador and a friend of mine: "I remain hopeful for Burma and believe that people with so many good qualities must eventually profit by their mistakes and make a going concern of a country so well endowed."

But a large question mark hung over the future of Burma. In particular, would Ne Win, now 66, stay or go? Some ambassadors – the veteran Sri Lankan and the Indonesian – thought change was in the air. The American Ambassador thought the current trial of the young captains was providing a useful textbook for the next coup attempt which was bound to come before long. The British Ambassador thought Ne Win would carry on indefinitely – and that's about what happened. Ne Win wasn't pushed out and he didn't step down for another 12 years, by which time he was 77.

No one could have predicted what eventually happened. Even into his nineties, Ne Win's military successors continued to visit him regularly at his home (where I had called on him) and he continued to some extent to be a power behind the throne. Then bizarrely, in March 2001, he was put under house arrest following the arraignment of a daughter's husband and their three sons, for plotting – wait for it – to put the old man back in power. Or was he, in turn, being framed? The son-in-law and three grandsons were condemned to death. Ne Win died the following year, still under house arrest, aged 92.

In the intervening years, under successive military juntas, Burma sank further and further into the mire of economic decline, xenophobia and international pariahdom.

Knock Five Times and Ask for the President or King

I. THE ITALIAN JOB

We began to like, admire and wonder about the Italians even before leaving Heathrow on 7 March 1980.

The departures board indicated that the flight to Rome would be half an hour late. The half hour became an hour, the hour two hours. Then I was summoned to the Alitalia counter where the manager explained apologetically that the air traffic controllers in Rome were going slow. They were handling only one international flight every two hours. If we waited our turn, the flight wouldn't leave for another six hours.

So, he said, the flight would leave immediately and go to Pisa instead. "And then," he added, "we will see what happens."

Three years in Moscow, in the secretive, slothful, Cold War, Brezhnev time, had taught me not to ask too many questions. On the contrary, it struck me as absolutely bloody marvellous that Italians admitted they were going slow and one of their countrymen could tell a foreigner.

So we set off for Pisa to see what would happen. We were approaching the Alps when the pilot announced, without mentioning Pisa, that we were going to Genoa; we would only touch down there and then proceed immediately to Rome. By touching down in Genoa, were we, in the eyes of air traffic controllers in Rome, being converted from a questionable international flight into an acceptable domestic one? Was that it?

Subsequently, however, without any further reference to Pisa or Genoa, the pilot announced we were going straight to Rome. This we did. Had the air traffic controllers been stunned by the pilot's audacity? Had the industrial dispute been settled? Never mind. Here we were on the fringe of the Eternal City.

We were met by members of the embassy staff and two charming Italian Protocol Officers, one about 55, the other in a post-retirement job (the retirement age was 65), exclusively meeting and farewelling diplomats and official visitors at the airport. Such is the multiplicity of international relations now.

Next day, a more senior and even more charming Protocol Officer called on me and arranged for me to call the following day on the Deputy Chief of Protocol (who was shortly to become the Ambassador in Dublin).

Finally, the following week, I made it to the Chief of Protocol – indeed, 'Prince Charming' himself, draped, as it were, with his arms entwined over the back of the fireside chair he sat in – in the most elegant office I've ever been in. He apologised for the delay in arranging for me to present credentials. I brushed this aside but he protested: "Oh, it's all rather Third-Worldish. But be assured you are not forgotten. On the contrary, you are on my mind *every minute*!"

There was no need for either of us to say what the circumstance were making for delay: the Government was toppling; the President was trying to form another government – the 39th in 35 years. He was, moreover, attending functions in various other parts of Italy, including the funerals of assassinated judges, three in four days that week.

One after another, the succession of protocol officers had emphasised how informal the presentation of credentials had become under President Pertini. No speeches were exchanged. It seemed that all I had to remember was to wear a dark suit, with tie and white shirt, and bring along three or four members of the embassy staff. The advice was so vague that I began to worry that I'd somehow misunderstood. So when I got to Prince Charming, I asked if (as in other capitals) there was a piece of paper setting out the procedure.

"Oh, no!" he laughed. "It's all much too informal for that!" But then he added a rather ominous warning: "You'll find that the President is a very nice man. Everybody likes him. But in one respect he's showing his years …" He was 83 and known affectionately to Italians as 'Il Nonno' [Grandpa]. "He has no sense of time, none at all. If there's any lull in the conversation, he'll conclude it's time to end it. Some ambassadors are offended by being dismissed so quickly but there's nothing I can do about it. It's up to you. You just have to keep the conversation going."

So, on the appointed day, 26 March, one of the charming Protocol Officers called for me in a Presidential Lancia limousine, which is far grander than a Russian Zil, and far rarer. "There are only three of them left in the world," said the Protocol Officer, "in fact, only two. The third is being cannibalised to keep the other two going – and they only just go."

We set out with two motorcycle outriders who were studiously ignored by all the other traffic. But such disdain had been more than taken into account. We arrived early and had to fill in time by going round the block. Finally, we drove into the vast and splendid courtyard of the Quirinale Palace, inspected a guard of honour and then walked into a portico area where there was a far more impressive display of Italian manhood in the form of Presidential Guards, every one of whom seemed to be at least eight feet tall and broad in proportion. They were dressed in a uniform of medieval magnificence, topped off with a helmet of gleaming brass adorned with black feathers.

We paused in an anteroom. Prince Charming emerged from an inner sanctum and passed the time of day with me. Eventually, the doors of the inner sanctum opened and I was ushered in, introduced to the President, a spry, twinkling-eyed, instantly likeable little old man. In the prescribed manner, I gave him envelopes containing letters which recalled my predecessor and accredited me. The President introduced me to his entourage and I introduced mine to him. He paused to admire "the youth and undoubted competence" of my staff and in particular, noted approvingly Geoff Randall's "beard in the modern style".

He then took me, on my own, into his innermost sanctum where we sat with an interpreter perched between us. I said I was honoured to meet him and be assigned to such an important and beautiful city. But he appeared not to be listening. As if speaking a little absently from a prepared script, he said he was sure there would be plenty of future opportunities for us to chat in a leisurely manner and he looked forward to that. And he was already beginning to rise from his chair.

Having thus exchanged two sentences each (my British colleague said later he wasn't sure whether he'd got in two or three), the President escorted me back to the anteroom where everyone shook the hands they had shaken less than two minutes before.

And it was done. Well, not quite. Before we were out of the anteroom, the President barked, "Who's next?"

And an aide shouted, "Madagascar!"

And the President did Guinea, too, before lunch.

* * * * *

In the three years which followed, I often met President Pertini briefly in reception lines but the only 'leisurely' conversation I ever had with him, and it was highly congenial, was in a farewell call in February 1983. I don't think anyone in the diplomatic corps in Rome ever met his wife. She was a professional psychiatrist, many years younger. 'In the modern style', with his support, she declined to take any part in the presidency. She said it was he, not they, who had been elected president; and it was she, not they, who had elected, and had qualified, to practise psychiatry.

He used the Quirinale Palace only for official purposes and lived with his wife in a nearby apartment. Everybody loved him for his exceptional human warmth, his fearlessness in condemning the terrorists (who had killed the judges) and in upbraiding wayward politicians and dilatory bureaucrats. He died in 1990, aged 93.

II. YUGOSLAVIA

Yugoslavia has such a mixture of people, so long at such odds with each other, it was said that, in World War II, more Yugoslavs died fighting each other than in fighting the German invaders – communists against monarchists, Serbs against Croats, Macedonians against Bulgars. When, at the end of the war, the communist partisan leader, Tito, took command of the country, he saw no other way but to rule with an iron fist, as his Russian mentors had taught. He imposed a dictatorial, centralised system of government tied closely within the Soviet bloc. He was Stalin's blue-eyed boy. Then, in 1948, he played Luther to Stalin's papacy, declaring there were different roads to socialism.

In June 1980 when I went to Yugoslavia to present credentials, I immediately began wondering if the Yugoslavs had left anything of the Soviet way of doing things. En route to Belgrade, the plane touched down at Split, on the sun-drenched, tourist-beckoning Dalmatian coast. The border control officer, a handsome young man, was casually bare-headed and smiling, as his Soviet counterparts never were. He took our passports and that of our daughter who was accompanying us for a couple of days in Belgrade. The officer glanced cursorily at the passports, handed ours back, then made a little play of holding on to our daughter's passport, saying with a faint but unmistakably lecherous grin, "Right! You two," – meaning my wife and me – "can go on to Belgrade and your daughter can stay here with me!" We laughed and said she was married. "Never mind," said the young man, "I am single. She can make divorce!" Then he winked at her and slowly handed the passport back. Crack jokes at border control? How far could you get from the Soviet way?

There was a similarly light-hearted approach to the presentation of credentials on 18 June 1980. The procedure provided for an ambassador to be accompanied by "a suite" of up to five members of his staff. But however good a First Secretary might be – as Laurie Markes, who was also accompanying us, most assuredly was – could he, laughed the Yugoslavs, constitute "a suite"? Couldn't the Ambassador's wife and daughter come along, too? So they did.

The little ceremony began with a guard of honour in a uniform of bright blue – Tito's Guards, they had been called and were now simply Presidential Guards. The stocky Tito's narcissistic imprint nevertheless remained: none of the guards could be taller than he was.

Under the post-Tito arrangements of rotating collective leadership, I was received by the current year's President, who had his Foreign Minister and two senior officials with him. There was an exchange of speeches, reciprocal introduction of "suites", then I had half an hour alone with the President and his advisers, the conversation flowing easily, everyone chipping in. Separate calls on ministers rarely ran to less than an hour.

There was a good feel to Belgrade. New Zealand trade prospects looked promising. But what of the future? Could the charismatic iron man, Tito, be replaced effectively by a faceless, rotating collective leadership?

III. MALTA

"You mean to say we're going by Air Malta!"
"Oh, but they're bound to have a British pilot."
"This is your Captain, Dayfid Williams speaking …"

* * * * *

For several thousand years, Malta was in the middle of the known world, a nodal point of trade, a pivot of grand strategic design. Occupancy of Malta changed with the changing fortunes of seafaring powers: Phoenician, Carthaginian, Roman, Turk, Arab, Norman, the Knights of St John (the Crusaders), Spanish, French, British. Occupancy was measured grandly in centuries: the Romans staying by far the longest, for 700 years, the French, under Napoleon, a far shorter time than anyone else (1798–1800). The Crusaders, drawing talent from all over Europe, although not Britain after Henry VIII broke with the Pope, left the greatest tangible imprint, in monumental ramparts and astonishingly numerous and splendid churches.

The Crusaders stemmed Islamic encroachment westwards. The British used Malta as a lynch-pin to enforce their worldwide Pax Britannica. The opening of the Suez Canal (1869) so enhanced the importance of Malta that, in 1888, 12,000 ships called there. In 1929, there were 86 warships at anchor in Malta and 21,000 troops in the garrison.

But when I called on the British High Commissioner in Malta in August 1980, he was standing forlornly at his office window, looking out at the aptly named Grand Harbour. The British had done so much to develop it but the Prime Minister of Malta, Dom (Dominic) Mintoff, was now demanding that the British clear away all their old shipwrecks and spent target-practice bombs. Mintoff was also demanding that Commonwealth war graves in Malta should be consolidated. Failure to get agreement on such issues had led Mintoff to declare that he wouldn't receive the British High Commissioner until his government came to heel.

Mintoff was offside not only with the British. In the 18 months the American Ambassador had been there, he had refused to receive her and said he wouldn't till the United States Government acceded to demands which they found unacceptable. From the Australians Mintoff was asking compensation for the loss of so many Maltese migrants that there were now about as many Maltese in Australia as there were in Malta. Mintoff was also at loggerheads with Italy, France, Germany and the Vatican.

Nor was New Zealand spared the insistent, peremptory pressure. From us they expected a formal aid programme, notwithstanding that their per capita income was far above the normal criterion for international aid; and our aid programme was, for good reason, concentrated much nearer home. Mintoff also wanted us to establish joint ventures on the island and use it as a trans-shipment centre for New Zealand trade throughout the Mediterranean. He wanted us to quote for Malta's state-controlled bulk-purchasing of meat, butter and cheese at 'friendly prices' and so on. Malta, in short, under Mintoff, had become increasingly volatile, petulant and importunate, and difficult to deal with.

On 28 August 1980 when I presented credentials, it was in the great salon where the Grand Master of the Knights of St John had received envoys in the 16th to the 18th centuries. They came bearing gifts of competitively large portraits, which were still there, of such patrons as Louis XIV and Catherine the Great. My gift from New Zealand was a sheepskin rug.

But the elderly President was kindness itself. He changed arrangements for a formal lunch which we were scheduled to have with him and his wife (his third, a Scot) later that day to make it "Sports-shirt-in-the-garden-and-come-half-an-hour-early-and-have-a-swim-first", which we did and greatly enjoyed the occasion, chatting apolitically about this and that, including the memoirs he was writing in six volumes. Similarly, on another day, when I called on the Speaker at 11 am, he got out his bottle of whisky and yarned for two hours.

So, like St Paul, who visited Malta in AD 60, we could feel that, despite other aspects, we had been shown "no little kindness," as he recorded of his experience there in Acts 28:2.

* * * * *

During his term as Prime Minister of Malta (1971–87), the fiery Mintoff expelled the British armed services, declared Malta's neutrality and signed agreements with Libya, the Soviet Union and North Korea. Then in 1987 the Government of Malta changed and in 2004 Malta became a member of the European Union, settling into an even-tenored relationship with traditional friends.

IV. EGYPT

At first glance, President Sadat was surprisingly sphinx-like. His face had the same lines and similarly gave nothing away. His body was lean and taut. When he smiled, as he quickly did, it was almost surprisingly as if the Great Sphinx had done so. And it was an extraordinarily benevolent smile, bringing a remarkably bright glint to his eyes. There was extraordinary gentleness and courtesy in his manner. He moved briskly, not a superfluous ounce of flesh on his sparely built frame.

He listened attentively and responded warmly, speaking so fluently that it might readily have been assumed that English was his mother tongue. He looked what he was – a man of habits so ascetic that, if he attended a state dinner on a day he had chosen to fast (quite apart from the requirements of Ramadan), he would sit through it comfortably while taking nothing but water. Without doubt he was heeding medical advice that if, at 62, he was to avoid further heart trouble, he had to take exceptionally good care of his health. One could easily conclude that, barring the unpredictable, Sadat was going to be at the helm in Egypt indefinitely.

As he talked, he quickly confirmed this conclusion by the pyramidal strength of his motivation. He had a job to do and it was not the job of any ordinary head of state or government. In his case now, he was both. He had a mission, an assignment with destiny, his mind riveted on 'the peace process'. It would have been an obsession bordering on lunacy if it had related to some lesser objective than to bring about an enduring settlement of problems of peace and war which had festered in the region for 30 years.

Knowing he had a sympathetic listener, he invited me, momentarily and in the manner of a well-intentioned father sorely tried by wayward children, to consider how obdurate and egocentric the Prime Minister of Israel, Menachem Begin, was; what obstreperous adolescents all the other Arabs were, squabbling among themselves, Iraq now senselessly at war with Iran, and all of them peevishly thumbing their noses at him. And the acerbity of these words was not his; it is mine as I try to sharpen the focus of what he said.

Publicly, he had spoken more harshly than that but he spoke to me with words of tolerance and understanding, almost with a tinge of sadness, it seemed, from an awareness that he was trying to bridge a generational gap of 6,000 years because he embodied the wisdom of ancient Egypt while all the neighbouring countries were mere 20th-century creations. He spoke quietly, with even greater certitude and sense of responsibility than the Pope. He personified the conviction that a majority can be one man who had firmly made up his mind. "The peace process," he declared, "is irreversible."

In this, there was neither arrogance nor any illusion that it was going to be easy. It would take time and, he indicated, careful, skilful, even manipulative manoeuvring. Some delays would be inevitable. Ronald Reagan, the newly-elected President of the United States, would have to be brought up to speed. But there must not be undue delay, exacerbating the problems. It was a many-faceted operation. He had to maintain the exchange of confidence he had with his own people. He had to cultivate his special relationship with the United States, undermining but also using their special relationship with Israel. If need be, he had to publicly admonish both "that mad boy" Colonel Gadaffi, in Libya, and "that upstart king" in Saudi Arabia.

The essential ingredient in this complex and ceaseless endeavour was concentration. It was so intense I felt sure that if I didn't watch carefully and assume responsibility for sustaining the conversation (which, although entirely cordial, was, from his point of view, peripheral), I would find that the glazed, communing-with-Allah, drawing-on-the-inner-strength-acquired-in-a-prison-cell look would come back into his eyes, the face again become expressionless, as I had first encountered it, and there I would be, trying to make headway with a sphinx.

Ten minutes, on 4 November 1980, were enough to provide answers to various questions. Why was it that he kept a petulance of ambassadors waiting, one of them for more than four months, to present credentials and then suddenly, at short notice, on two successive mornings, receive 14 of them, one by one, and every one of them divested of his customary retinue? Why was it, to admit my own petulance, that, encouraged by the Egyptian protocol people, I had previously gone to Cairo, expecting to see Sadat and present credentials, only to find I couldn't because he was too busy? (Busy? But he and Mrs Sadat spent a whole morning with a gabby American woman who told my wife all about it, after they'd chummed up in the lift at the Nile Hilton, letting it be known she was Rosalyn Carter's cousin. To prove it, she gave my wife a gold-plated or, more probably, brass-plated peanut to hang on a pendant chain. She might not have done had she known that in 1977 our Prime Minister, Rob Muldoon, had referred to the President of the United States disparagingly as "a peanut farmer from Georgia".)

Why was it that, when I called on the Minister of Agriculture on 1 November, he nervously enjoined me to write and tell President Sadat that he was doing what Sadat had just that day instructed him to do and was proceeding, as hard as he could, to buy 500 breeding cows in New Zealand?

In theory, ambassadors might have presented credentials expeditiously to the Vice-President – which had been Tito's practice – but, in reality, they much preferred to wait and see him because he counted for more than the rest of the Government put together. From his point of view, neither the

Ambassador of the Central African Republic (the first of today's 14) nor of New Zealand (the 14th) would spread the good word about Egypt, in quarters critical to Sadat's lofty, single-minded ambition, as effectively as any Jew or gabby American woman. The short notice ambassadors were given? The ban on retinues? Only someone who, on the way up, had himself taken part in an assassination knew how careful you had to be.

And he knew his own people only too well. If he barked loud enough at his Minister of Agriculture to buy 500 breeding cows in New Zealand, the outcome would almost certainly be some lesser number in some much longer time, which would be none too soon to help relieve Egypt's shortage of food at rapidly rising prices. The people had to be decently fed and not just because occasion might demand – as it had when he went dramatically to Israel in 1977 – that he go over the heads of his advisers and get the people's support for his grand design. As John Gunther said of Mahatma Gandhi, Sadat was a combination of Jesus Christ, your own father and Tammany Hall.

He relished the expression that New Zealand's attitude towards the peace process was 'quasi-identical' with Egypt's. He appreciated that New Zealand's agricultural efficiency could help make good the main deficiency in Egypt. He knew, moreover, where New Zealand was. As he put it, it was the second stop past Indonesia, where he'd been.

* * * * *

When an Alitalia flight landed, it was the invariable practice of the passengers, presumably mainly Italian, to burst into loud applause, sometimes, especially if there'd been turbulence on the way, with a few 'bravos' thrown in for good measure. There was premature applause when we were going into Cairo the other night in the dark. Misled by the sound of the wheels being let down prior to landing, some passengers assumed the plane had already touched down and started clapping, and were severely scolded by those better informed.

On the return journey, when the plane came in to land at Rome, the air hostess gave the usual announcement in Italian. In the subsequent English version, it emerged as: "Ladies and Gentlemen. In a few minutes, we'll be landing at Leonardo da Vinci airport in Rome. Would you please extinguish your seats, fasten your seatbelts and return to your cigarettes."

V. SAUDI ARABIA

Rome–Jeddah

We left Rome on Sunday 9 November 1980 and five hours later arrived in Jeddah on New Year's Day, 1400. That's how it was recorded in the hotel register. And we were not without warning that something like this was about to happen. For an hour or so before the plane landed, a succession of heartless women had monopolised the toilets, which they entered as well-heeled members of the modern world, with all the latest trimmings from St Laurent and Gucci. After an intriguingly long time behind closed doors they emerged as different women from a different time – even, perhaps, a different planet – clothed shapelessly from head to toe, chadors in place and opaque, full-face, black veils at the ready. They were now prepared for their Saudi role which left only the hands of a woman showing in public, when, that is, she appeared in public at all.

For hundreds of years, Saudi Arabia was internationally significant only as the place where the holiest of Muslim shrines existed, at Mecca. Apart from that, it was a backwater beguiling a handful of intrepid explorers but playing virtually no part in international commerce or other affairs. Even in Muslim affairs its influence was slight. Their morbidly stern interpretation of Islam was far too much for most other Muslims to stomach. Tunku Abdul Rahman, a bottle-of-brandy-a-night-over-poker man and disarmingly self-confessed philanderer, was as popular as Secretary-General of the Muslim League, stationed in Jeddah in the early 1970s, as he had been as Prime Minister of Malaysia and notwithstanding that he made no secret of his conclusion that, as he said, the Saudis were "impossible". It was the least of their oddities that they clung to the Muslim calendar (dating from the Prophet Mohammad's retreat from Mecca to Medina), as well as the Thursday–Friday weekend.

We have tended to forget how recently the West (and the communist world) has been, to a large extent, secularised and how recently women have been emancipated and society has become so permissive. I was taken aback by Saudi society which goes to the other extreme and banned singing, dancing, music, liquor, cinemas and insurance; sequestered women so that they were forbidden to drive or take paid employment except in medicine or education; and where everyone in the (womanless) Ministry of Foreign Affairs dropped everything they were doing to participate in prayers broadcast at 'High Noon'. On a subsequent visit, I arrived at the appointed time to call on the Governor of the Eastern Province and his secretary said, "You will have to wait. His Highness is saying his prayers." And at moments like this, I sometimes wondered whether people in Wellington realised how different things could be beyond Tawa.

The differences really hit home when there was a New Zealander involved. In a case which made international headlines early in 1980, a young English nurse and her Dutch boyfriend, both naked, fell to their deaths from the balcony of a fifth-floor apartment in Jeddah. There had been a party and the Saudi police moved in quickly to question everyone there. This included a young New Zealand man, Jeremy Smith, and an English woman, Gwendoline Jones, whose husband, also English, was working in Jeddah as a doctor. (These are not their real names. They may well be living now in respectable obscurity which should not be disturbed.)

Later, I talked about the case in Jeddah:

"I can't understand why the New Zealand bloke, Jeremy Smith, and the English women, Gwendoline Jones, *volunteered* to the Saudi police that they'd been in bed together …"

"Oh, they weren't in bed. They did it on the floor."

"Surely they must have known that adultery was a capital offence in this country?"

"They hadn't been here all that long, some months, I think. Anyhow, they apparently didn't realise that adultery was a capital offence, or, probably, perhaps, didn't realise that this could apply to foreigners. And, mind you, all this happened about dawn and there'd been a hell of a lot of booze flowing. And they were putting forward this alibi to clear themselves of what the police suspected was a double murder … To give Smith his due, it wasn't he who volunteered the adultery. It was *her*. And she couldn't have been more explicit: 'How could we have had anything to do with the deaths? We were in there making love.' 'You mean you were in the bedroom talking together?' 'Oh, come off it, chum. We were fucking.' 'You mean you were having sexual intercourse?' 'Yes, I mean he had his penis in my vagina … Hey, chum, you're spelling 'penis' wrong.'"

"It must have been utterly incredible to the Saudi police, putting her head into the noose like that … and her husband there in the next room all along … What a horrible clash of the extremes of two different cultures."

"And in this case there's nothing in ours to be proud of."

"On the contrary."

"When they were arrested, she engaged a lawyer who pointed out that, in Saudi law, a confession of adultery was sufficient grounds for imposing the death penalty. 'Oh, my God,' she said. 'What have I done?' So, she changed her story and got word to Smith to change his to coincide with hers … They were eventually released and they all left the country."

I digress. The first sign of Saudi Arabia's significant modern role in the world appeared in 1938 when Americans discovered oil at Damman in the Eastern Province. The resulting oil wealth enabled Ibn Saud to consolidate his authority over a country in which he had been proclaimed, in 1932, the first King. In the 1970s, in particular, Saudi Arabia became a vital part of the modern, Western world, its supply of oil accounting for a fifth and more of 'free world' production. And, as a result, further of the ten-fold increase in the price of oil since 1973, the Saudis had money running out of their ears. So, with the exception of the sacred shrines in Mecca and Medina, everything from the past was being bulldozed and replaced. Broad new roads, with elevated highways, had become essential for men who had left their camels in the desert and taken to duty-free Cadillacs and Mercedes.

Saudis were the product of a pitiless desert, a land without lakes or rivers and with an average annual rainfall of four inches. They have close to a million square miles but, even with modern desalination and artesian bores, less than one percent of the country could be cultivated. Bore for water and the chances were that you found only oil. Until the oil was found, life was so nasty, brutish and short – Lawrence of Arabia observed it was "death in life" – it had to be assumed that another, happier life followed death. On earth, the least a bloke was entitled to expect was that his home comforts were always readily available, from four wives for those who could afford it, and, in his absence, were not disturbed by other blokes. Continence, celibacy, were ridiculous; but not homosexuality.

Precepts developed in a harsh desert were not easily reconciled with modern Saudi affluence. Urbanisation demanded multi-storey apartment buildings; the old precepts demanded separate lifts for men and women, as well as separate compartments on buses. Affluence brought in many foreigners whose quiet drink at the end of the working day was very much part of their lives, but the ancient Saudi precept banned liquor in all forms. Some foreigners brewed beer in the bathtub. Diplomatic missions found an exporting agency in Europe ready to falsify shipping documents. (I asked the Ambassador of a two-man mission: "How do you get on for liquor?" and he replied, "Bring it in by the container lot as conserves.") There was reliable evidence that some wealthy Saudis were up to this game too. And, from whatever sources, there was by common account among expatriates, a flourishing black market in liquor.

Much, probably most, of the work in Saudi Arabia was now being done by expatriates. The hotels were staffed by Filipinos, supervised by Lebanese, with Swiss chefs, or some such combination. On the numerous construction projects, it was impossible to discern anyone who looked like a Saudi. The Americans estimated that the foreign community (mainly on two-year contracts, unaccompanied by dependents except at the managerial or highly qualified technical level) included 300,000 Egyptians, 5–7,000 Yemenis, 120,000 Indians and Pakistanis, 600,000 Palestinians, 30,000 British, 30,000 Americans, as well as many Koreans (mainly on construction work), Thais, Eritreans and others. Only eight percent of the doctors in the country were Saudis. It was a common assertion among expatriates that they now outnumbered the Saudis but this was impossible to prove because official population statistics were secret.

In short, there were all sorts of stresses and potential sources of trouble in Saudi Arabia. But I must get back to our arrival in Jeddah. We were met on the airport tarmac by Sheik Simbol, an elderly man who has been Chief of Protocol in their Ministry of Foreign Affairs for 16 years. He wore flowing, Persil-white robes, with a white head-piece kept in place by a black circlet and, over his shoulders, a ground-length nut-brown cape embroidered in gold. He whisked us away into the most splendid VIP waiting room I have ever been in, decorated in the colours of sand.

Our passports were taken and the entry formalities quickly completed. Then Sheik Simbol floored me utterly by saying nonchalantly, "You may have to wait 30 days [to present credentials]." I was speechless, thinking of all the things to be done, the commitments already made elsewhere. Then I tried, as politely but firmly as possible, to make it clear that I very much hoped it could be sooner, much sooner.

"Well, of course," he explained, "only after you have arrived and given us the copies of your credentials – I do hope you have remembered to bring them? – can we even begin to make arrangements for you to be received by the King. He is very busy. He has Trudeau at the beginning of next week … and I've heard, although I'm not sure whether it's correct, that the King then has in mind to go camping in the desert outside Riyadh. I'll get in touch with Royal Protocol in the morning and see what I can do. Now, let me take you to your hotel. The Sheraton? That's quite nearby. Your baggage? Oh, let's not worry about details like that. You can send a boy back from the hotel to collect the baggage. Your colleague from Bahrain who was to meet you here at the airport? Oh, he probably hasn't arrived yet or perhaps he's got lost. Come on, let's go."

So, there being no scope for any further discussion on these issues, we were whisked away in Sheik Simbol's beautiful white Mercedes, upholstered in royal blue velvet.

We checked in at the hotel. Peter Rider, from the New Zealand Consulate General in Bahrain, soon turned up, having arrived in Jeddah just before us, as planned, but then had been unable to get into the VIP room.

So Peter and Geoff Randall, who had accompanied me from the embassy in Rome, became 'the boy at the hotel' who went back for the baggage. Then we started living as riotously as you ever can on apple juice.

There followed a week of polite persistence on our part, inventing all sorts of excuses to call repeatedly on the Protocol people to remind them of our continuing existence and concern to present credentials ("You've got to put the pressure on a bit," counselled the Danish Ambassador); a week in which I was incommunicado, unable to make calls on any other Saudis until I had presented credentials to the King – indeed, Sheik Simbol questioned the propriety even of calling on diplomatic colleagues until I had presented credentials to the King, which was technically correct but a formality now rarely observed. At close of play, two o'clock in the afternoon, on Monday, 17 November, he became more hopeful than ever that the King would receive me in Riyadh on Wednesday.

"We'll fly you and your colleagues up on Tuesday and you can stay there overnight, all at our expense. It looks very promising now. But it's not certain. I'll be in touch with Royal Protocol again in the morning and then let you know definitely. In the meantime, have a good rest." (These were his parting words after every encounter or telephone call, just as the hotel staff invariably said, "Have a nice day," even at ten or 11 o'clock at night when we were going to bed.)

On Tuesday around noon, Simbol rang again. "I'm sorry. It's just not possible. And next week the King is going on tour in the Eastern Province … so I suggest you go back to Rome and have a good rest."

So we packed our bags, to catch the overnight flight to Rome, scheduled to arrive there at 4.30 am. Meantime, we checked out of our rooms at the hotel in Jeddah, and had a leisurely meal there, after leaving the bags in the lobby by the entrance door.

"I suppose the bags are all right here, right by the entrance door?"

"Oh, yes, they'll be all right, Ambassador. They think twice about pinching anything in this country when a thief can end up unable to feed himself or unable to wipe himself." (A recidivist thief could be punished by having a hand cut off, an outrageously barbaric practice especially in a society where people ate with their hands, reserving one hand strictly for eating and the other hand strictly for toileting.)

* * * * *

The phone rang when we were having breakfast on 13 December, a Saturday.

"This is the Ambassador of Saudi Arabia. I've just had a ring from Jeddah to say the King can receive you, in Riyadh, on Tuesday. You'd need to be in Jeddah on Monday and there's a Saudi Airlines flight from Rome tomorrow afternoon. May I say you'll be on it? … Are you there? … Are you there? …"

"Er, yes … Well, er, there'd be a lot of things to get done if I'm to get away by tomorrow afternoon… and our embassy isn't open today, Saturday … and I haven't got a valid visa for Saudi Arabia …"

"Oh, don't worry about details like that. They'll give you a visa when you arrive in Jeddah." (Didn't he know that at the airport in Rome the Saudi Airline counter checked not just once, but twice, to ensure that you had a valid visa before letting you on a flight to Saudi Arabia?)

"And I'll have to see if I can get a seat on that flight."

"Oh, don't worry about details like that. If you have any trouble in getting a seat, just give me a ring and I'll get someone else offloaded … Can you ring me back in an hour and let me know how you're getting on, so I can tell Jeddah."

"Yes, all right."

And if he thought I was taken aback by the suddenness of all this and sounded only half awake and at a loss to understand the extremely short notice, he was absolutely right. But I knew well enough that I hadn't been sent there to stand on my dignity, least of all with the King of Saudi Arabia. I rang Pia, the bilingual secretary-stenographer at the embassy and, by a stroke of good luck, just caught her before she went out shopping. And Barbara Barriball, the New Zealand stenographer, went into the office, too. On the way in, I jotted down a list of about 30 things to be done. It wasn't simply a matter of booking Rome–Jeddah–Rome. I'd already arranged to go to Cairo the following week for trade talks, then on to New Zealand. It took the three of us about four hours, flat out, to get through the list. After the first hour and a half, the essentials were clear enough for me to ring the Saudi Ambassador and report: "I'll be on that flight tomorrow."

I set out the next day, alone; Geoff Randall, who had become fluent in Arabic, having now left the embassy without being replaced. I'd arranged by phone for George Horsborough, New Zealand Consul General in Bahrain, and Peter Rider, who spoke Arabic and had recently arrived there, to join me in Jeddah – both of them being accredited there, too – and to bring plenty of money. Those were the days when traveller's cheques were very commonly in use, but not credit cards, at least internationally.

Then I confronted the problem of the two checkpoints at the airport in Rome where they made absolutely sure you had a valid visa before letting you board a Saudi flight to the Kingdom. Fortunately, the Saudi Airlines counter was manned by an Italian who inspected my passport, found a Saudi visa, but because he couldn't read Arabic, assumed it was valid which it was not. I was blessed with the same ignorance on the part of the Italian manning the baggage and check-in counter. So instead of the half-expected hassle, I had a leisurely beer.

I was duly met in Jeddah by a tall, handsome Protocol Officer, of about 35, in a white galabeih (a full-length, flowing robe) and red and white checked headpiece. He arranged for a new visa to be put in my passport and we collected the baggage. As we were waiting for a car to take us to the hotel there was a pause in the conversation. We gazed into the black night across the tarmac and I wondered what he was thinking about. A hard camel ride he once did in the desert? Then he suddenly broke the silence by asking, "What is the capital of New Zealand – Morocco?"

We flew to Riyadh next day, together with the new Belgian, Portuguese, Burundi, Mauritian and Bahraini Ambassadors who were also to present credentials on the Tuesday.

I asked the Belgian if they had much trade with Saudi Arabia.

"About 500 million US dollars a year – exports, that is."

"That's a lot."

"Yes – it includes a lot of NES."

"NES? I'm sorry. I don't get it."

"NES. Not elsewhere specified. Arms."

The Portuguese Ambassador lived in Jeddah and I asked whether there were many of his countrymen working in the kingdom.

"Between seven and eight hundred, mainly working on construction projects. That includes four in jail; three for making and selling liquor and the fourth for murder. He was a construction worker who dropped a rock on his foreman, also Portuguese, from some scaffolding. At first, everyone assumed it was an accident. But when the Saudi police inspector came on the scene he very quickly declared: "This is not an accident. This is murder." And he assembled all the men on the construction site and said, "This is murder. I give the culprit ten minutes to own up or I arrest every one of you." And the guilty man stepped forward immediately. "I did it," he said and then asked, "What will it mean?" The inspector said, "The death sentence," and the man said, "I would like it carried out immediately." "But it couldn't be, of course," added the Ambassador. He was engaged in protracted negotiations with the Saudis, aiming to get the man extradited.

I was the first of the six to be done next day. At the palace there was a guard of honour to inspect in the courtyard, then a long period of waiting. No specific time had been set for the little ceremony ahead. Meanwhile, there was much anxious murmuring about the King's health and firm instructions, repeated several times, to keep speeches, customarily made when presenting credentials, confined strictly to one sentence and, in conversation with the King, to avoid all questions of substance, presumably to avoid any possibility of upsetting him and triggering a heart attack. "And never, *never* mention women, not even your wife."

These instructions were repeated so often and so anxiously I began to feel a bit anxious myself, wondering whether, if I strayed even just a little, inadvertently, from the straight and narrow, the King might shout, "Off with his head!" There were all sorts of functionaries milling about in the corridors of the palace which, although recently refurbished, was not especially grand, having been built before the great influx of oil wealth in the past decade. Not a woman in sight.

Eventually I was ushered in, past a squad of tightly packed and brutally tough-looking guards, in working uniform, rifles with fixed bayonets at the ready, sitting on benches around three sides of the King's antechamber. (His predecessor, another of Ibn Saud's 300 sons – they didn't seem to count daughters – had been assassinated.)[41]

In the prescribed manner, I spoke my one sentence and handed over the credentials and the letter recalling my predecessor. To illustrate the quaintly archaic language used in such documents, let me quote the letter which recalled me, when my turn came:

Sir My Brother,
My Trusty and Well-beloved Mr James Harrison Weir who has lately been accredited to Your Majesty in the character of My Ambassador Extraordinary for New Zealand being on the point of retirement from My Diplomatic Service, I cannot omit to inform you of the termination of his Mission in that capacity.

Having Myself had ample reason to be satisfied with the zeal, ability, and fidelity with which Mr Weir has executed My orders on all occasions during his Mission, I trust that Your Majesty will also have found his conduct deserving of Your approbation and esteem, and in this pleasing confidence I avail Myself of the present opportunity to renew to You the assurances of the invariable friendship and cordial esteem with which I am,
[hand-written]: Sir My Brother
       Your Majesty's
       Good Sister
       Elizabeth R

cont...

---

[41] *The Times* (London) obituary of 10 November 1953 said King Ibn Saud was "personally a man of commanding presence and of a stature exceptional in Arabia … remarkable for a gentle and equable temperament capable of sudden transition under provocation to heights of indignation truly majestic. Uxoriously inclined, he took the fullest advantage of the social code of Islam … to marry frequently and to divorce freely. He is believed to have had no fewer than 150 wives, by whom he had a large number of acknowledged children."

Buckingham Palace
30 December 1982
To
My Good Brother
King Fahd bin Abdul Aziz al Saud,
King of the Kingdom of Saudi Arabia.

Thirty years later, such documents are no longer signed by the Queen but by the Governor-General and the wording is not nearly as grandly colourful:

His Royal Highness King Abdullah Bin Abdulaziz Al-Saud
Custodian of the Two Holy Mosques
Your Royal Highness
Having need elsewhere for the services of ……, who has been residing with You as Ambassador Extraordinary and Plenipotentiary of New Zealand, I wish to notify You of his Recall.

…… has carried out his functions during his assignment. I hope that his conduct has also merited Your approval.

I take this opportunity to renew to Your Royal Highness the assurance of my continuing friendship and of my interest in and good wishes for the welfare and prosperity of the Kingdom of Saudi Arabia.

(Signature)
At Government House in Wellington
The …… day of …… two thousand and ……

I introduced George and Peter and the King introduced the three of us to his retinue. The room was then cleared of everyone except the King and me, an interpreter (who sat on the King's left, while I sat on his right) and, sitting some distance away, the Saudi Foreign Minister (a tall, good-looking, young-looking man), and – so it seemed – Colonel Kentucky-Fried-Chicken Saunders, a twinkly-eyed, grey-bearded, elderly man with the most benevolent smile. He had been with the Royal Household for many years, listed as Special Adviser to the King. He was, in fact, a medical doctor, a Syrian. I assumed he was there today in case the King suddenly dropped dead. He certainly looked as although he might. (Not until after the King died did I know that he had suffered from heart trouble for 20 years and was also crippled with arthritis.)

We talked about the weather, flora and fauna. He asked if we practised falconry in New Zealand and made various references to Australia which the interpreter, presumably a little stronger on geography, refrained from translating. Throughout this conversation, which lasted perhaps ten minutes, a servant hovered about, serving Arabic coffee in very small porcelain tumblers. The coffee was light brown, rather sweet and highly aromatic. The servant wore flowing white robes with a revolver in a holster attached to a long leather strap slung diagonally across one shoulder. As he stopped to fill and subsequently refill the tumblers from a heavily embossed coffee-pot with an elongated spout, the revolver dangled menacingly between us, like a disembodied penis prowling with intent.

* * * * *

Peter and I returned to Jeddah that evening and were up early next morning to go to Cairo for trade talks. We'd had trouble getting hotel bookings in Cairo and found ourselves rather inconveniently well away from the centre of the city at the Holiday Inn Pyramids. And there they were, in all their ancient splendour, right outside our bedroom windows. After the dreariness of Saudi Arabia – where every waiter and room-boy, all of them an expatriate, sought to engage me in conversation which invariably in ten seconds flat, became the wretched, unstoppable saga of how much he hated Saudi Arabia and was only there because the money was so good and it was 136 and a half days or whatever till his contract ended, the Saudis gave him back his passport and he could get back to his homeland.

For me it was a marvellous relief to get back to the cheerfulness of Cairo, especially to encounter two young bellboys who, as it emerged in subsequent conversation, were fourth-year university students. When the one carrying my bag unlocked the door to my room, he put his hand in and switched on the light, but nothing happened.

"Something wrong with the light?" I asked.

"Oh, no," he grinned, "we only do it that way because we've hidden a girl in here for you."

And he burst into prolonged peals of deep-throated laughter, meanwhile going into the room and turning on the light at a switch by the bed, to reveal a very pleasant room (and no girl).

VI. KISSING HANDS

So there it was. After presenting credentials in Riyadh, I'd completed the process of establishing myself to operate in five countries which formed a kind of private little Roman empire – not extending westwards as the ancient Roman Empire had but, by taking in Saudi Arabia, going much further east. Neither the Romans nor any other power had thought Saudi Arabia worth occupying. The five-in-one New Zealand arrangement was greatly envied by colleagues stationed in Jeddah, Cairo and Malta. They wished that they too could spend most of the time in Rome and just visit the countries where they were actually posted from time to time, as I did. The interests and resources of the countries they represented, were, of course, much greater than ours, although eventually New Zealand established posts in both Riyadh (1984) and Cairo (2006). In my time it was rather like five for the price of one.

There'd been an interesting little prelude to the presentation of credentials in these five countries. When we were en route to Rome from Moscow, where we'd been for three years, it was put to me, "How would you like to kiss hands with the Queen?" I had to ask what that meant. I was told it was something regularly done by British Ambassadors just before they set out for a new post. The British had only recently realised, the Queen being Queen of New Zealand, that this access should also be available to New Zealand Ambassadors setting out for a new post. We found out more, at first hand, on 6 March 1980.

"Are you nervous?" asked my wife, a little daunted by being about to meet the world's best-known face.

"No. Well, only about that bloody car," I grumbled. There'd been a last-minute change at New Zealand House and we'd been left not quite knowing which driver was coming to collect us, as arranged, or at what time. Indeed, as time passed, I began to wonder if there'd been a thorough cock-up and the driver wouldn't turn up at all.

"If it weren't raining, we could walk," I brooded. "But I suppose if we arrived on foot they wouldn't let us in … If only we had Yuri (the splendid driver in Moscow). *He'd* get it right … he would have stayed up all night polishing the car till he thought it good enough …"

The New Zealand House driver came in good time, of course. Indeed, we had time to spare and drove round the block, actually round the Palace where crocuses starred the lawn outside the walls. At the entrance gate the driver announced, "Mr and Mrs Weir for an audience … Yes, a private audience. They're from New Zealand."

The policeman on duty checked by phone and let the car pass. We drove through the forecourt, under an archway to the left, into a gravelled inner courtyard which was entirely bare and the thought flashed through my mind, "Now, if that were mine, I'd grow ferns in there … they'd do well in that shade…"

The car stopped at a doorway under a large portico where we were greeted by Colonel What's-his-name (I didn't catch his real name or perhaps he didn't give it) but he quickly proved himself a master of the art of chattering pleasantly to put people at ease. "… I was with Her Majesty in Lusaka [where there had recently been a Commonwealth Heads of Government meeting] and I came down with the most frightful bout of hepatitis. It was all my own silly fault. I decided, one evening, to have a Scotch while I was in my bath before dinner. It's always rather nice, isn't it, to have a Scotch while you're in the bath? We'd been warned, of course, not to drink the water in Lusaka so I had the Scotch with soda and it seemed the most natural thing in the world to do in that heat, to add some ice. It just never occurred to me that there could be trouble in a couple of lumps of ice – but that's where the hepatitis came from …"

In a while he went off to await the arrival of the Ambassador of Portugal who was coming to present credentials and we were taken over by Lady Thingamabob who was dressed more elegantly than anyone in *Vogue* and won my wife's heart instantly by admiring her hat. Then, in no time at all, she was on to "the Ballantraes", as she said, meaning Sir Bernard and Lady Fergusson. He had been Governor-General in New Zealand, 1962–7, and was now Lord Ballantrae. "Absolutely devastating, of course, that Laura was killed by a tree brought down in that awful storm in Scotland. But have you heard? Two most marvellous New Zealand girls turned up and knocked on Bernard's door and said, 'This is just too awful for words and we just can't bear to think of you here trying to manage on your own, so we're moving in to look after you.' So they did and won't take a penny for it. So there he is with these two marvellous girls looking after him. Now, isn't that absolutely splendid …"

Then, on our left, double doors were opened by footmen and we were motioned to go through. We stopped, as we'd been instructed, at the edge of the large rug covering most of the room. I bowed and my wife curtseyed. The double doors were closed behind us. And there we were, alone with the Queen. And having so recently emerged from three years of Russian paranoia, where I was rarely able to meet even quite junior officials on their own, it seemed astonishing to be alone with the Queen. Moreover, no one had asked us for positive identification. They only assumed we weren't armed. For all these people knew for sure, we could be imposters, nutters.

As we entered, the Queen was standing, leaning over a side table, reading something – no doubt a list of the day's engagements, with explanatory notes. She looked up and eyed us rather quizzically, I thought, as we advanced toward her. We shook hands, bowing and curtseying again. The Queen smiled a little uncertainly, it seemed, and motioned us to sit, my wife to my right, the Queen to my left where she had an electric bell on the table beside her.

She began the conversation by remarking that they were going to Rome in October. "I suppose they'll put us up in the Quirinale Palace again. We're used to living in biggish houses but the Quirinale is *enormous*. You have to walk a mile from one room to the next …" and she smiled warmly.

The conversation then turned to the Soviet Union. "Philip has been there twice and Anne once …" And we thought it thoroughly endearing that she spoke so matter-of-factly about them, not using any honorifics nor referring to Philip as "my husband". It was almost as if we were being treated as part of the family circle. Sir Bernard Fergusson, when Governor-General of New Zealand, had been pompously unbending in such matters, invariably referring to his wife as "Her Excellency".

"I sometimes wonder," said the Queen, "if half the people in the Soviet Union live underground, listening to what the other half is saying, above ground." Again she smiled warmly. "Is it like that?"

"Well, they do put an extraordinary effort into such things …" And I found myself chattering and telling her little anecdotes which I thought she might find amusing. And I suddenly realised that I was, indeed, nervous, very nervous, and I cast my eyes down to concentrate on what I was saying, rather fearing I might freeze and not be able to say anything at all. When I came towards the end of it, I raised my eyes again and found the Queen had cocked her head and was leaning forward, looking up into my face, listening intently, smiling radiantly and then breaking into a very jolly laugh.

She went on to talk about the proposed boycott of the Olympic Games to be held in Moscow later in the year. Speaking with real spirit, she said she thought "the politicians" were "meddling". "I don't know why they pick on sportsmen. I'd be very annoyed, indeed, as a mother, if any of my children were going to participate in the games and then suddenly had it all cut short by a boycott, after all those years of training so hard. Why pick on sportsmen? Businessmen are continuing to make lots of money out of doing business with the Russians …"

After 20 minutes or so (no cuppa, let alone any kissing of hands), she let us know deftly that it was time to leave. We shook hands, bowing and curtseying as before, and turned to go back to the double doors where we had come in. Incidentally, we were not required to walk backwards, as the

Knock Five Times and Ask for the President or King

British Prime Minister, Tony Blair, was shown as doing in the 2006 movie *The Queen*. Indeed, as we had our backs to her, walking across the vast expanse of rug, she called out, thoughtfully, in a completely unexpected and thoroughly engaging way, "Mrs Weir, I do hope your unpacking in Rome goes much more smoothly than your packing up in Moscow."

And there was enough enchantment in that brief encounter to last a lifetime.

Departures

I. A SILENCE IN BELGRADE

Arriving in Belgrade for the funeral of President Tito on 8 May 1980, the diminutive President of Italy, Sandro Pertini, strode up to the guard of honour waiting on the dais to receive him, and, momentarily in tears, took the colours in his hand and kissed them. He paused, head bowed, then, head back, strode on resolutely. This was the way for one old soldier President to farewell another.

Pertini was fairly new in the presidential role and the wary constitution of Italy allowed him style and influence rather than power. The other old soldier, Tito, could have said, for the better part of 40 years, "I am the State." On a conventional view he had got there by being twice a traitor. With indispensable help from the Russians, he had betrayed his King. Then, in short order, as Stalin saw it, he betrayed the Russians.

The son of a poor Croatian villager, Tito came to live it up, like an Austro-Hungarian emperor in whose domains he had been born. In government, he had been as merciless in cutting down opposition, including any old comrade who eventually questioned him, as he had been in resisting German occupation during World War II. He was finally merciless even with his wife, Jovanka, who, to all appearances, had been devoted to him for 25 years. In his last two and a half years, he had banished her from public view.

He could not admit he was old. At 60, he had divorced his wartime wife and married Jovanka, a comely woman in her twenties. I met him in a reception line, when he visited Moscow in 1977. He was then 85, dressed like a rock star, with brightly hennaed hair, a youthful tan, diamonds, opaquely dark glasses worn indoors, a natty suit – a mysterious-looking, inscrutable figure.[42]

Yet, when he died (4 May 1980), the world paid homage. In his own country, he was revered. In Belgrade, one sensed that the correspondent of *The Times* of London was absolutely right in finding, on the day Tito died, that "every Yugoslav today feels a personal, family loss".

As his body lay in state for three nights and two days, his country-men and -women filed silently and respectfully by in two queues, in numbers which must have run into millions, converging on either side of the catafalque in the entrance lobby of Parliament House. Throughout that time, the most honoured Yugoslavs – many thousands of civilians and military people, men and women – kept vigil by the catafalque, eight at a time, in three-minute shifts.

The quiet, often tearful, homage of ordinary Yugoslavs – mainly, it seemed, in the current generation, aged between 20 and 40 – was interrupted only by the homage of illustrious queue-jumpers representing 127 governments. There were four kings, 31 presidents, 24 prime ministers and 47 foreign ministers. These included the New Zealand Minister of Foreign Affairs, Brian (later Sir Brian) Talboys, who attended the funeral en route to pre-arranged meetings in Europe, accompanied by Ian Stewart, Deputy Secretary of Foreign Affairs, and the Minister's Private Secretary, Ken Richardson. As ambassador-designate, I had gone ahead to Belgrade.

There were so many representatives of international organisations and communist parties that the Yugoslav authorities and foreign correspondents lost count and could say only that they were numerous. It was the largest assembly of world leaders the world had seen. On the day of the funeral, the most eminent among them were seated at the foot of the steps leading into Parliament House. The rest of us stood behind them. Behind us and on either side were what seemed to be millions of Yugoslavs, so thickly packed in that vast concourse that few of them could see much, if anything, of the funeral service conducted on the landing at the top of the steps. Yet everyone in that enormous crowd remained so uncannily silent throughout the service that the chirping of sparrows became obscenely intrusive. And the millions, as it seemed, of Yugoslavs who assembled on either side of the three miles of the processional route, were silent, too.

There were some very moving moments: when the old warrior's medals

---

[42] In Tito's Flawed Legacy (London: Gollanz, 1985), pp. 40–1, Nora Beloff remarked: "Under his command during the Second World War, the Partisans exercised no discrimination and women were treated as equals, killing and being killed. Yet in his personal relations, he stuck by the old-fashioned view of them as mistresses or servants, preferably both."

(including the Order of Lenin conferred by a forgiving Brezhnev in 1977) were borne ceremoniously down the steps of Parliament House; when eight guards officers carried the oak coffin down the steps to the waiting gun carriage; when the grief-stricken widow appeared and came down the steps, flanked by Tito's two sons by two previous marriages; when Tito's ancient, gnarled, comrades-in-arms assembled to walk in a hot sun, behind the family, three miles to the grave; when, at the end of that long walk, on an uphill grade, the widow Jovanka, a handsome, heavily-built woman, faltered in her grief and her high-heeled shoes but her two stepsons, one on either side of her, offered no hand to help her. (The official attitude towards her was uncertain; foreign missions were requested not to address condolences to her personally.) And, most moving of all, were little children who sprang to attention and saluted as the gun-carriage went by.

The heads of foreign delegations were taken by car from Parliament House to the gravesite and other members of these delegations were taken to a promontory overlooking the final stage of the processional route. The procession was thus exclusively Yugoslav, with only one honoured exception: a fit-looking 69 year old Scot, Sir Fitzroy Maclean, marched with Tito's veterans. In 1943, at the age of 32, and with the rank of brigadier, he had been secretly dropped by parachute into German-occupied Yugoslavia, as Churchill's personal representative and commander of the British Military Mission to the Yugoslav partisans. He remained in Yugoslavia till 1945. His estate in Scotland adjoined Sir Bernard Fergusson's and, he told me, when we first met, in Moscow, "During the war, we competed for airdrop supplies – he behind Japanese lines in Burma, I in Yugoslavia."

What had Tito done to command such acclaim? His first great achievement was to forge, during World War II, the most successful resistance movement in history. Tito's partisans began in the forests and mountains with little more than old sporting guns and farm implements. They depended for further equipment on what they could capture from the enemy. Only when they had proved themselves did they get Allied supplies. Keeping on the run, as hard on themselves as they were ruthless with the enemy, they held down 20 German divisions for the best part of four years – a fact which, from 1948, the Russians must have considered repeatedly. The essence of Tito was defiance. As a young man, he had used six years in jail (for communist activity) to further his education.

His second great achievement was to forge a united, purposeful nation out of a heterogeneous collection of people with a turbulent history, traditionally divided by ethnic origin, religion, language (pulled apart by different alphabets) custom, disparity of regional development and factionalism. "Two Yugoslavs, three factions," Stalin had sneered. Tito held

Departures

this polyglot country together and gave it a far higher standard of living than that of his original mentors, the Russians, and a far better quality of life.

Tito's third and probably his greatest achievement was to defy Stalin and get away with it. Until then (1948):

> Soviet power had been securely based on the absolute authority and absolute infallibility of the Kremlin. Tito challenged both and survived. The fact of his survival pointed a moral and exerted an influence which were to extend far beyond the frontiers of his own small country and the span of his own lifetime. It showed what a small country, well led, courageous and independent-minded, could do. The events of 1948 and the whole sequence of results that have flowed from them mark a turning point in history.

So wrote Sir Fitzroy Maclean in the *Daily Telegraph* (London) on 5 May 1980.

I still treasure the memory of my first evening, alone, in Yugoslavia. On entering the hotel dining room, I was a little startled to see waiters wearing maroon jackets – exactly the same as the jackets worn by waiters all over the Soviet Union. But it was about the only vestige of Soviet communism to be found, either on that occasion or in travelling, in the following three years, in every constituent state of Yugoslavia. During that first evening in Belgrade, I was bombarded with what were, by Soviet standards of that time (and such standards could only be better in post-Soviet Russia), one surprise after another: on entering the dining room, I was immediately noticed and shown to a table; it was clean and set; a waiter came to attend to my needs immediately; he smiled; he quickly dispelled my assumption that the menu would be a hoax and the only thing readily available would be the dish of the day; I asked for a beer and he brought it promptly, ahead of the meal *and* the beer was cold; I chose lamb (unobtainable in the Soviet Union) and it was a New Zealand-sized serving of meat and excellent (Yugoslavs being a nation of six-foot protein-eaters[43]); and I signed for the meal (which was then beyond the accounting capacity of any Soviet hotel). Outside the hotel, there were even more startling surprises: the shops had lots of things to buy. Yes, it was a little wonder that Yugoslavs queued all night to bless Tito.

---

[43] The tallest of them all, it seemed, were the Montenegrins. A few years ago in Wellington, I asked a taxi driver where he was from and when he said "Montenegro", I remarked flippantly that he wasn't tall enough. But when we got home and he got out of the car, it was easy to see he was well over six feet so I could happily declare, "Oh, yes, you're from Montenegro all right."

Tito's fourth great achievement was to help found, at a meeting in Belgrade in 1961, the non-alignment movement which, at times, irritated both super powers but, over the years, became more genuinely independent and more favourable to the interests of the West. In his 87th year, Tito, now long the doyen of the non-aligned, was obliged to strive, still with vigorous tenacity, to keep the movement out of Russian clutches by Cuban proxy.

It was, in all, a dazzling performance. He balanced Yugoslavia's fervent wish for peace against the cold reality that, from 1948 onwards, the Soviet Union could seek to crush his infectious heresy, as they later came to crush heresy in Czechoslovakia and Hungary. If Soviet forces had intervened in Yugoslavia, moreover, no one would have gone to Yugoslavia's aid. Yugoslavia's own regular forces, although tough and well trained, would have been numerous and equipped enough only to form a kind of tripwire. And it might have been reasonable to assume that, the longer Yugoslavs enjoyed the good life which Tito gave them, and the better that life became, the less inclined would they have been to abandon it and take to the hills and forests again as partisans.

In domestic affairs, Tito sought to balance the requirements of the individual and the state, of defence expenditure and consumerism, of central and local authority. He sought the middle ground between state control and private enterprise, authority and liberty, conformity and diversity. He insisted on pragmatism, not doctrine. "Will it work?" was his test. Although he lived it up, he sought neither preferment for his family nor any grand monument for himself. The marble slab on his grave says only

Josip Broz Tito
1892–1980

* * * * *

In the years which followed, especially when world economic conditions deteriorated, with successive sharp rises in the price of oil, and when the Soviet Union crumbled, removing pressure on Yugoslavs to stick together, Yugoslavia too, collapsed. By the end of the 20th century, upwards of a million Yugoslavs had died fighting each other in five wars, and Yugoslavia had broken up into six (by 2008, seven) separate states.

* * * * *

Departures

Wherever you go, there's a New Zealand connection. A nephew of Tito's, Franjo Broz, born in 1918, was vice-consul and second-in-command at the Yugoslav Consulate-General in Wellington for four and a half years from 13 February 1954. He looked very much like Tito. Indeed, there was a stronger resemblance to Tito than in Tito's two sons, judging by what I saw of them at Tito's funeral in 1980.

Also working at the Yugoslav office in Wellington at the same time was a highly personable young man of Yugoslav descent, but New Zealand born and raised. This was Jim Belich who became Mayor of Wellington (1986–93). He was knighted in 1990. He was fond of recalling that when the Yugoslav Consul-General, a Mr Popovich, left New Zealand at the end of his posting in January 1955, Franjo Broz remarked to Jim Belich and me, "Well, if Yugoslavia declares war on New Zealand now, I'll have to do it!" As Jim Belich tells it, I was not amused, although he was probably more put out by his colleague's faux pas than I was. (Fresh in our minds at that time was the ominous convergence of Yugoslav and New Zealand forces on the disputed territories of Trieste in 1945. The status of Trieste was finally settled only in 1975 when the city became permanently Italian, the countryside around it, Yugoslav.)

II. THE LIGHTER SIDE OF DARKNESS IN CAIRO

It has long been an axiom of diplomatic practice that many a useful friendship was first forged in a convulsive handshake at a funeral. And the opportunities have been greatly extended by capacious jet aircraft converging quickly from the furthermost parts. And, nowadays, on the death of a head of state or government (and Sadat was both), his peers converge by large jet aircraft which are at their personal disposal. So the planes are filled up with bodyguards, wreaths and subordinate handshakers. The number, size and exotic beauty of wreaths, brought from afar, along with the number and seniority of delegations bringing them to a funeral, have become a new test of relations between states. Conversely, *not* to attend a funeral (and almost all the other Arabs chose not to go to Cairo when President Sadat was assassinated) is an acerbic new mark of displeasure with the deceased and his state.

The funeral of a head of state or government, moreover, has come to be judged not simply by the ceremonial or the assembly of mourners but even more, perhaps, by the amount of business it is possible to transact on the side. The handshakers converge to sympathise with the bereaved but also to shake the hand, convulsively, of the successor and confer with him. They also confer bilaterally with each other, too, applying to funerals the same serious and insensitive concern for maximum utilisation which has become the preoccupation of a commercial airline. At Tito's funeral, Mrs Gandhi won the bilaterals, numerically. At Sadat's funeral (10 October 1981), tight security obscured the bilaterals but, pretty clearly, Italy (run a close second by China) won the wreath section, with a matching autumnal pair, each measuring, perhaps, 50 feet in circumference. "We did it first for Tito," said Prince Charming, the Italian Chief of Protocol, "and decided we couldn't do any less for Sadat."

An obligatory new chapter has been added to the contingency planning of every well-organised capital: how to cope with several hundred (or, depending on the importance and popularity of the deceased and his state, several thousand) official visitors who arrive suddenly to attend the funeral of a head of state or government. No matter how much lead time the deceased may have given, the contingency planning can only be taken so far till he (or she) actually dies. A great deal then still remains to be hurriedly done. Accommodation must be commandeered (tourists and businessmen brushed ruthlessly aside) and allocated according to precedence which can only be determined when the bereaved state knows who is to attend, and whether they are idiosyncratic. Prime Minister Begin, for instance, was so much of a fundamentalist, in his fashion, that, on the Jewish Sabbath, which

Departures

the day of Sadat's funeral happened to be, he would go nowhere except on foot. So he had to be accommodated within easy walking distance of the grave.

No one would ever have supposed that Egyptians were up to contingency planning of this order. Every Egyptian would laugh, with the utmost good humour, at any suggestion that Cairo is well-organised. ("In this country," remarked an Egyptian friend, on a subsequent occasion, "you can rely absolutely on one thing. Inefficiency. That's how Sadat was shot. And consider," he added, to my dismay, at a dinner he had taken us to, in the countryside some miles from Cairo, "at that roadblock on the way here, how the police checked the boot of my car for arms. Of course, they didn't find anything. And I could rely on them, absolutely, not to look in the glovebox where I keep my revolver. If they'd found it, we'd have been in trouble.") Sadat's death, moreover, was the work of lunatics, to whom, alone, it was predictable. It was widely expected also that fellow lunatics would use such a well-publicised occasion as the funeral to strike again.

My own concerns on arriving in Cairo late in the evening of 8 October were petulantly self-centred and mundane: of waiting an hour, as usual, for the baggage to emerge; of spending another hour (as I had when arriving in Belgrade, in advance of the main New Zealand contingent for Tito's funeral) lugging this baggage around the airport, looking for someone – anyone – who knew something relevant and, in particular, where the New Zealand team was to stay; of spending another hour getting into the city … In fact, within half an hour of arriving in Cairo on this occasion, I not only had my baggage but was ensconced in a hotel room. I also had a retinue of five Egyptians, headed by a 'chamberlain'. (We would call him a liaison officer, but, for two days, I quite shamelessly enjoyed the notion of having a chamberlain.) The speed and efficiency of these arrangements prompted the reflection that, perhaps, after all, it was the Egyptians who had invented contingency planning, it having been a major preoccupation of the pharaohs to supervise the construction of their own extraordinary tombs.

Subsequent reflection was earthier: it was the lunatics who were setting the pace or, rather, the fear that they would strike again. Apart from the idiosyncratic Begin and those staying at the homes of their ambassadors, all official visitors were accommodated at the Sheraton Heliopolis, five minutes from the airport, well away from the city and now heavily guarded. And we were all, in effect, put under house arrest. My grey galabeihed (i.e. plain clothes) bodyguard shadowed me everywhere for two days, except into my room and except outside the hotel building into the hotel grounds, where a burly police officer (the third in the retinue of five) took over. I wished to order a wreath and, there being no florist's shop in the hotel, I suggested to the chamberlain that I go out somewhere and organise it. He hesitated, went away and eventually came back with a little man who took E£50 (about US$45) from me in exchange for a receipt. (It's a bargain, I thought. We paid US$350 in Belgrade. Subsequently, however, I could reflect that we had *seen* the wreath in Belgrade.[44])

I needed a haircut and, there being no barber's shop in the hotel, I suggested to the chamberlain that I go out somewhere. He hesitated, went away and eventually came back to say a barber would come to the hotel. But he never materialised. (Incidentally, an unexpected departure from Balmoral posed a similar problem for Prince Charles. In his case, as he told me, the problem was solved by a young wife getting to work with her nail scissors.) And I had a parcel – in truth, fabric to re-upholster an old Regency sofa (you see what I mean about maximum utilisation?) – which my wife was sending to an Egyptian friend, the wife of a former Egyptian Ambassador. I told the chamberlain about this and asked whether I could deliver the parcel or could she collect it from me at the hotel? He hesitated, went away and eventually came back: *he* would deliver the parcel *after* the funeral. So I rang the woman to let her know what was happening. She, normally the blithest of spirits, ended the conversation by saying, "We shall pray for your safety tomorrow." I went out into the hotel grounds to have a swim but found the pool closed, so I went for a stroll in the hotel grounds – but a policemen hurried me back indoors.

Next morning, the driver and outrider who had brought me from the airport (and who completed the retinue of five) re-appeared. The official visitors were marshalled, delegation by delegation, and despatched, not in a slow procession, as might have seemed appropriate for a funeral, but in one or two cars at a time, at high speed, through streets cleared of all other traffic and uncannily deserted, in a city normally bustling with – as Cairenes put it – ten million people by night and eleven million by day. There was one exceptional corner, where we turned off the highway, at the closest point we came to the inner city. A crowd of perhaps 2,000 ordinary Egyptians, exclusively, I think, men – had assembled and, just as we passed, they broke the crowd-control barriers, surged forward, gesticulating and wailing, primevally demanding, so it seemed, some part in honouring their dead leader. But shots were fired, presumably over their heads, to keep them under control. Security determined that Sadat, a man of the people, was to be buried by foreigners (from 80 countries) and the Egyptian Establishment.

---

[44] When I remarked on this later to the British Ambassador, he said, "You're in good company. Our people from London brought a wreath from the Government but we realised there should also be one from the Queen. So we ordered it locally – but never saw it."

Departures

They assembled in the outskirts of the city, at the end of the military parade track where Sadat had been shot. The coffin arrived by helicopter – a final, bitter aloofness.

The new President, Hosni Mubarak, led the procession of several thousand, walking 20 to 30 abreast, down the dusty track, heavily guarded on either side, for the better part of a mile, everyone chatting, hailing old friends, changing places in the procession to walk with them and, subsequently, other old friends – all rather like a cocktail party on the march, without refreshments and with sweat trickling down the spine in the midday heat. And I found myself with a hang-up problem: the chamberlain and the police officer, walking on either side, concluded that the best way to look after me was to hold a hand each. This was against my determination that, although it may be a local custom for men to walk hand in hand, this just would not do. The freeing of hands at least enabled the police officer to carry on fingering his worry beads feverishly, as he had done from the moment he had met me on the tarmac, and when to his apparent surprise, everything remained in order, he could now also, every few minutes, scratch his genitals.

Mind you, there were a few startling moments about halfway through the march, when it seemed that this twitchiness had been justified. Ahead of us, for several yards, and all around us, everyone suddenly ducked – as I did, too – and all but threw themselves in the dust. A row of Egyptian soldiers had suddenly taken up a position, across the path of the procession, and pointed their bayoneted rifles at us. And you could sense everyone thinking, "Christ, there're more of the bloody lunatics!" It turned out, however, that these soldiers were simply checking that everyone in the procession was entitled to be there, as indicated by identity badges issued for the occasion.

Finally the procession converged on the reviewing stand where Sadat had been shot and opposite which he was to be buried in a newly constructed tomb. And what happened then was a shambles. At the top of the reviewing stand was a small room where President Mubarak, Mrs Sadat, her children, and others, had lined up to shake hands. The trouble was that every member of the Egyptian Establishment, along with most of the handshakers from abroad, conceived it his duty and right to be first into that room. The crowd surged forward in a most unseemly mêlée, pushing, shoving and shouting abuse at each other and at the police who tried to restrain them and who eventually succeeded in doing so only by shutting the doors and allowing people in one by one.

The pushing and shoving to be first in the queue nevertheless continued. The chamberlain pulled me out of this scrummage while the police officer simultaneously took the other hand and pulled me into it. His strength being greater than mine and the chamberlain's combined, the police officer won. More than that, he now turned his back on the congestion, forcing a way through with brute strength, convinced that anyone wearing a purple badge, denoting that he was the leader of a delegation – in my case, a delegation of one – had a right and responsibility to get into that reception room ahead of anyone with some lesser kind of badge, even if they had once been President of the United States (and there were no less than three former Presidents of the United States, as well as the current Secretary of State, in that ruck.[45])

Eventually, I insisted, again, that this just would not do; I had no wish to be in such a competition. In only a few minutes, anyhow, I moved into the small room and went down the reception line, shaking hands, then out the door on the far side, from whence Muslims went to the graveside for the burial service and others found their cars pointedly waiting, with outriders revving up.

The culmination of tragedy, it was an extraordinary piece of organisation: tightly, effectively and, in the circumstances, appropriately arranged to prevent further tragedy which, apart from anything else, would have hurt Egypt even more.

When we went back to the hotel, the chamberlain wandered off somewhere and, while he was away, I set up a beer for each of us. When he returned and saw what I'd done, his jaw dropped. I assumed that, in declining a beer the previous day and now being put out when given one, he was, in fact, a strict Muslim teetotaller. I apologised and offered to change the drink. "Well," he grinned, "after a posting of four years in New York, I prefer a Bloody Mary."

Over lunch, he could then confide, to a delegation of one, pointing contemptuously at the delegation from Zaire, "Look at them! Forty of them! Drinking and stuffing themselves silly! They only do it because it's free!" Because, with that generosity of spirit which Sadat had declared was the essence of Islam (and which he extended to the deposed Shah of Persia [now Iran] by granting asylum to him and his family when all his other old friends didn't want to know him any more), the new President of Egypt made all official visitors attending Sadat's funeral, guests of the Egyptian Government.

---

[45] The United States delegation was led by the Secretary of State, Alexander Haig, and included three former presidents: Richard Nixon, Gerald Ford and Jimmy Carter.

III. AN UNMARKED SAUDI GRAVE

When President Tito of Yugoslavia and President Sadat of Egypt died, a great assembly of world leaders converged to pay homage and sympathise with the bereaved. But when King Khalid of Saudi Arabia died on 13 June 1982, there simply wasn't time for world leaders to assemble. Within hours of his death, the King was buried, without a coffin, in an unmarked grave – a pauper's grave – in a public cemetery. Besides, the funeral of a King was not to be regarded as a state occasion. All this was in accordance with the austere code of Islam – Wahhabism – practised by the House of Saud. The funeral prayer lasted just two minutes. Government offices stayed open and flags remained at full mast. Mourning was forbidden because death was to be regarded as the will of God. To mourn was to suggest displeasure or discontent with God's wishes. And, in death, all men were equal.

Italian Days

EXCERPTS FROM A DIARY

9 July 1980

There are all sorts of good reasons for not keeping a diary. There isn't time. It's a severe discipline. The truth, although freshly recorded, remains elusive. Keeping a diary, moreover, invites ego-tripping. Worse, it's a trap for plaintiveness when things go wrong. And God knows they've been going wrong with us.

Between Moscow and Rome our personal effects were badly pilfered. It's an occupational hazard. Then, when we arrived in Rome, we found we'd inherited live-in domestic staff who seemed to be playing roles in an incredibly bad farce. Maria, usually known as Momma, had the role of cook. A toothless septuagenarian, completely illiterate, completely unsmiling, completely determined to have her own way. The leading role in this built-in farce was taken by her daughter, Mimma, a martinet and, not surprisingly, unmarried. Between the two of them, in the course of eight years, Momma and Mimma had seen two previous New Zealand ambassadors come and go until, by now, it seemed, they had perfected the art of ruling the household with a rod of iron, to suit their own convenience and advantage or, in some respects, merely to satisfy some strange eccentricity.

Pleading lameness, Momma never left the house. Mimma went out only to the market, a chore she insisted was hers alone. M might say we'd like steak for dinner and Mimma would buy the best, most expensive cut. But then it was handed to Momma who decided how it was to be cooked. Obviously, it had to be minced because of her toothless gums. Never mind

Italian Days

that ours were in better condition. She couldn't be expected to cook different meals for such a small household. Momma and Mimma had absolutely no social life; never went to church or the movies or visited friends or relatives. They had no visitors coming to the house. They lived with and for each other, padding the marketing bills to feather a retirement nest. We pleaded with them to take time off. We certainly didn't expect them to be on duty seven days a week. We pleaded for time to ourselves, especially at the weekend. But it all fell on deaf ears.

Well, it took quite a while to sort all that out, and to do it smoothly, with compassion for them, lost souls as they were, as well as consideration for ourselves. Because God knows what they might have got up to if we hadn't arranged an amicable departure. This was finally organised by latching on to the incontestable point that, under Italian law, Momma was obliged to retire because of her age. To this we added, to ourselves, the fervent hope that, if Momma went, Mimma would opt to go too. Which is how it worked out.

It was a great weight off our minds. Momma and Mimma hadn't actually gone yet. They had to give notice to the tenants of their apartment. Meantime, summer had come and we swam every day and felt friskier for it. And the urge to keep a diary returned.

* * * * *

But that strays from today which included a lunch at a restaurant straggling into a piazza, as many of them do, in the middle of the old part of the city. Then, after five, M came to the office, after a further valiant three hours at Italian. She changed in the office, there being no time to go home before we went to the private showing of a film, at the invitation of a cocker spaniel-friendly American named Steve Barclay[46] whom I'd met at a reception some weeks ago. He said he'd come to Rome 30 years previously, working first as an actor, "in the big-time costume movies of that period", as he put it, and then in production. He's a large, well-built man, handsome, photogenic and very active although probably well into his sixties. He said he'd been out of films for 15 years and, these days, was "a contact man". Somehow, he had access to a posh theatrette, with a well-stocked bar, in a basement in downtown Rome. He'd contacted mainly newly-arrived ambassadors and their wives to see an English-language movie this evening. It turned out to be *1941*, which was dreadful.

Steve left us wondering what his contacts are for and how much to

---

[46] *The New York Times* reported on 4 February 1994 that Steve Barclay had died of cancer in Rome, aged 75. The report confirmed the outline of his career as he had told it, including his association with Sophia Loren.

believe. But there could be no doubt that he had some good lines, such as, "I gave Sophia Loren her name." He said that, when she first appeared in a movie, it was to play opposite him and his standing was such that she had to change her unpronounceable Italian surname to ensure the film was a box-office success. To replace her real surname, he chose 'Loren', for its simplicity. It was the name of a mate of his. And he said he'd decided to get out of movies "while the going was good, while I was still rich and famous" – although we had never heard of him. And he said, too, "My wife was Miss France". He didn't say which year but his claim was entirely believable – and that it had been a vintage year.

After the dreadful movie, we went to another of Steve's contacts for dinner. I think his name was Pellegrini – an Italian lawyer. We didn't meet him till we'd been there an hour or more. He had a plump, pleasant wife and we didn't meet her until we were leaving, three hours after we'd arrived. There was also a winsome daughter, divorced after a year of marriage.

The Pellegrinis lived in a luxurious ground-floor apartment opening on to a large terrace covered with bright yellow awnings. The terrace opened onto a much larger lawn which was kept immaculately and enclosed by a high wall which muffled the sounds of traffic. In this outdoor area there were round tables and chairs under large umbrellas in yellow to match the awnings. We arrived about 9.30, along with others who'd been at the movie and there were several people already there. Still more people drifted in for the next hour or so until there were at least a hundred. And finally we were invited to help ourselves to a buffet dinner, which was absolutely delectable. Meanwhile everyone had been gently sipping wine which, the Pellegrini daughter informed us, came from their country estate.

But the really remarkable thing about this evening was the attire of Italian women. You know those way-out dresses which most women pass over quickly, thinking 'Not for me', when looking at *Vogue*, or stop only to glance at in the windows of the most exclusive, most expensive boutiques, wondering who on earth could afford to buy them and on what occasion they might be suitable to wear? Well, there they all were, this balmy summer evening, drifting into dinner with the Pellegrinis at 10.30 pm. There were hemlines plunging up and necklines plunging down, with row upon row of flounces and a floor-length feather boa to match; a fried-blonde countess sheathed – but only just – in shocking pink and … M touched my arm and said, "It's time to go home."

10 July 1980
Last night we met an Italian woman in yellow to match the Pellegrinis' awnings and umbrellas. She divided her time, she said, between New York

and Rome. She had a villa in Parioli, a fashionable inner suburb of Rome but was thinking of selling it and putting the money into the expansion of her farming activity. "The EEC is giving such marvellous subsidies these days, you know. It's money for jam." She rang at nine this morning, inviting us to dinner next Thursday; "just a few of us and sit-down". Well, that was unexpectedly kind of her but we'll be in Padua next Thursday, which I couldn't help thinking was rather a blessing. I could scarcely look forward to a whole evening with a woman who gushes so much in praise of agricultural subsidies which are squeezing New Zealand out of the European market.

Called on the Saudi Arabian Ambassador whose chancery is in a palace built by the Duke of Alberoni. It is an architectural gem, now owned by the Saudis, the oil-rich dukes of the modern world. (They own a separate building as the Ambassador's residence.) As palaces go, it's not all that large, but large enough to provide the ambassador with a room, which may have been the ducal ballroom, with a floor area bigger than our entire office and a ceiling more than twice as high as ours. The room, moreover, is adorned with two magnificent chandeliers. The circular hallway upstairs, from which other rooms radiate, has a marble floor with a large central mosaic medallion made mainly of lapis lazuli.

Wellington has in mind that Brian Talboys, Minister of Foreign Affairs and Overseas Trade, visit Saudi Arabia in October. I'd questioned the proposed timing as likely to coincide with the Muslim equivalent of Christmas, the birth of Mohammed. The precise timing of this is variable, which scarcely helps forward planning – and, in any event, falling within the period of the Hajj when the Saudis, whom BT would most wish to see, would be preoccupied with leaders of fellow Muslim states, going about their worldly as well as spiritual affairs. Wellington nevertheless asked me, in effect, to press on with Christian resolve. So I did today. The Saudi Ambassador was at first inclined to dismiss the proposed timing as altogether too difficult for his government. He didn't even want to ask them. But he finally agreed to do so. (The Saudi counsellor rang a week later to say curtly that the timing was "unsuitable".)

We then went on to talk about other things and, on instructions, I told him of New Zealand television's decision not to show *Death of a Princess*, a highly controversial television drama-documentary which showed Saudi Arabia in a bad light – in some respects, it appears, unfairly so – and which the Saudi Government found highly offensive. I suppose I expected the New Zealand decision would produce some favourable reaction from the Ambassador. Not at all. Not even the faintest glimmer of a smile. For a few moments, he looked down blankly, his hands on his knees, then abruptly got to his feet and, without saying a word, turned his back on me and paced about the large room, head down, for what seemed like an eternity, although it was probably just a minute or so. Then, as abruptly as he had left me, he came back and sat beside me again and immediately began talking about something else, making it abundantly clear that he simply didn't wish to talk about *Death of a Princess*. What was I to make of all this? I could only speculate. How do you interpret silence?

(It is probably worth giving more of the background and going on to speculate a little. *Death of a Princess*, regarded as one of the most controversial films of all time, was a docudrama, a dramatized television film based on real events. It centred on Princess Masha'il of Saudi Arabia and her lover, who were publicly beheaded for committing adultery. The film did not name Princess Masha'il or identify the country the film's princess belonged to. It was produced by ATV, a British television channel, in cooperation with an American one, and funded by television channels in Australia, Britain, Canada, Japan, the Netherlands, New Zealand and the United States.

(The film was first shown on television on 9 April 1980 in Britain. It provoked a swift and very angry Saudi response The Saudi Embassy in London called it "an unprincipled attack on the religion of Islam and its 600 million people, and on the way of life in Saudi Arabia, which is the heart of the world of Islam". On 23 April, the British Ambassador in Saudi Arabia was expelled. Then Saudi Arabia cut off the supply of oil on which Britain was largely dependent and stopped the purchase of arms, which were a major British export.

(Strangely, the Saudis weren't at all miffed with the immediate public conclusion that the film's fictional princess could only be their Princess Masha'il. What really troubled the Saudis, it seemed, was that the film mocked the Saudi way of life and was based on gossip as well as fact. In one scene, Saudi princesses were shown being driven down a desert road looking for lovers. In another scene, an Arab socialite was asked what rights were accorded to Saudi women and she answered bluntly, "Sex".

(Confronted by the vehement Saudi reaction, the British Foreign Secretary, Dr Owen, apologized publicly. Foreign ministers elsewhere followed suit. Gradually, things were patched up though it took a (rather courageous) visit by the Queen to restore British–Saudi relations fully. The film was never shown publicly in New Zealand, though it was shown at the time in all the other countries which had provided funding. This suggests that, in my encounter with him on 10 July 1980, the (Westernised) Saudi Ambassador's odd behaviour was prompted by the thought that the New Zealand television people were rather contemptibly two-faced, having funded the film but not shown it like all the others.)

15 July
No local newspapers today. Journalists and other newspaper workers are on strike. Italians seem to get their strikes over and done with quickly. In strikes, as in other things, they have an extraordinary capacity for suddenly flaring up and then, just as suddenly, calming down. My Italian wasn't nearly good enough for me to follow the issues closely but I could be confident the newspapers would be back again next day – and they were.

There's a wonderful abundance of flowers in Rome – for sale (and not expensively) in numerous little shops or at wayside stalls, as well as growing in parks, private gardens and, as avenues of flowering trees, in the middle of the city. The city authorities put out large pots of flowering azaleas to adorn the Spanish Steps and other prominent places. Wisteria trails over fences and terraces and, with latticework support, grows up the exterior of buildings for several storeys, some of the plants having trunks as thick as that of a tree, indicating they've been there a very long time. Then, when it comes their time to bloom, roses ramble over fences and archways.

Best of all, perhaps, are the oleanders, now in bloom all over the city and, in the old part, in clumps so huge they must have been there for hundreds of years. (The species originated in the Mediterranean area.) Remarkably, they grow not only as shrubs but also, in the mid-city area, as trees, planted in avenues, and the flowers come in white, cream, pale yellow, salmon and every possible variation of red, from the palest pink, through cerise, to the darkest blood-red. And planted among them, in some avenues, and blending perfectly with them, are mauve hibiscus, also grown as trees.

In arranging flowers in bouquets as gifts, Italians use strong colours – purple, orange, blue, yellow, even black – boldly, mixing them together as they do in designing fabric for women's clothes. But for the exterior of buildings, an entirely different approach has applied for well over a thousand years and remains in force: make the façade any colour you like so long as it's mellow.

A funeral cortège commands attention for the flowers. Through glass-sided hearses, higher than those used in New Zealand, the wreaths are usually so large they have to be put on the roof of the hearse or the roof of a following car. Skipping ahead a few days: in Padua, we saw a bridal car completely covered in white flowers, the radiant bride and groom both dressed in white.

17 July 1980
We set out around 9.30 am for Padua. The highway (autostrada), a double lane each way, skirting Florence and Bologna, goes all the way (490 km) from Rome. It's a remarkable feat of engineering, with many viaducts and

tunnels, the long tunnels often curved and inclined, and there is always a separate tunnel for each flow of traffic, the surface of the road always excellent. This highway and others like it have all been built in the past 25 years – a unifying factor in a country with marked regional differences and which, in the modern era, achieved political unity only 1861. The highway is also remarkable for creating such little disturbance to the landscape. In places where it has been necessary to cut into hillsides to make way for the road, trees and shrubs have been planted, including the golden yellow Spanish broom (which has been in flower for several months) and oleanders. For about a hundred kilometres north of Rome, the median strip has been planted with a kaleidoscopic array of oleanders.

There are many forested areas, the commonest tree being the Italian pine which grows in an umbrella shape. Also common are plantings of dark green yews, often on either side of a driveway leading to a villa or leading to and then surrounding a cemetery. Hay is being cut. There are vineyards everywhere. Fields of sunflowers stare at the sun. Medieval towns perch on hilltops, guarded by walls to keep out marauders and sited to get away from the stifling heat of mid-summer and the malarial mosquitoes which used to breed in the valleys and marshes.

Such is the immensity and sameness of the Russian landscape and the frequently poor conditions of the roads – which make the going slow and cautious – the traveller has a sense of arriving in the evening where he began in the morning. In Italy, by contrast, you have a sense of arriving before you should, such is the relative smallness of the country, the great variety of the landscape – the cultivation intense, in microscopic, extraordinarily well-tended plots, by the standard of Soviet collective farms – and the excellent condition of the roads. Nazzerano, the embassy driver, drove at 145 km an hour most of the way. Nor is there any need, as there is in Russia, to worry about where the next petrol station will be or, even more to the point, whether it will have petrol. And you don't even think, as you must in Russia, of taking a picnic lunch to eat by the side of the road. There are service areas scattered at frequent intervals along the highway. In two respects, however, the Italian and Russian landscapes are remarkably similar, in the abundance of wild flowers and the dearth of animals.

As we drove into Padua, we saw a high double gate made of timber, recently painted green. Scrawled across it, in white paint, were the words (in Italian), "Don't spoil the green places." There's graffiti on almost every writeable wall in Rome. Not even the walls of the Vatican are spared. How's this for good wishes to a chum on his 18th birthday, on a wall by a secondary school and in Italian: "Long live Angelo and may he inseminate many". Then there's the mysterious "We are magic", the explicit "Fuck Nato", and across the street from our office, "Country bastards". The only real answer to graffiti is to grow ivy or other creepers over the walls – a common practice, especially in suburbia.

Friday 18 July
Bridling mutinously at Nazzerano's advice that I needed to take six bottles of whisky to reward the succession of police outriders who, he said, would escort us in Padua, I put in only two, albeit in large bottles which is all I had in stock. When I emerged this morning and looked about for the motorcycle outriders, I noted smugly that there weren't any. But Nazzerano pointed out that Butch Cassidy and the Sundance Kid – as I thought of them – two lively-looking, moustachioed young men casually dressed in jeans and sports shirts open to expose a chest forest of hair, waiting nonchalantly beside a pea-green Fiat with ordinary number plates, were 'plain clothes' police, Italian style. I shook hands and found them instantly likeable.

Padua, I'd been told, but had refrained from telling M, is a centre of terrorism. Someone blurted it out, obliging me to say, well, it was where they masterminded, rather than did it. Anyhow, I set out, with Butch and the Kid leading the way in their pea-green car and called on the prefect (the regional representative of the central government) and the mayor, both of them very pleasant, keen to chat and, to judge by the number of police guarding their premises, neither of them taking any chance that Padua could be relied on for the theory rather than the practice of terrorism.

Apart from being an industrial and servicing centre, Padua is a university city, with the second-oldest (AD 1222) university in Italy. In population, Padua is about the size of Wellington (250,000) but the university has 60,000 students. A tremendous influx occurred in the post-war period when university education was made cheap and the entrance exam abolished. Now there's a heavy failure rate at the end of the first year and heavy graduate unemployment. Included among the 60,000 are 11,000 doing psychology. In such various ways, Italy emerged from authoritarianism at the end of the war and went overboard to protect minority interests. Such were among the worries of the prefect and mayor, although their central concern was terrorism.

As I was about to leave, I remarked that Padua was perhaps best known in the English-speaking world as the setting of Shakespeare's *The Taming of the Shrew*, which had recently been made into a highly successful musical called *Kiss Me Kate*. The mayor (a professor of mathematics) looked at me blankly and, in rapid-fire Italian, conferred with his colleagues, a man in charge of the city's cultural affairs and an utterly charming contessa who appeared to be the city's public relations officer. Then the mayor said, "You are telling us something we do not know." In short, my observation, intended to be light-hearted, fell appallingly flat.

Later in the day, M and I met the contessa just off Dante Street, where she lives, and she took us on a walking tour of the city, firstly to see a 12–13th century 'communal palace' which has market stalls at ground level and, above it, a breaktakingly huge and remarkably well-preserved, frescoed hall, 260 feet long and with a commensurately high ceiling unsupported by interior columns.

As we walked through the streets, it seemed that every man turned instinctively to look at the contessa. She's in her fifties, a grandmother, but so comely, so elegantly dressed and wearing such a fortune in jewels, she seemed accustomed to the role of head-turner and rather enjoyed it.

Just on five, she took us to an ancient frescoed church, no longer 'working', but used for exhibitions, such as *Tangata*, a showing of photographs by Brian Brake of pre-European Maori art, formally opened this evening, and the reason for our visit to Padua. There was a very good attendance, including the prefect, the mayor, the chief of police, the local military commander and several young men who had played against the All Blacks. One of these lads whipped off his Padua Rugby Club tie and gave it to me. His club is one of the foremost in Italy, he said, and went on to explain that rugby was a post-war development, largely confined to the north.

After the opening of *Tangata*, we walked on to another exhibition, the work of an Italian architect (Albini), in a museum made out of an old monastery. On the way, the contessa slipped us into a coffee shop for a cup of coffee (which you almost invariably have to drink standing up as there is rarely much, if any, seating available) and then into a church to see frescoes by Giotto, a master of that art in the early 14th century.

When going for a walk by ourselves early this morning, we came upon a restored church which had two plaques by the entrance – one recording that it had been damaged by Austro-German bombardment in World War I, the other that it had been damaged by Anglo-American bombardment in World War II.

We drove then into the countryside, for a superb dinner put on by the mayor, with his councillors and the contessa, at an elegant restaurant beside a track where trotting races were being held. At dinner I pursued with the mayor a question I'd given him notice of this morning: "Why, in this affluent society, do 30 percent of the people vote communist?" "But in Padua," he protested, "it's only 24 percent." "But," I laughed, "that's almost 24 percent more than I can understand." He countered by saying that, in Italy, political affiliation was inherited and communist affiliation began in the 19th century, when factory conditions were appalling. "But surely,

Italian Days

in this country, as in ours, a factory worker's son can become a doctor?" But the mayor said that, in fact, there was little social mobility and, even when it occurred, political affiliation tended not to alter. "What you do not understand," he chided, "is the cohesiveness of the Italian family." All this in the utmost good humour. (We left around midnight but I was proud of Laurie Markes,[47] the embassy's second secretary, not only for having set up the *Tangata* exhibition so well, but even more for his stamina in staying to drink with the mayor, closer to his age than ours, till 3 am.)

Saturday 19 July
This morning we visited the huge basilica which is the burial place of St Anthony, whose name is invoked for things mislaid and whose pickled tongue is on view as the centrepiece of much finely-wrought gold ornamentation – not one of the things from the past which we can admire or even want to see; and the university, mainly to see Galileo's perfectly preserved anatomy (operating) theatre (made of timber), the first in the world (1594). Then Butch Cassidy and the Sundance Kid almost jumped for joy with the whisky I gave them.

At the dinner last evening, we met a Mr Piva, fortyish, a city councillor and architect, who invited us to afternoon tea at the family holiday home, about 40 minutes out of Padua. And it wasn't at all what we expected although it provided a great example of Italian family cohesiveness, such as the mayor had been talking about last night. It certainly wasn't a cottage but a large house, fronting directly on to the street of a small village and opening, through a high timber gate and an archway, into an area where you could see that the house sprawled in an L-shape around a large lawn enclosed by a high brick wall decorated with marble statues. The original house, now with mod cons and greatly extended, was built in the 18th century. It was acquired by Mr Piva, Senior, 25 years ago. He's an antiques dealer, hence the marble statues. He and his wife had seven sons – no daughters – all of them now married and, among them, have 14 children. This extended family spends the summer here together and, indeed, frequently gathers here at other times of the year as well.

We were met by a flurry of little children impatient to show us their baby rabbits in a cardboard box and baby thrushes in a cage. We were shown the main rooms of the father's part of the house, where the walls were stuccoed in lace-like patterns, one room with mirrors inset in patterns, amongst the stucco work. Some walls and ceilings were entirely frescoed. Then we went to that part of the extension to the house occupied by the architect son and his family. It had separate cooking and other facilities and overlooked

---
[47] Lately in Rome again, this time as ambassador.

a goldfish pond which the architect had made. We had tea, first iced, with lemon, then hot, served with apple strudel which the architect's wife had made and decorated with red currants from the garden. We ate with sterling silver cutlery, which the architect had designed, and sat at a table he had also designed, with a glass top supported by legs of painted steel and leather devices coupling the glass to the steel. It was all utterly enchanting. Not at all what a New Zealander thinks of as a holiday home. Nor could we imagine young men in New Zealand always wanting to have long holidays with mummy and daddy.

Then we had to hurry away to get to Carla's place at the appointed time – Carla being the sister of Stephania, wife of the Italian Ambassador in Kuala Lumpur when we were there. They were good friends of ours there and continue to be now they live in retirement in Rome. We found Carla's place in a narrow, winding street where all the buildings fronted directly on to the street in what was one of the oldest parts of Padua. From the outside, it looked rather seedy. A concierge let us in and we found ourselves in a cobbled courtyard with about half a dozen doors. Carla greeted us warmly, took us through a succession of rooms, all of them elegantly proportioned, elegantly frescoed and elegantly furnished, introduced us to another, older sister – both of them are widows – and other guests including a retired general who plays golf four days a week. On Stephania's instructions, Carla had an ice-cold lager waiting for me and the others had punch.

Carla's home is a wing – two storeys and an attic – of what had been built as the palace for a cardinal in the 17th century (or was it the 18th?). The twinkly-eyed general said that some of the frescoes were not at all the sort of thing a cardinal should have had about. Then we were all invited to go into the garden where we sat on cherry-red canvas chairs round a table covered with a cherry-red table cloth, beside a matching oleander and under an apricot tree laden with ripe fruit, some of which were piled in a sterling silver dish for us to eat. It seemed miraculous that, after entering from a narrow, rather seedy, mid-city street, there could be such a large garden with an extensive lawn and magnificent old trees at the rear, the street sounds blocked out by the intervening buildings, the only sound to intrude being the chiming of bells at St Anthony's.

How civilised these people were, in their conversation, manners, dress, the simplicity of their pleasures. We could reflect, too, that here, in one day, we had been warmly welcomed into the homes of two comparative strangers whereas we'd been in the Soviet Union for three years and only one Russian had ever been allowed to invite us into her home – presumably because it enabled her to keep up to the mark with her qualifications as a professor of English. These Italians are remarkably abstemious in their drinking habits,

Italian Days

too. They always drink wine with the evening meal but we have never seen any sign of drunkenness. Recently, we had the Italian rugby team to drinks at the house, before they went on tour in New Zealand. They each had a glass of lager or wine, then put the glass down and seemed surprised when offered another, which not all of them took. And that's how it was at Carla's this evening. (How could such people be compatriots of the Mafia, the terrorists?)

Sunday 20 July 1980
Padua–Rome, getting home about 2 pm. We were scarcely out of the car when Maria came scolding about something we did not understand. Damn Maria and Mimma. In the marvellous sunshine on the day of the week we had tried hard to have by ourselves (and our pool not being overlooked by any of the neighbours), I swam and sunbathed starkers. ("Well, it's no more than they can see on television almost any night of the week." There's an awful lot of pornography on television, some of it amusing, most of it sick.)

21 July 1980
The Turkish Ambassador called at the house, accompanied by two armed Turkish guards and with an Italian police car, with two policemen, following his car, which has windows of dark glass. The Turks are prey to Armenians here. (The most notable event in the long history of bad relations between the two countries was the Turkish massacre of two million Armenians in 1915 – about one of every two Armenians in the world.) The present Turkish Ambassador's predecessor was assassinated in Rome. Recently, the Turkish Ambassador to the Vatican was shot but not killed. When I went to the gate with the Ambassador today, it was to find that his car had broken down. So he left in the Italian police car, sandwiched between his Turkish armed guards.

23 July 1980
After months of extensive negotiations about continuing access of New Zealand sheepmeats and butter to the EEC market, all that was agreed at the EEC Council of Agricultural Ministers yesterday was an arrangement for our butter, up to the end of this year: quantity down by 20,000 tonnes, price up by 50 percent. (Even that, however, fell apart later.)

24 July 1980
At 8.30 am we picked up Peter Dolan, a Brit who is in charge of the Commonwealth War Graves Commission cemeteries in this area, including parts of north Africa, and set out for the Sangro war cemetery, where 350

New Zealand servicemen are buried, along with several thousand others. It is by the Adriatic coast, 250 km away, through steep hills, many of them barren. The highway, a double lane each way, is an even more spectacular feat of engineering than the highway north, with longer tunnels and longer and higher viaducts.

The cemetery is in a natural amphitheatre. From the top of it you get a glimpse of the sea and it overlooks the Sangro River. The lawns are now parched and the strips of cottage garden flowers are past their best. At either end of cemetery, the Indian and Pakistani dead are buried in separate areas, behind hedges. Hindus, having been cremated, are commemorated on a granite column. The others have the Christian cross.

I find these cemeteries deeply moving. So many of my contemporaries were cut down in their prime. I have to hurry ahead of the others, blinking away the tears.

The best of today was Peter's fund of anecdotes. A Sicilian, employed as a gardener, had complained that his gun had been stolen while he was working at the cemetery. Peter had demanded, "But what were you doing with a gun at the cemetery, anyhow?" And the Sicilian retorted, "But I wouldn't go *anywhere* without a gun. Would *you*?"

This evening, Maria and Mimma departed – civilly, shaking hands.

A few hours later, there was another departure. After a marriage of ten years, Geoff, aged 29, took his wife, Sue, and their two children to the airport, to see them off on their way back to New Zealand. He is leaving her for Linda, an English woman of 30 who, until recently worked in the Embassy, having been recruited locally. And Linda has left her Italian husband and their two children, including a three-month-old baby! – for Geoff. She is now in England, instituting divorce proceedings and waiting for Geoff. I suppose you could say we've got through all that appalling development smoothly enough: none of them had a nervous breakdown, as each of them, by turn, seemed likely to do; and Tino, the Italian husband, didn't come rampaging into the office with a gun, as I feared he would, and as Geoff might justifiably have feared even more.

26–27 July 1980
A report rightfully on page one of the London *Sunday Times* makes me glow with pride in being accredited to Italy. Thousands of cleverly imitated copies of *Pravda* have been printed in Italy, smuggled into Moscow and distributed during the Olympic Games. This edition of *Pravda* announces the fall of the Soviet regime and the promise of free elections.

29 July 1980
"I don't know what's got into Picco – biting and scratching – not at all herself."

"Did she have her swim today?"

"Come to think of it, no, she didn't."

"Well, no wonder she's out of sorts."

M had been looking in pet shops for a kitten and found the prices astronomical. She happened to mention this one day to a Little Richard – which means I must tell you about him before going on about Picco. The Australians must be given the credit not only for discovering Little Richard but for sharing this remarkable discovery with us. This is against the background of great difficulty in finding Italian tradesmen to come and do minor jobs. But Little Richard is a rare phenomenon in the modern world, a jack-of-all-trades and competent in them all, who comes promptly and when he says he will, whose charges are remarkably reasonable, who swears like a trooper, at himself, when on the job and, when he's done it, likes nothing better than to sit down with me and yarn about ecology or something like that.

By conventional standards, he's a nut. He's a wiry Englishman in his early thirties, who has lived here for ten years. I once asked him what brought him to Rome. "Oh," he said, "I just arrived." He is married to an English lass who works as a stenographer with FAO (the Food and Agriculture Organisation) and they have two children, now both at school. His wife is the regular wage-earner and he's the house husband. He assumes primary responsibility for looking after the children and cooking the meals and he supplements the family income by doing odd jobs for embassies (which keeps him within the law). His passion in life is competitive bicycle riding. He almost certainly arrived here from England on a bike, just as he does at our house, sweating profusely after his stiff climb up the hill, which he enjoys as part of his training. To engage him, therefore, is to encounter a higher level of body odour than you're likely to find anywhere outside Russia. When summer came, M overcame this problem by inviting him, to his delight, to cool off, as she put it, by having a swim before he started work.

Little Richard is likely to arrive with a little present in the knapsack strung across his back. In the spring, it was wild white irises for M, gathered from the side of the road. Another day, he brought a book on organic gardening to lend to me. Then one day he brought a kitten which he'd found in the yard of the school which his children attend. We didn't know whether to thank him or not. The kitten was so sick it seemed doomed to die within hours. In her distress, M rang Little Richard who put her on to a vet, with whose help the kitten began to shake off its sickness overnight. She became 'Picco' and, even when very young, would respond to the name.

She became fond of gardening and would accompany me for hours as I pottered. She showed no reaction at all if distant dogs barked but flared up in anger, even as a small kitten, if a stray cat came into our garden. She liked to be with people but was easily excitable; nipping and scratching. When reprimanded, however, and gently cuffed, she would be conscience-stricken, hiding her head in shame and soon coming back to apologise.

When summer came, Picco took to swimming every day like us. She especially liked her rub-down afterwards. Then, having sunned herself dry, she resumed her place by the zinnias, guarding them from butterflies and, when relieved of this responsibility by the setting of the sun and the disappearance of butterflies for the day, she would pretend to be a crab, running sideways, or a Lipizzaner horse, prancing in all directions.

30 July 1980
When we came, we found a job-lot garden, almost everything planted in multiples of five, presumably bought at bargain prices by the speculator who had built the house and landscaped the grounds at minimal expense. All the multiples of five had been planted in rows. M took one look at it and said, "I don't like it." I heartily agreed. "Of course not. That should be a herbaceous border – can't you just see it?" So, the first weekend, I took out four scruffy spruces, digging over the ground as I went. The second weekend, I took out the remaining six spruces and all the bronze-coloured flaxes planted between them. And you might think it would be a problem to dispose of ten scruffy spruces and all those bronze flaxes in suburban Rome. Not at all. I just threw them over the fence. Everybody else who didn't want something just threw it over the fence. The people next door had thrown two large armchairs over their fence, into the alley between us, and there was a discarded motorbike there, too. We were appalled, when we first came, to see how much litter there was in Rome.

There were hundreds of large plastic bags of rubbish piled on the side of the road, in particular parts of the city, remaining there as an apparently permanent part of the landscape. It seemed no wonder that archaeologists always had to dig down a surprisingly long way to find the remains of ancient cities. They'd buried themselves in their own rubbish.

One could cheat in establishing a new garden quickly. A marvellous array of plants are sold here in small plastic pots and already coming into bloom. So, by the second Monday morning, the first section of reorganised garden, by the front gate, had a clematis in bloom, a climbing rose and dahlia tubers planted, and daffodils, tulips, verbenas, forget-me-nots, pansies, violas and polyanthus already in bloom. It was instant gardening. Some plants were from the garden of the Japanese Ambassador and his wife, who lived down the street and who used to be in Wellington, where we'd also known them. On the second Monday morning, I found Nazzerano inspecting what had been done. When I appeared, he laughed and clapped, in that ebullient Italian way, declaring, "It is very, very beautiful! It has been transformed!" And it became his routine to inspect the garden every Monday morning, to see what else had been done.

The lower level of garden was dominated by four Italian pines at one end. At the other end was a small swimming pool. Between them were five job-lot yews which I took out and replanted in large earthenware pots to put on the balcony. Then, in the gaps left in lawn, I sowed grass-seed to extend the area of lawn, opening it up to more sun, and to more people coming to swim. And I took out 50 or so paving slabs which had encircled the lawn and replaced them with a narrow strip of garden which seemed the obvious place for wisteria and a climbing rose to help themselves to a four-foot-high wrought-iron railing fence.

In the months which followed, most things flourished in the wonderful sunshine and even more wonderful absence of strong wind. Ivy geraniums, planted outside our bedroom windows on the third floor, tumbled voluptuously three or four feet to the level below. In summer, we harvested more tomatoes from the six plants I'd put in than we could possibly use, and gave the surplus to Nazzerano and folk in the office. But my greatest pride and joy was a thicket of hollyhocks, which grew from a scattering of seed and became well over six feet tall but remained unstaked. They held each other up like good companions and bloomed better than the seed packet said they would.

31 July
Workmen began installing new doors, with combination locks and bulletproof glass, in the lobby of the office and an enclosure of bulletproof glass for Lidia, the receptionist, whose desk is in the lobby.

1 August
Through an Irish priest who is a friend of the Irish Ambassador, who is friend of ours, a Sri Lankan, a fine-looking young man of 29, came looking for a job, together with his plump little wife. They are in Italy illegally but look good and have excellent references and can regularise their status by working for an Embassy. We snapped them up. They say their names are Sena and Kamala but I think of them as Saner and Caramel. Today they moved into their quarters in the attic, together with their seven-month-old baby.

2 August
A revolutionary start to the day. Saner had the terrace swept before breakfast. Caramel boiled an egg to perfection.

At 10.25 am, tragedy struck in Bologna. An explosion ripped through the restaurant and second-class waiting room at the railway station killing 76 and injuring nearly 200 – the bloodiest act of terrorism in post-war Europe. It was generally assumed to be the work of neo-fascist terrorists who favour massacre, aiming to undermine faith in democracy.

The leftist terrorists, such as the Red Brigade, are more discriminating. They favour murder of selected individuals, or the maiming of them (notably by 'knee-capping') – politicians, judges, magistrates, policemen, businessmen. Their most infamous achievement was the assassination of Prime Minister Aldo Moro in 1978. (Nazzerano re-enacts the crime every time we go by the site which is not far from our house. "Boom! Boom!", brandishing an imaginary gun in the air.)

3 August
There has been no rain for weeks. The temperature hovers in the nineties (Fahrenheit) with high humidity. It's essential to water the garden every day to keep plants alive. We have several swims a day, ending with one around 10 pm. From time to time during the day, especially at weekends, we have 'Dad's half hour' (i.e. starkers), when the womenfolk are obliged to find things to do indoors. (Daughter Brendy has been staying.)

7 August
A day off for an excursion to Pompeii, 250 km south of Rome. The highway is as good as that north to Padua or west to the Adriatic but it runs through gently undulating country without the need for spectacular viaducts or tunnels. It was prudent to avoid the coast road which would be clogged with holiday traffic. (Rome has become astonishingly unclogged. Traffic is now so sparse that my commuting time has been cut 75 percent. Two million of Rome's three million people are said to be away, mainly at the beach, escaping the heat. Many of the little shops and cafés have closed completely for a month or six weeks. Those who remain in the Italian ministries knock off for the day at 1.30 pm.)

At Pompeii, we hired a guide to show us the ruins – a wizened little old man who had learnt English, he said, by listening to the BBC news during the war.

Pompeii was a town of 25,000 people buried in AD 79 under hot ash from an eruption of Mount Vesuvius, four miles away and long thought to be extinct. The town lay buried for almost 1,600 years. Then excavation began under the French (Bourbon) rulers of Naples. From the 19th century excavation has been continued, more scientifically, by the Italians, and is still continuing.

At first, the ruins seem unimpressive. A jumble of narrow streets lined with the shells of cheek-by-jowl buildings of stone blocks or brick, very few of them anywhere near intact. Then gradually and increasingly, one is impressed. The Pompeians built to last and had a remarkably high level of civilisation. Pavements of flat-topped, interlocked boulders, interspersed with white boulders to mark the way at night, will be good for at least another 2,000 years. They had running water, channelled in pipes made of lead imported from Britain, "then a province of Rome", the guide said. And because they knew that lead contained poison, they had water filters, some of which are still there. They had one-way streets, pedestrian malls, blocked to chariots by upright boulders, underground septic sewage tanks beneath the houses, upstairs toilets and a central town square which takes little imagination to see was architecturally finer than anything which exists in New Zealand.

When you enter the best-preserved buildings, you have an uncanny sense of intruding in the lives of people who have simply gone out for the day. In a men's communal bath-house – one of four in the town (women's were separate) – plaster reproductions of men (who average five feet) dramatise their agonising death in hot ash 2,000 years ago. A fountain in the 'cooling-off room' spurts water in the air from a round bowl, perhaps eight feet across, carved from a single block of white marble. And it becomes easy to imagine young men cavorting there in unabashed nakedness, bragging even more outrageously than a man their poet, Catullus (c. BC 84–54) had written about, entreating his wife to "Stay at home and prepare nine good fucks for me, one after another."

The ebullient hedonism is confirmed in the best-preserved house. In the entry is the fresco of a man thoughtfully weighing, on a pair of scales, his erect and greatly exaggerated penis. At the rear of the house, the guide pointed out "… excuse my words … a pleasure room for bachelors … and, you see, language was no barrier. A man just pointed to whichever fresco on the wall showed … excuse my words … the position required."

We had lunch outside the walls of the old city, under the trees of a restaurant which sprawled out on to the pavement. The house wine was 'Tears of Christ', which comes into the same curious Italian category as 'The Bank of the Holy Ghost' and 'Jesus Jeans'.

9–10 August

Something's gone wrong with the mechanism which operates the swimming pool. The water has stopped circulating and is starting to smell. And, of course, anyone who might be expected to know something about such things is away at the beach for a month or six weeks. The swimming pool maintenance company which the embassy has dealt with for years simply doesn't answer the phone. Locally recruited staff at the office kindly found an electrician, then a plumber, to come and see if they could solve the problem, but they couldn't.

On Sunday evening we went to a spectacular outdoor performance of the opera *Aida*, with a cast of hundreds and six magnificent white horses, against the backdrop of what remains of the Baths of Caracalla, begun by the Emperor Septimus Severus in AD 206 and inaugurated by his son, Caracalla, 11 years later. (The baths continued in use until the sixth century when the Goths cut the aqueducts which supplied the water. They were the second largest, probably the most luxurious, baths in the city, able to accommodate 1,600 bathers at a time.) The opera is staged there every summer, it being 99.9 percent certain it won't be rained out.

11 August
The water in the pool had become foul and as brown as roast beef gravy. It is being emptied.

12 August
I took the day off and we went to Siena, about two hours' drive. Just beyond Siena, in the countryside, Neil, our trade commissioner, has rented an apartment in an old farmhouse now subdivided and let to holidaymakers in summer and university students for the rest of the year. Neil is having a month there, to relax and take a course at the university to improve his Italian. It's a charming house, with beamed ceilings, antique furniture and splendid views over the Tuscan farmland. We wandered briefly in the old part of Siena, an entrancing medieval city with narrow, winding streets, a little church at every corner and a wonderful cobbled square encircled by breathtakingly beautiful façades. But mainly today was a long and excellent lunch – Neil is a first-rate cook and we left him with enough tomatoes from our garden to see out his stay.

When we returned, Saner said of one of the men who came to look at the pool, "I don't like that man! He wanted to look all over the house and I wouldn't let him. He asked where the alarm system is and I said I didn't know." No wonder he doesn't. There isn't one.

13 August
At last we've tracked down someone from a pool maintenance firm. He came early this morning and quickly discovered a faulty valve and blocked

outlet. He fixed things in no time at all and, assuring us we'd have no more trouble, began refilling the pool.

15 August
M and B left for Venice by train.

16 August
When I came down this morning, Saner was not about and Caramel looked uncharacteristically sad. The baby, she said, was sick and Saner had taken it to the hospital. "Has fever. All night, won't sleep. Won't eat. All night, cry. All night, running pooh-pooh, sir." The baby has been admitted to the hospital and is expected to be there for several days.

The long spell of hot, dry weather has ended with a violent thunderstorm and prolonged heavy rain.

17 August
The sun returned. It took me more than an hour to skim the pine needles and other debris, brought down by yesterday's storm, out of the pool. The water now has the delightful fragrance of pine.

M and B returned.

18 August
On 10 August, a 20-year-old New Zealander I'll call John Smith, was arrested at the airport in Rome after attempting to bring in 2.3 kg of marijuana in the false bottom of his suitcase. David, our administrative and consular officer, went to see him in jail and found he was most insistent that his parents in New Zealand should not be told what had happened. He had £380(Stg) in traveller's cheques, as well as a camera he could sell, to buy 'extras' while in jail. He was fit, in good spirits, had no complaints. It had been a fair cop, he said. His case can't be heard in court for quite a while because the marijuana has to be analysed first by the State Laboratories, which are closed till 15 September.

We have a surprising number of birds in the garden and living in the trees in the valley below: tiny birds with a full-throated, melodious song; even tinier hummingbirds who, in a remarkable feat of aerodynamics, gather honey from the zinnias; owls which, at night, hoot in the valley; and nightingales who, it seems churlish to record, have understandably fallen in love with their own voices but don't know when to stop.

Dinner at a restaurant in a plaza, with strolling players, in the middle of the city.

20 August
B left for New Zealand.

21 August
Italian statistics show that the value of New Zealand exports to Italy increased 80 percent in 1979 (over 1978) and Italian trade to New Zealand 50 percent. No doubt reflecting Italy's leading role in the fashion world, the main New Zealand export to Italy is in hides and skins, increasing 176 percent in volume in 1979, followed by wool.

23 August
The baby came home from hospital.

24–30 August
In Malta presenting credentials etc.

1 September
Dorothy Atherton and her brother Ronnie arrived to stay.

3 September
Denis Walton arrived to stay.

4 September
Two MPs, Trevor Young, with his wife, and Dr Shearer, came to lunch, from which they left, with Laurie, on an official visit to Yugoslavia.

5 September
Called on Zamberletti, Under-Secretary of Foreign Affairs, a pleasant man who talked frankly.

7 September
Ronnie left by cab at 5 am to catch a plane to London. Denis left by cab at 9.30 am to catch a train to Portugal.
　The days are getting shorter, the nights chilly.

11 September
Negotiations, centred in Brussels, about continuing access for New Zealand butter and sheepmeats, go on and on and on, as they have for many months, without any definite conclusion about a single thing.
　Laurie returned from Yugoslavia. The two parliamentarians he accompanied there were teetotallers when they went, he says, but not now.

12 September
Mexican National Day reception at noon, the first such occasion for many weeks.

A late, excellent dinner at the "Prison" restaurant, in a courtyard, with strolling players and waiters dressed as convicts and exposing chest forests of hair. At 1 am we saw Dorothy onto the airport bus at the city terminal. The cheapness of excursion fares London–Rome–London is accounted for by the departure of such flights at an ungodly early hour in the morning. Best left to young backpackers. (Dorothy is 70.)

15 September
Went to Rinascente, the largest department store in Rome, to buy a new summer-weight suit. They had none in my size and directed me to another shop which, they said, catered for "overseas figures". And there I struck it lucky and bought two suits, one light, one heavy, from a charmingly helpful and persuasive assistant who, like the police escorts in Padua and the waiters at Prison restaurant, was exposing what appears to be the regulation chest forest of hair.

Rome goes in for small shops, and lots of them. Department stores are small even by New Zealand standards.

16 September
I went back to collect the suits today. Ready-made suits are on sale with the trouser legs unhemmed. One pair, when I went today, had still not been hemmed because there had been other adjustments to make (including taking in the waist – mark that) and the tailoress wanted to check that this was right before doing the hems. So I said I'd go back some other time to collect that suit. She said, however, if I could wait five minutes, the job would be done. And it was.

17 September
A Commonwealth ambassadors' lunch at the Australian Ambassador's. The Brit remarked that planning for the Queen's forthcoming visit to Italy – and the British plan such tours in the finest detail, accounting for every minute of every day – had so far proceeded with "up to five or six letters a day, on different aspects of the tour" from the British Embassy to the Italians, without a single letter of acknowledgement or reply.

The comely contessa from Padua and the Rinaldis, an Italian diplomat with a New Zealand wife, came for drinks at the house, then we all went to dinner at another of those charming restaurants in central Rome, outdoors, with excellent food, service and wine. The conversation was good, too, the contessa as witty as she is comely.

18 September
To the bank to collect traveller's cheques. This always takes at least an hour. Employment in banks in Italy is almost exclusively a male preserve and much sought-after occupation. Employees get 17 months pay a year, plus another month's pay, on retirement, for every year of service. Tellers are casually dressed and also exposing chest hair. Today, one of them was in a tailored version of a rugby jersey, with wide horizontal bands of alternating red and blue.

19 September
We're going to Egypt by ferry, run by a Danish shipping company and manned by Danish officers and Egyptian crew. It's an economical, relaxing way to go. Many European tourists take their cars. The cabins and bunks are surprisingly small. Meals are pay-as-you-go. But nothing to really complain about, although a German engineer, who shared our table for dinner tonight, complained about everything and said of Egypt, where he works, "Those people is crazy ... Baksheesh, baksheesh ... you go through a revolving door and there's someone on either side of it wanting baksheesh to let you pass."

The urge to write graffiti extends to the alteration of signs, although two I noticed today seemed more likely to have been the work of English-speaking rather than Italian larrikins. 'Arsoli' seemed improbable as the name of a town. When I checked on the map, I found it was meant to be 'Carsoli'. And, in the men's toilets at the wharf, the English version (there was also an Italian version) of "It is forbidden to shave and undress" had been changed to "It is forbidden to shit and to piss."

Saturday 20 September
The sea as calm as a millpond. A bright, warm sun. Dolphins alongside. A boy of about three spent the morning drowning his doll in the paddling pool and, when that was done, he washed its clothes.

21 September
A three-hour stop at Patras, Greece. We teamed up with an elderly Swiss couple to see the sights. Poked our heads into a Greek Orthodox Cathedral where a service was being held – uncannily similar to the Russian Orthodox – but the Swiss woman was mortified to be told very firmly, indeed, to get out immediately because she was wearing slacks.

Today, near the bar on the upper deck, several German lasses were sun-bathing topless. A young Egyptian barman was goggle-eyed, only able to glance momentarily, now and then, at what he was supposed to be doing.

Italian Days

Basking in the sun, we wondered, idly, whether the first snow of winter was falling in Moscow as it usually does on this day.

22 September
Stopped for an hour at Iraklion, Crete, but were not allowed off. Three hundred more passengers, mainly German, got on. Again it was calm and sunny and these days have allowed me to read up on Egypt.

23 September
Awoken at 5 am to be ready to disembark at Alexandria at 7 am but when the ship docked at this time, it was found to be only 6 am local time, so we had to wait an hour for customs and suchlike officials to come on duty. An elderly deaf-mute Egyptian porter took our luggage and, for a little while, disappeared. For ever? No, there he was, grinning, bobbing up and down as he pushed the trolley with our luggage and being enormously helpful in getting us through customs. But there was no sign of Geoff, who'd gone ahead by air on Friday to start making arrangements. Then, after we'd waited only a few minutes, a car pulled up right beside us, the driver got out, clipped a New Zealand pennant to the car, and in a courtly manner, invited us to get in. We found Geoff outside the gates at the entrance to the wharf. He had not been allowed in without a pass, which he didn't have and couldn't get till 8 am when the relevant office opened for business (in half an hour's time).

The Nile Hilton – a quiet room at the rear although overlooked by workmen constructing an extension. (Next day, M rightly insisted on moving to a room overlooking the Nile, which was well worth it despite the noise of the traffic below. It was high enough up for M to "put the pyramids to bed" as night fell over them every evening before we went to have dinner in the coffee shop.

2 October
Cairo–Rome by air and, although, in eight days, I saw more ministers and senior officials in Cairo than I've been able to see in Rome in seven months, I failed to see the man I most wanted to see, President Sadat, who, in May, had also become Eygpt's prime minister.

In Rome the government has fallen.

In Brussels, after millions of words in telex exchanges among our EEC posts and Wellington in recent months, arrangements for entry to the EEC market of our sheepmeat and, to the end of 1980, of our butter, have been concluded. What happens to our butter after 1980 remains completely undecided, due solely to the French.

Gillian George, a lass from our embassy in Baghdad, came in to chat. She'd been evacuated by way of the 800 km road to Amman, in Jordan, under cover of darkness, the airport in Baghdad having been closed by bombing.

At 5.30, a showing of New Zealand films, with dubbing in Italian, by the Dante Alighieri Society – a full hall and everyone agog with excitement because an Italian Princess was present. (Such titles were abolished many years ago. But so what?) And, with everything else that's been going on and my mind full of Egypt, I'd completely forgotten about this function. Pia reminded me only just as I was leaving the office. So I arrived at the hall without the faintest idea what I would say in the speech I was expected to make. The Rector of Perugia University spoke first. He was a roly-poly, charming old man who spoke solemnly, unaware that his fly was undone. Then I got up, took a deep breath and drivelled. And everybody laughed and intermittently clapped and the chairman said it was "brilliantly witty". There are times when you have to bluff your way through.

A dinner with the Dutch.

Sunday 5 October

Geoff came to the house to chat. He doesn't now plan to return to New Zealand, as he'd previously proposed. He's prospecting for a job in the UK so as to be with Linda and is applying for leave without pay from the New Zealand Public Service. (This was granted.) An ambassador in his time plays many parts … today Father Confessor.

"Baghdad has today been calm and there have been no air raid warnings at all," reports our embassy there.

9 October

It's been a busy week in the office, catching up on all the problems and paper which accumulated while we were in Cairo and completing the record of all our discussions there. And we had three dinner engagements this week.

10 October

Rome–Udine, 800 km north, setting out at 8.30 am. The countryside surprisingly green. After the summer dryness, recent rains have quickly restored the grass. There were several small mobs of sheep with young lambs. Lambs in autumn? Yes, they're being fattened, milk-fed, for Christmas. When their lambs are taken away, the ewes are milked to make cheese. (Imagine how all my sheep-farming forebears and other relatives in New Zealand would guffaw.)

Italian Days

11 October
In 1976, there was a severe earthquake in northern Italy and the New Zealand Government gave NZ$50,000 for relief activity. To the dismay of our embassy and even more of officialdom in Wellington, the Italians announced subsequently that they were going to use this money to restore a museum in the earthquake-stricken area of Friuli. On the New Zealand side, the expectation – indeed, the specific terms of the Cabinet approval – had been that the money would be used to re-house earthquake victims or for other humanitarian relief purposes of that kind. My predecessor accordingly made representations (as the diplomatic jargon puts it) to Zamberletti, then Under-Secretary, Ministry of Internal Affairs and concurrently Special Commissioner for earthquake relief in Friuli. At that time, he said, placatingly, that our donation would simply be put into the General Relief Fund.

And that's the last we might have expected to hear of it. Then, in July, I received an invitation to the opening of the museum, now restored. New Zealand, moreover, was being given great credit for financing the restoration. In the meantime, Zamberletti had become Under-Secretary of Foreign Affairs, with special responsibility for EEC matters, an appointment highly significant for New Zealand's need to secure continuing access to the EEC market. Here was an excellent opportunity to get alongside him. So, in brief, we attended the opening of the museum this morning.

The museum is described as one of the most important ethnographical museums in the world. It certainly has a remarkably extensive collection, dating mainly from the 16th century, although some items are older and one, a religious carving, dates back a thousand years. And it seems that, wherever you go in Italy, there are surprises. When we got to the clothing, M asked, "A bride would have worn a purple dress?" "Oh, yes. They always wore strong colours but with a white lace shawl over her head and with a white lace apron …" and, after pausing to give us an 'excuse my words' grin, added, "and, the following Sunday at church, she would wear a black apron, like that one." The opening of the museum today was attended by several hundred people and celebrated with a lunch for over a hundred.

The credit given to New Zealand was astonishing. It was reported not just in the regional press but acknowledged in a marble plaque, which M was invited to unveil, at the entrance to the museum. (Whispered aside: "Next week, my darling, you'll be able to compare notes with the Queen.") In all, the restoration cost NZ$480,000 so New Zealand's donation accounted for only about a tenth. And there was the particular bonus that, in Zamberletti's mind, New Zealand would have been indelibly inscribed as a country which had helped Italy in a troubled time. Now, serendipitously, he was in a position to help New Zealand. By speaking on the same platform at the opening of the restored museum and again at the ten-course lunch, where I sat next to him, my superficial acquaintance, based on a brief introductory formal call, became a friendship. In short, New Zealand's grant for earthquake relief turned out to have all sorts of unexpected results.

12 October
Udine–Rome

15 October
Ambassadors assembled in the gilded and frescoed splendour of the Quirinale Palace from 9.30 am onwards. We were put in line, checked eight times to ensure the order of precedence was correct and, at ten, we filed in, one after another, each one announced by some stentorian Italian voice at the door, before going forward to the centre of a grand salon, to be received by the Queen and the Duke of Edinburgh. Just a handshake, a few words and out. Subsequently, the Queen had a photograph taken with the Commonwealth Ambassadors, then mingled for half an hour, and later autographed the photo.

17 October
A truly marvellous display put on for the Queen by the Italian mounted police: 180 horses, chestnut, grey and white in equal numbers, led by a commander on the most beautiful black Irish charger. They were led, even further out in front, by a brown mongrel dog who adopted the unit four years ago, sleeps with the horses, parades with them wearing the colours of the Italian flag, takes up the most prominent position of all when the horses are being sedate but knows only too well to get out of the way when they perform at a lively pace. There were some spectacular movements, the most dramatic when the unit divided in two, each half taking up position at opposing ends of the field, then charging at one another, full tilt, with drawn swords. In the silence which this spectacle produced among everyone observing it, you could hear people sucking in their breath, absolutely convinced that there could not possibly be enough space, order or discipline to avoid the chaos and disaster which seemed inevitable. But suddenly, when the opposing teams of galloping horses were within inches of each other, they were brought simultaneously, miraculously, to an abrupt halt.

20 October
In the June year, 1979/80, Italy edged ahead of Germany to become New Zealand's seventh-largest market.

23 October
Noon reception for ambassadors (no spouses, and in fact, all the ambassadors at that time were men) at the Papal Nuncio's, to celebrate the second anniversary of the Pope's accession. In Rome, the Papal Nuncio is ex officio Dean of the Diplomatic Corps but he never assumes the usual responsibilities of that role in taking up issues with the Government on behalf of the Corps, arranging presentations for departing ambassadors and so on. Some ambassadors grizzle that there's a kind of conspiracy between the predominantly Italian Vatican and the Italian Government. It suits the Government, they say, to have a weak, divided Corps. However that may be, the fact of the matter is that the Diplomatic Corps, as an entity and as it operates, I think, in every other capital, scarcely exists here.

24 October
Dinner at home for Commonwealth ambassadors. Since coming here, I've attended a couple of stag Commonwealth ambassadors' lunches – which some, such as the Australian and the Brit, have lamented because the Asians and Africans have been reluctant to engage in anything but small talk. So tonight we tried a different tack, making it dinner instead of lunch and including wives. And it worked. Discussion flowed freely over a wide range of topics and the party didn't begin to break up till after midnight, which is highly unusual among ambassadors, and understandable when it can take upwards of an hour to get home. But why did the different formula work? Did they drink more freely on a Friday night? Did M's excellent dinner help? Were ambassadors wanting to show off in front of their wives?

25 October
Spent most of the day in the garden. It's been quite a while since I had time for it. Picco couldn't have been more delighted.

28 October
Stan and Pam Quill, old friends from our time together in Singapore, arrived to stay. Pam had written beforehand to say they were coming here after visiting Greece where her brother, Lindsay Buchanan, then with the RAF, had been stationed briefly at Paramythia in 1941 and had gone on a mission to bomb the Monastir Gap, aiming to stop German forces pouring through into Greece. But all the six Blenheims in the squadron Lindsay was with were shot down. He was eventually posted missing, presumed killed. His name was engraved on the El Alamein War Memorial as having no known grave. In the years since 1941, Pam had the nagging thought at the back of her mind that she should go to Greece to see if she could find out

anything about her much-loved brother's death.

Stan, a retired Air Commodore (RNZAF) wrote to the RAF people in London to see if they could help. They replied that Lindsay's plane was known to have gone down in a lake but, beyond that, they knew nothing. Then, about two months ago, the Quills received a letter from an Englishman named Bryce, whose brother had been killed on the same mission as Lindsay. Bryce had visited Greece last October and, after talking to local people, discovered that his brother had been buried near Lake Mikna Drespa, about 40 miles from the wartime air base at Florina.

On their way to Greece, the Quills met Bryce in London and he teamed up with them in Greece. They discovered that the lake in which Lindsay's plane had crashed was not in Greece as they thought, but just across the border in Albania. So, Albania then being a dormouse-in-the-teapot country, they slipped across the border surreptitiously, a local Greek rowing them out into the lake in a small boat. The Quills thought this little expedition should proceed as quietly as possible. The Englishman, Bryce, thought quite differently, talking loudly every inch of the way. "I'm not going to kowtow to any bloody Albanians." They found the remains of the aircraft sitting on dense reeds. Stan took small parts of the plane to see if British experts in London could say for sure whether it was the one Lindsay had been in. Then they erected a plaque in Lindsay's memory, on the Greek side of the lake. He was 23.

31 October
We began our required annual medical check on 23 October with Dr Rosemary Harris, the English wife of the No. 2 in the Canadian Embassy. Today we went for the blood test, X-ray and cardiograph part of the check-up at the clinic run by the Little Sisters of Mary, an Irish order whose hospital, including the clinic, is set in spacious grounds in the old part of Rome. While M was being X-rayed, a nun came up to chat and, intrigued by her accent, I asked where she came from. She said, "Wellington."

She stayed with us during the series of tests which were conducted in different parts of the clinic, which also has a hospital wing and residential quarters for the nuns. We hadn't gone far, in walking from one part of the place to another, when I was moved to exclaim, "I've never seen a place as spotlessly clean and shining as this!" "Yes," said the nun, "we used to employ a local staff of 48 but ran into trouble with two or three of them who weren't doing an honest day's work and, moreover, they were creating trouble with others. We wanted to dismiss the few troublesome ones but the union declared we couldn't, under Italian law. But we went ahead and sacked them anyhow. The union then pulled all 48 local workers out on strike. For six weeks, our handful of nuns did all the work of these 48 people, cooking, cleaning, gardening, as well as our own regular work in running the clinic and hospital. The problem was finally solved when we dismissed all 48 members of the local staff and re-organised the whole place on a contract basis. The cleaning and so on are all done on contract now. The doctors, too, now work on contract."

Which suggests that Italian law protects unduly. It just shows, anyhow, that, when push comes to shove, Italians are no match for the Irish, especially nuns.

On 29 October, three bandits, as they were described, seized Dario Giaschi, the 18-year-old son of a wealthy builder in Florence. It was Italy's 34th kidnapping this year.

Sunday 2 November
To Cairo with Geoff to present credentials.

4 November
"Do you realise we're competing with Jimmy Carter and Ronald Reagan for international headlines today?" "Yes. And I guess they'll win." But, in a way, they didn't, but only because Egyptian time is so far ahead of American time that the American election results hadn't even begun to come through when we turned on the six o'clock news in Cairo this evening. And there, the very first item gave a list of the ambassadors who'd presented credentials at Abdin Palace in Cairo today. "But what was that he called me? The Ambassador of New Zealand, Jimmy Harrison?" Arabist Geoff nodded and grinned.

5 November
Up at 4.30 am to get the flight back to Rome. Meanwhile, Pat and George Laking had arrived to stay.

6 November
The new coalition government in Rome is dominated, like all the others since the war, by the Christian Democratic Party but this new government is radically different in composition; a new faction has taken over. The Prime Minister is new. So are the Minister of Agriculture and the Deputy Foreign Minister responsible for EEC affairs. (My friend, Zamberletti, has gone!) In other words, three of the four Italians responsible for the decisions about New Zealand's continuing access to the EEC market, have changed. Colombo, the fourth, remains as Foreign Minister. So we have to make a concerted effort to ensure that the new ministers are aware of our trading problems, and as sympathetic as their predecessors have been. So I called on

the new Minister of Agriculture this evening. His predecessor, Marcora, was that rare phenomenon in Italian politics, a minister who stayed in his job for seven years at a stretch. He had become an expert in agriculture, thoroughly familiar with and sympathetic to our interests and, moreover, he was 'a character' – energetic, ebullient, full of laughter, highly respected and well-liked in the EEC and by Italian farmers and New Zealand ministers. His successor, I found, was disconcertingly different: a schoolteacher, colourless, with no officials in attendance as there almost always are when you call on a minister. He was pleasant enough, of course, and I'd brought a piece of paper, setting out our problems.

Sunday 9 November
Rome–Jeddah, with Geoff.

18-19 November
Jeddah–Rome, arriving at 4.30 am.

At their meeting in Brussels last week, the EEC Council of Agricultural Ministers failed to reach agreement on access for our butter after 1980. So the issue now goes to the EEC Council of Foreign Ministers who meet next Monday or Tuesday. I tried to see the Foreign Minister, Colombo, but he's away in Greece on a state visit with President Pertini. This evening I called on his deputy, Speranza, who replaced my friend Zamberletti, but only two or three days ago and, like the new Minister of Agriculture, had not held such a position before. Fortunately, however, Speranza had with him an experienced official well known to us. In the event, at the council meeting, Colombo not only spoke in our favour but went one step further than we'd requested. But, again due solely to the French, the council's discussion on this issue was entirely inconclusive.

23 November
Around 7.30 this evening there was a disastrous earthquake in southern Italy.

25 November
Helen Neilson, a stenographer from our embassy in Tehran and now on her way home, came in to chat, furious with Wellington for pulling her out after only a year in Tehran (but a turbulent, difficult year) and irritated that she'd missed out on a posting in Moscow. "I suppose I'm a nut but I enjoy a challenge, unusual places. I wouldn't want to be posted in New York or Paris." "In fact, New York can be a very lonely place for single girls whereas, in Moscow, there's a very active social life among the Embassy lasses." "Yes,

Italian Days

I know." "And the lads." "I should hope so." The airport in Tehran had been closed so Jean travelled by bus to Turkey, with two suitcases, and caught a plane from there. She doesn't know when, or even if, she'll see the rest of her effects again.

26 November
Around noon, I went to the Canadian Embassy to sign a book of condolences opened after the death of a former governor-general. As Nazzerano was away doing something else, Sergio drove. "Sergio! Sergio! Why are you crying?" "The earthquake, sir. I just heard this morning … four of my relatives were killed." He sobbed quietly all the way to the Canadians and back.

27 November
They passed the hat round in the office. Over $500. To make the money go further, Laurie shopped at Metro, a wholesale place to which embassy people have access. Tomorrow at 5 am Sergio will set out in the embassy station-wagon, to take food and other supplies to his stricken village and attend the funerals of his relatives.

28 November
M left this evening to have Christmas with the children in New Zealand. And Geoff left this evening – left Rome and left the New Zealand Foreign Service for at least a year, to join Linda and look for a job in London.

13 December
A telephone call today from the Saudi Ambassador summoned me to present credentials in Riyadh and I caught a flight there next day. There's a lot to do when you're going away, rather unexpectedly and certainly at remarkably short notice like this. And I wasn't going to be away for just a few days in Saudi Arabia. I was slotting that assignment in with pre-arranged trade talks in Cairo and then overdue leave in New Zealand to be with the family for Christmas. Getting away was a sort of round-the-clock operation. Well down the list of things to do or to be done after I'd left was a note for David, asking him to take liquor from the stock at our home to give as Christmas cheer to various embassy contacts, some of whom had made their annual expectations clear, as in a note from five "Porters of the Ministry of Foreign Affairs" wishing the embassy "a Good Christmas and a Happy New Year". And I scribbled another note for David: "I'd like you to go and see John Smith [the young New Zealander jailed for attempting to smuggle marijuana into Italy] before Christmas. Please buy him something with the attached. *Not* marijuana."

Monday 18 May 1981
I returned from New Zealand in early February but all the good reasons for not keeping a diary prevailed until today when I began again, reflectively.

The telex rules our lives. The first job of the day is to read the traffic – the outward traffic to make sure it's been correctly sent, the inward to see what's new. Until recently and for many months there had been a continuous flood of messages headed "Sheepmeats" and "Butter" – tiresomely jargonistic, wordy (never using one word if six could be found), repetitive, anxious. Now, thank God, we have some respite from it, our problems of access to the EEC market having been largely and satisfactorily resolved for the time being.

Included among the sheaf of otherwise mundane traffic this morning was a rather startling message from the General Manager for Commercial Affairs of some state organisation in Tripoli, complaining to me (although I'm not accredited there, our Trade Commissioner, Neil Wilson, goes occasionally to explore prospects for trade) that, during a call there on 10 May, Neil had been "very nervous and acted in a non good manner and bad behaviour …" and on and on in this vein.

"What's this about?"

"I asked them for some statistics and they accused me of spying. They were just so rude."

"Well, please draft me a reply. You know the sort of thing … regrettable misunderstanding … mutual advantage in developing trade … assurance of my highest consideration …"

"I feel like telling them to get fucked."

"By all means but put it *politely*."

And when he brought the draft reply, I could see, as I hadn't before, how the misunderstanding had arisen and the accusation of spying levied by the prickly (but oil-rich) Libyans. Neil had been passing on a request from Graeme Harrison (of whom, more later) seeking information about Libya's importation of meat (much of which is in the highly lucrative form of live animals for slaughter) and plans for storing and handling frozen meat. It was understandable that a Libyan who probably had little idea where or what New Zealand was, should, when confronted by a request of this kind from out of the blue, wonder whether it was any business of ours, notwithstanding that the main statistics requested would eventually be published by the Libyans themselves. So I fiddled with Neil's draft to smooth things over even more than he had done and, far from being irritated and displeased, as he might have been, he said, surprisingly, "Thank you for extricating your trade commissioner from difficulty."

After the telexes, the mail. And today there was a letter from Norman McCrae, Deputy Chairman of the New Zealand Meat Board:

Although somewhat belated, I wish to express warm appreciation on behalf of the recent Joint Board/Meat Exporters' Council Mission for the splendid hospitality and support given by your staff and yourself during our stop-over in Rome …

We all thoroughly enjoyed the luncheon you gave with representatives of the Italian trade. From my viewpoint, it was the most enjoyable and relaxed Embassy function I have been to. I know Graeme Harrison greatly appreciated the chance to catch up on some family history with you …

There'd been 14 of us at the lunch. This included Giulio, the embassy's marketing officer, locally recruited, a bilingual Italian. We had the lunch at Hostaria Villa Massino, a charming old restaurant a few minutes' walk from the office. We sat at a long table in a room we had to ourselves and I began by saying, "Norman, you sit on my right … the most senior Italian guest [to whom I'd only just been introduced and whose name I didn't catch] on my left … Dr Bunyon opposite me … and Graeme next to him … and I put you all on notice that I have no intention of spending all our time together just talking shop. I'm going to spend part of the time talking family with Graeme, a cousin I've never previously met."

So we had a four-course lunch and I had a four-way conversation. (Beforehand, I'd had a heated exchange with Giulio about the menu. I'd begun by thinking we'd have a 'main' and dessert – a light lunch such as most of us in the embassy had. Indeed, what I had in mind was more than we normally ate at lunchtime. But Giulio insisted we couldn't possibly do that. Italians, he said, had their main meal in the middle of the day and would think us incredibly mean to provide no more than I'd suggested. So I gave in, having in mind that the New Zealanders would be leaving the lunch to catch a plane on the long journey towards home and no doubt wouldn't mind passing the time by sleeping off a hearty lunch washed down with Italian wine.)

First, I had a conversation with the Italian meat importer on my left. Then I turned to Norman McCrae. Then I had a brief exchange with Dr Bunyon, a Harvard-educated Saudi and New Zealand Meat Board representative in the Middle East, resident in Dammam, on the Persian Gulf. He's a rather odd-looking man of perhaps 45. Although the citizen of a strictly teetotal country, he began lunch – as I couldn't help noting – by asking for a gin and tonic and later agreeing readily to wine. This confirmed the report of our Meat Board people, who'd enjoyed his hospitality in Dammam, that (illegally) he had a stock of liquor in his home worth, so he'd told them,

US$60,000. (It didn't seem to add up. Was he a black-market marketeer? And were the Meat Board wise to retain him?[48] And did my ears deceive me? Were my countrymen from the Meat Board taking mateyness a bit too far in calling him not "Fahd", but "Fart"?)

I hadn't got far in a family conversation with Graeme, when Dr Bunyon broke in by saying, "Your Excellency, I'd like to tell you this story about a Saudi Prince ..."

There was a chorus of disapproval from the New Zealanders. "Oh, not again, Fart!" "You don't tell a story like that to the ambassador!"

I intervened placatingly, "Why not?"

"Well, it was like this, Your Excellency. A Saudi Prince was visiting the United States for the first time. He was given an entry card to complete and, in the part where it asked for sex to be specified, he wrote, "Twice a day". The immigration official was very cross with him and pointed out he must specify male or female. And the Prince said, "Oh, I don't mind. Either will do.""

Then Dr Bunyon quickly followed up with a much juicier, obviously apocryphal, story about King Faisal.

* * * * *

In the mail which came in the bag from Wellington this morning was a letter addressed to M, the name and address on the envelope typed and the envelope emblazoned "OHMS ... Prime Minister's Department". And my curiosity got the better of me. For the first [and only] time, I opened a letter addressed to my wife. Oh! A mantilla required when they call on the Pope on 15 June. "She is very petite so, if there's a choice of sizes, would you please select the smallest. Her size in dresses is 8."

20 May

5.30. *Breaker Morant* at the Australian Embassy. Superb. Dinner with the Danes – our first 'black tie' occasion in Rome. The Italians go in for elegant, often highly expensive, casual.

"Do you understand Italian politics yet?" a retired Italian ambassador asked me.

"No, I don't."

"Neither do Italians."

"I am intrigued, however, to hear so many Italians say, 'We can't go on like this', but no one ever suggests what the remedy might be. Is the secret of this country its ingenuity?"

---

[48] Shortly after this visit to Rome, the Meat Board terminated their contract with Dr Bunyon.

"Absolutely – the art of compromise in all things – morality, religion, politics."

21 May
"What shall we do today?"

"I don't know. You're the teacher. But I suggest we move on from that lesson we had on Tuesday. I very much doubt that I'll ever have occasion to use the Italian words for 'brassiere' and 'petticoat'."

Twice a week, we plod on.

13–15 June (Saturday–Monday) 1981
My first encounter with Rob (who became Sir Robert) Muldoon was in the (northern) spring of 1965 when he came through Washington DC in the course of a United States State Department 'foreign leader' grant, which gave him three months in the United States, all expenses paid. At that time, it was the custom for the men in the New Zealand Embassy – but not the ambassador, who had lunch at home, next door to the office – to operate on a regular schedule of places to go for lunch. On Monday we went to The Greasy Spoon (although that may have been a nickname) about a hundred yards away and, when the weather allowed, we took our purchases away to eat sitting on the ground under the trees on New Zealand property where a new chancery was built many years later. On a Wednesday, we walked across a park and then across Wisconsin Avenue, to a pizza parlour, as Americans called it, about two hundred yards from the embassy. It was there that Rob Muldoon went with us one day. He had little to say, seemed tense, perhaps missing his wife and young family. But a memorable thing happened during that lunch. A large rat ran diagonally across the length of the restaurant and Rob Muldoon snarled, "Typical!" – as if to say, 'Nothing in this country is as good as it looks'.

I didn't meet him again till he came through Kuala Lumpur in 1975 when I was high commissioner there and he had become leader of the (National Party) Opposition in New Zealand. And, with the possible exception of Norman Kirk, Rob Muldoon was, on that occasion, the best official visitor I ever encountered, before or afterwards, at any post at which I served. (I say Norman Kirk was only a possible exception because, when he came through Kuala Lumpur early in 1974, he was already showing signs of being seriously ill. He died in August of that year, aged 51.) In 1975, Muldoon greatly impressed Malaysian Cabinet ministers and others he called on. He had an admirable grasp of issues, a nice dry wit. Socially, he couldn't have been better. He was completely at ease with the Malaysians – as Keith Holyoake never was with Lee Kuan Yew in Singapore – and made a point of chatting separately with all those we invited to dinner to meet him.

My next encounter was in 1980, by which time he had become Prime Minister. In January of that year, the Soviet Ambassador in New Zealand was caught passing funds to the Socialist Unity (Communist) Party and the New Zealand Government accordingly expelled him. The Russians then played tit-for-tat with me, as Ambassador in Moscow, by asking me to leave within the next few days. As I was due to leave, anyhow, in six weeks, at the end of a three-year term, the Russians took their tit-for-tat a bit further by cancelling the approval they had already given for my successor's appointment. The expulsion of an ambassador being highly unusual at that time and, in this case occurring when the Soviet Union was New Zealand's fifth-largest market and just after the Soviet Union had invaded Afghanistan, there were many things to consider and I was asked to return to New Zealand briefly "for consultations".

All the Cabinet ministers I called on at that time were intensely interested in the Soviet Union. So, too, was the Governor-General, Sir Keith Holyoake. My call at Government House, scheduled to last 20 minutes, ran on for two hours. And, when I went to see the Prime Minister, he greeted me warmly and *apologised* for keeping me waiting, although it had been no longer than five minutes. He was not to know that, in Washington DC, the New Zealand Ambassador could be kept waiting for upwards of an hour to see a senior State Department *official*. When we sat down to talk he began by saying, "Well, I'm not much interested in the country you're going to [Italy]. I want to talk about the country you've just come from." And, in half an hour, he plied me with such pertinent questions that the long, tiring journey back to New Zealand seemed thoroughly worthwhile.

But when he came to Italy for a long weekend in June 1981, it was very different. He was over-tired, querulous, abrasive, irascible. I was left wondering what had happened to the man I'd previously encountered. I was certainly left wondering if any of those accompanying him would vote to re-elect his government at the upcoming elections in New Zealand. (The moment his back was turned, the Secretary to The Treasury, Bernie Galvin, mimicked his mercilessly.) And, as they muttered to each other, the New Zealanders he met on this visit seemed to reach an even more critical verdict.

The main purpose of the weekend in Italy was to enable the Prime Minister to re-visit the area he'd been in, heroically, during World War II. This now meant going to Trieste, where he'd ended up in the closing phases of the war. In organising the visit, we engaged the services of an Italian, who'd become a close personal friend, as a local guide. He'd been a partisan leader, the equivalent of a brigadier, who'd fought alongside the New Zealanders and had a great regard for them. He would glow with pride in saying, "I once had the Maori Battalion under my command."

This Italian was completely bilingual, a man of the world. On the day of our tour he carried out his guiding assignment in exemplary fashion, quick to grasp that the Prime Minister couldn't recognise a particular area he'd been in during the war simply because the roading network had changed so much. The Prime Minister let out a whoop of delight when we got on to the old, familiar roads. ("Look, Tam, that's where I got out of the truck …")

During the day, the Italian ignored the Prime Minister's extremely cutting anti-Italian jibes. At the end of the tour, the Prime Minister stalked off without a word of thanks. I thanked my friend myself when we had a nightcap together. We chatted for a while, and then he gave an impish grin. "You know, I've been thinking your Prime Minister should give his lance corporal's uniform to the museum in Trieste!" We both laughed heartily. The Prime Minister's jibes weren't worth a second thought. What mattered was that New Zealand forces had played a key role in "saving Trieste for civilisation," as this Italian put it – keeping it out of the hands of Tito's men.

* * * * *

On retirement in 1983 we returned to New Zealand by sea, travelling from Genoa to Auckland, through the straits of Messina and the Suez Canal, in the *Tolaga Bay*, a British-owned and British-crewed container ship of 60,000 tons. The crew was remarkably small – about 30 men, most of who worked in shifts. They were all highly qualified and every one of them was excellent company. We were the only passengers, ensconced in one of two suites: one for the captain, the other intended for the shipping company's top brass; notably directors of the board, who often went on voyages to the Mediterranean, but rarely, if ever, could spare the time to go as far as New Zealand.

For us, there could have been no better way on winding down, taking a complete break after ten years continuously abroad and before settling back in New Zealand to a very different and even more congenial life. We would again be in the same country as our children, one of whom now had a child, our first grandchild. On board the *Tolaga Bay* we walked around the deck every day, clocking up the miles. In the tropics, the ship's very small swimming pool was filled and we swam once or twice a day. We read a lot – the ship had a surprisingly good library and, in Perth, we replenished our own stock of books. Across the Great Australian Bight, albatrosses kept their beady eyes on us, almost, it seemed, within touching distance and without moving their wings, just gliding gracefully, majestically, day after day, one of the wonders of the natural world.

Index

Abdul Rahmin, Tunku 99, 158
adultery, death for 159–60
Air Malta 153
Alderton, Biddy 54–5
Alderton, Lisle 54–5
Alexandra, Princess 101
Alitalia 147, 157
Ananda Mahidol, King of Thailand 29
Aorangi 41
Armstrong, Dr Val 41 fn
Armstrong, Wade 41 fn
Australian School of Pacific Administration 61
authoritarianism 87–8
autostrada, Italian 189–90
aviation in New Guinea 58, 65

banking, Italy 206
Barclay, Steve 185–6
Barker, Eddie 113
Barraclough, Moira 33
Barriball, Barbara 163
Barton, Ailsa 47
Barton, George 47
Begin, Menachem 155
Bellamy, Rose June 143

Bennett, General Gordon 102
Berendsen, Sir Carl 17, 25, 30–4, 36, *123*
Berendsen, Ian 47
Biak 65
Blake, Douglas 135
border control 151
Brake, Brian 192
Browne, Madie 15
Broz, Franjo 177
Buchanan, Lindsay 211–12
Buddhism 139–40
Bunyon, Dr 217–18
Burma, 110–46
Burma Airlines 142

Cambodia 29–30
Campbell, Duncan 8
Canberra 50–6
Canberra Pact 53
Carver, Lord 92–3, 106
Casey, N.V. 101
central heating 40
Channing, Carol 35
Cheng, C.K. 101
Childs, Colonel Frank 135

Churchill, Sir Winston 30, 103
Cleland, Brigadier Donald 61
Collins, Dick 34
Colombo Plan Conference, 1967 110
Commonwealth War Graves 195–6
consular work 48–9
Corner, Frank 23
Craw, Charles 14, 42–3
Craw, Evelyn 42–3
credentials, presenting
    Belgrade 151–2
    Cairo 148–9
    Malta 154
    Rangoon 117–30
    Riyadh 162–7
Crooks, David 7
culture shock 50
Cunninghame, Rex 13

Davin, Adelina 22
Davin, Antonia 22
Davin, Dan 21–2
Davin, Tom 21–2
Dawson, Bill 41 fn
Death of a Princess 187–8
Dewar, Francis Eric 135
diaper service 39

earthquake 209–10, 215
Ecafe meeting
    Bangkok 27
    Lapstone 26
education, Burma 133
EEC market 195, 204, 207, 214, 216
Eisenhower, President Dwight 80
Elizabeth, Queen 168–9, 210
Elworthy, Lord 102
Empire State Building 35, 42, 48
Evans, Sir Francis 48
Evans, Harold 12
exports to Italy 204, 210, 216–18
External Affairs Department 9–25
Eyre, Dean 80

Fairburn, Rex 46
Fergusson, Sir Bernard 13, 83, 120, 135, 145, 169, 174
Fergusson, Lady (Laura) 169
ferry, Italy–Egypt 206–7
Firth, Cedric 52
Fortune, Robert 97
Fraser, Peter 9, 15, 33, 37, 56

Gabites, Paul 13, 24
Gadaffi, Colonel 156
Gale, Glenda 8
Galileo 193
Galvin, Bernie 220
Gandhi, Indira 83
gardening 198–9
Garner, Sir Saville 84–5
Gentlemen Prefer Blondes 35
George, Gillian 208
German New Guinea 60
Giulio, marketing officer, Rome 217
Goh Keng Swee 83
Gold, Max 34
Goroka 57
Gorton, John 102
graffiti 190–1, 206

Hahn, James 94
Hampton, Helen 25, 53
Han Suyin 96, 99
Harland, Bryce 99
Harlem 35
Harriot, Bob 32
Harris, Dr Rosemary 212
Harrison, Graeme 216–18
Hasluck, Paul 54
Herrick, Admiral Terry 107–8
Hill-Norton, Admiral Sir Peter 107
Hislop, T.C.A. 21
Hollandia 65
Holyoake, Sir Keith 18–19, 99, 220
home brew 13
Horsborough, George 163
hospital charges 36

Index

Hughes, Sir Rochford 91, 101–2
Hunt, Brigadier Les 26–7, *121*
Hutchens, Dick 12
Hyde, Robin 46

insurgency 114–15
IQ test 23
Ishak, Rahmin 84
Israeli military advisers 88
Italian politics 218–19

Japanese occupation of New Guinea 60
Jeffery, Margo 12
Jeffery, Peter 12
Jones, Arthur 56
Jones, Fred 55–7
Jowve, Nicolas 66

Kennedy, Robert 73
Khalid, King of Saudi Arabia 183
King and I, The 35
Kipling, Rudyard 94
Kirk, Norman 120

Lae 57, 65
Lake, Doug 15
Laking, Sir George 9, 14, 35, 107, 213
Laking, Rob 7–8
Lange, David 6
Lake Success 39
Larkin, Tom 14
Law, Doug 8
Leahy, Michael 59
Lee Hsien Loong 82
Lee Kuan Yew 74–89, 92–3, 95–7, 99–103, 112–13, *125*
Letters from Moscow 7
Libya–New Zealand trade 216
Lim Kim San 92, 100
Loren, Sophia 186
Loveday, Max 53–4
Luxton, David 203, 215

MacArthur, General Douglas 72
McCarthy, Senator Joe 30
McCrae, Norman 216–18
McGregor, Bert 26–29, *121*
McIntosh, Sir Alister 13–18, 23, 56, *126*
McIntosh, Lady (Doris) 17, *126*
McIntosh, James 32
MacLean, Sir Fitzroy 174–5
McNamara, Robert 80
Madang 57
Male, Cathy 45–6
Male, Hilda 45
Male, John 45–7
Malta 153–4
Manokwari 65
Maoris 37, 75
Markes, Laurie 193
Marshall, David 98–9
Mecca 158
Menzies, Dame Patti 52–55
Menzies, Sir Robert 14, 55, *123*
Milner, Frank 47
Milner, Ian 47
Mintoff, Dominic 153–4
Montgomery, Field Marshal 92
Mubarak, Hosni, President of Egypt 181–2
Muldoon, Sir Robert 119, 219–221
Murray, Sir Hubert 60
Myitkina 140–2

Nash, Sir Walter 14, 43, 45, 55
Nazzerano, driver, Rome 190–1, 199–200
Nehru, Jawaharlal 98
Neilson, Helen 214–15
Netherlands New Guinea 59–60
Ne Win, General, President of Burma 110, 119–20, *127*, 129–32, 134, 136–46
New Zealand Insurance Company 101, 111
non-alignment 176
Northy, Jack 13

oil 133, 145, 160, 176
Osten, Bill 101
Owen, Alex 110, 114, 141

Padua 189–95
Papua New Guinea 57–71
   Australian administration 60–1
   Chinese 62
   diversity 57–9
   missionaries 62–3
   political development 63–4
   resident Australians 63
Parkway Village 39–46
Peeper, Jean 42
Perry, Agnes 21
Perry, Ray 9–10, 13, 21
Pertini, President of Italy 148–50, 172
pets 51
Plimsoll, Sir James 53
Poananga, Brian 74
Pompeii 200–1
Porritt, Lord 102
Port Moresby 57
Pritchett, Bill 92
prostitution 87
Protector of the Chinese, Pickering 95
Puttick, Beverley 11

Quill, Pam and Stan 211–12

Rabaul 65
race relations 86–7
racism 75, 80
Raffles, Stamford 89, 96–7
Randall, Geoff 161–2, 196, 207–8, 213–14
Razak, Tun 80
Reagan, Ronald, President of America 156
Reedy, Arnold 36–9, *122*
religion 87
rice 115, 129
Richard, Ivor 101
Richardson, Ken 173

Rider, Peter 8, 161–3, 166–7
Rillstone, Father Tom 139, 140 fn
Robb, John 83–4
Rofe, Wanee 24–5
Roosevelt, Eleanor 38–9
Rostow, Walt 80
rubber 97

Sadat, Anwar, President of Egypt 155–7, 178–82
Saker, Dorian 12
Saudi Arabia 158–167, 215, 217–18
Schouten, Hank 108
Scott, John 13, 30–1
security 83, 191, 199
Seaplanes 27
Seath, David 98
SEATO 43
Seddon, Mary 11
Sentimental Bloke, The 52–3
Sergio, Embassy driver, Rome, 215
sexual harassment 43
Shanahan, Foss 22–5
Shanahan, Joan 24–5
Sharp, Dick 20, 49
Shaw, Runme 97, 98
Shearer, Dr Ian 204
Singapore 28, 74–103
skyscrapers 34–5
smoking 19–20, 83, 120, 142
Sorong 65
South Pacific 35
Sparkman, Senator 22
Stewart, Ian 173
Stewart, R.H. (Sir Robertson) 81
Sukarno, President of Indonesia 73, 75
supermarkets 40
Sutch, Bill (W.B.) 44–5, *122*
Sutch, Helen 44

Talboys, Sir Brian 173, 187
tea 97
terrorism 200
Thomson, David 81–2

Index

Thorn, James 44
Thornton, General Sir Leonard 81–2
Tin Oo, General 143
Tito, Josip Broz, President of Yugoslavia 172–7
Tito, Jovanka 172, 174
Tolaga Bay 221
Trieste 200–1
tropical suits 29
Turner, Bruce 47–8
Twiss, Vice Admiral Sir Frank 104

United Nations Charter 9
United Nations Economic and Social Council 44
United Nations membership 36

Valiant, HMS 104
Virgona, Pia 163

Wade, Hunter 20
Walton, Denis 204
Wau 65
Wickham, Henry 97
Wild, Sarah 8
Wilson, J.V. 14, 16
Wilson, Neil 202, 216
Womsiwor, Herman 66
Woodward, John 12

Young, Trevor 204
Yugoslavia 151–2, 172–7
  break-up 176
  collective leadership 151–2

Zamberletti 204, 213